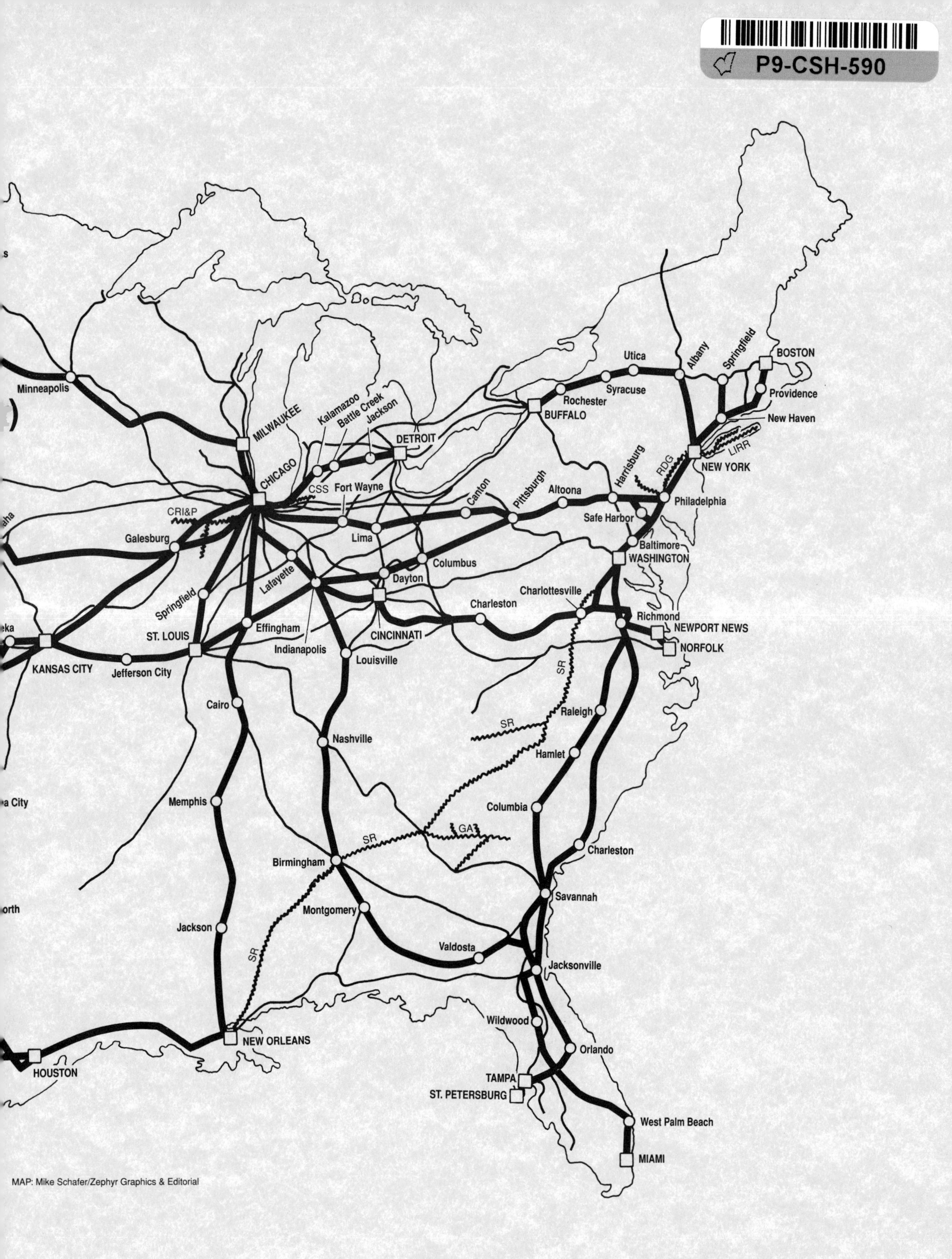

MAP: Mike Schafer/Zephyr Graphics & Editorial

ALL ABOARD

1971 AMTRAK 1991

BY MIKE SCHAFER

WITH BOB JOHNSTON AND KEVIN McKINNEY

FOREWORD BY AMTRAK PRESIDENT W. GRAHAM CLAYTOR JR.

ALL ABOARD AMTRAK 1971 1991

BY MIKE SCHAFER

WITH SELECTED CHAPTERS BY BOB JOHNSTON AND KEVIN McKINNEY

FOREWORD BY AMTRAK PRESIDENT W. GRAHAM CLAYTOR JR.

PUBLISHED BY

RAILPACE COMPANY, INC.

P.O. Box 927

Piscataway, NJ 08855-0927

ISBN: 0-9621541-4-8

COVER PHOTO: The winds of winter are pleasantly cool on this temperate February day in 1988 as the westbound *California Zephyr* approaches Emigrant Gap in California's Sierra Range.—*Mike Schafer* TITLE PAGE: Hitchin' a ride along the route of the *Coast Starlight* in 1973 is former Amtrak Passenger Service Representative and Seaboard Coast Line *Florida Special* hostess Patty Saunders.—*Mike Schafer* THIS SPREAD: Muffled by the snows of a wispy winter day near Rocky Prairie, Wash., the *Coast Starlight* heads into its overnight run to the Golden State on Feb. 18, 1990.—*Scott O'Dell*

Foreword

On May 1, 1991, Amtrak turned 20 years old. Twenty years in the railroad business is not a long time. Railroading is a mature industry more than 160 years old, and, compared to that long span of time, Amtrak might be viewed as an adolescent.

But just as a son increasingly approximates his father's age as the years and decades pass, so Amtrak has gained an ever-larger segment of railroading's total time line. It surprises us to realize that the National Railroad Passenger Corporation, as Amtrak is formally known, has occupied fully one eighth of the history of American railroading.

Since its first, tentative day in operation, Amtrak has earned a degree of stability and permanence few informed observers—even zealous advocates—might have dared predict during the company's early years. That it survived at all surprised some of the industry's most stout-hearted believers.

Amtrak's initial gloomy prognosis was understandable. In 1970, the last year before Amtrak operations began, some 27 different privately owned railroads ran up a total operating loss of $450 million—a figure that in 1991 dollars would translate to a staggering $1.5 billion.

There were many reasons for this state of affairs, but, contrary to popular lore, the blame did not lay primarily with poor railroad management or some inexplicable disenchantment with running good passenger train service. These were contributing factors in many cases, but they in turn were caused by far more pervasive and powerful forces external to the American railroad industry.

With the brief notable exception of the World War II period, the number of Class I railroad passengers and revenue passenger-miles declined slowly but steadily beginning in 1921, the rate accelerating in the postwar years. The temporary resurgence during the War was no aberration; gasoline and tires were rationed and the private automobile was dealt its only major setback to its otherwise inexorable climb to domination in U.S. passenger transportation.

While the auto possessed some of its own uniquely endearing characteristics from the very beginning—privacy, freedom from schedules and a certain panache—it gained its ascendancy only through public policy which permitted it to thrive and multiply. As with any major transportation mode, the auto needed an infrastructure: roads, bridges, tunnels, pavement and increased law enforcement. That infrastructure was largely provided by government as a matter of public policy, first through the early federal and state highway systems, and eventually through the massive federal Interstate highway program.

Amtrak President W. Graham Claytor Jr. in January 1991.—*Bob Johnston*

Other public policy ensured that gasoline remained artificially inexpensive, levying only minimal taxes on the increasingly popular fuel. The auto's ascendancy was assured and, not surprisingly in view of public policy, the passenger train's fate seemed to be sealed.

As highways continued to receive ever-increasing largess from municipal, state and federal treasuries, the nation's passenger train "subsidy" resided only in the railroad system's contracts with the U.S. Post Office Department. Even that revenue source was no gravy train: There were costs associated with operating the Railway Post Office service. When even this stipend was pulled out at the end of the 1960's, the demise of the passenger train was truly at hand.

Failure to mention America's excellent aviation system as a contributing factor in the decline of passenger-train service would be a serious oversight. Much of the railroad's business travel and considerable domestic discretionary travel took to jet planes whose tremendous speed made up for lack of amenities. Airlines, too, have their infrastructure largely provided at little or no cost to them: air-traffic control, tax-exempt airport construction bonds, and federally funded military research and development for advanced technology.

It was into this milieu that Amtrak hesitantly stepped on May 1, 1971. The day before, and for several months previously, the fledgling passenger railroad had been little more than a concept on paper. It owned no track and didn't have any operating employees. Although it had acquired ownership of a considerable number of old and mostly tired railroad cars and locomotives, it continued to be both operated and maintained by the same private railroad employees who had done so before Amtrak took over.

From the beginning, Amtrak was defined by Congress as a "for profit" railroad corporation and was not to be considered a government agency or entity. In fact, however, it appeared initially to be more a contracting organization than a railroad.

From this inauspicious start was expected to grow a successful passenger railroad which would prosper in a nation that had for a quarter century pledged its unwavering commitment to its automobiles, its sprawling highway infrastructure and its fascinating new jet airliners. The extraordinary thing is that this is just what, in due course, did take place.

A year before Amtrak, railroads carried intercity passengers 4.9 billion passenger-miles and lost the 1991 equivalent of $1.5 billion doing it. In Fiscal Year 1990, Amtrak carried its 22.2 million intercity passengers 6.1 billion passenger-miles and pared operating losses to about $330 million.

Ironically, it is the booming success of the passenger train's most-competitive rivals, the auto and the jet, that has helped bring about a resurgence of interest in U.S. passenger trains. People are flocking to Amtrak in part because they find trains to be a welcome relief from the stress of traffic gridlock and increasingly impersonal air service. The very things that once seemed to forecast passenger trains' certain doom are helping revive a time-honored mode of travel.

Amtrak is determined to continue to improve bottom line through better service and controlled costs until 100 percent of operating costs are covered by earned revenues. At close to 80 percent in 1991, we are nearing that goal.

To reach that goal, Amtrak will have to rely on the special attributes of rail passenger service—adventure, scenery, family, nostalgia and service—and on the special qualities that have characterized Amtrak's corporate culture in the first 20 years: experimentation, resourcefulness and tenacity.

ALL ABOARD AMTRAK does an admirable job of reminding us what is possible in the face of tough odds and cynical predictions of failure. Amtrak's next two decades are destined to be its most exciting.

—W. Graham Claytor Jr.
Washington, D.C.
August 1991

Introduction

Brad Joseph

Why would a devout student of the passenger train who was born in the 1940's be such a loyal follower of Amtrak? After all, it was the National Railroad Passenger Corporation's formation which ultimately doomed more than half of U.S. passenger trains on May 1, 1971, ending a colorful period of individualism, history and operation in railroading.

Indeed, several of my contemporaries lost interest in American passenger trains that fateful day, citing that homogenization of what was in fact the skeletal remains of a once-vast and amazingly diverse rail passenger transport system had taken the last breath out of a dying industry. It is easy for me to understand their feelings, and I must confess that at times I shared their cynicism as an infant Amtrak foundered through its formative years.

Perhaps this is all the result of a little mind game I play every so often—which involves some explanations. I rode my first passenger train (Illinois Central's *Hawkeye*) about 1953 or so and immediately fell in love with rail travel. With more personal freedom at hand in my mid-teens, I made passenger trains a quest, photographing and/or riding everything my paltry budget would allow.

My memories of those days in the 1960's were bittersweet. Although I reveled in the excursions my buddies and I took on the likes of Erie Lackawanna's *Lake Cities*, Monon's *Thoroughbred*, Milwaukee Road's *Arrow* and Gulf, Mobile & Ohio's *Midnight Special*, I knew at the time these conveyances were living on borrowed time. No matter how fine those rides were, knowing that these trains—indeed, perhaps all long-distance U.S. passenger trains—faced certain oblivion always seemed to cast a bit of a pall on such outings.

And that's the one thing perhaps many of us old enough to remember tend to forget about the 1960's, the final decade of the traditional passenger train: there seemed to be no hope. I wanted to see new trains inaugurated; I tried to imagine what it would be like if the railroads of 1967 actually ordered brand-new passenger locomotives and rolling stock. I wished I could have seen IC's *Land O' Corn* touted in a hometown TV commercial. Most of all, I wanted to see the trains full of customers.

So, I regarded Amtrak's arrival as a last hope—albeit with a high price for the devout passenger-train enthusiast what with fewer trains and standardization. And at the time, I was ready to embrace *anything* that appeared it might give new life to this industry I so love.

And that mind game? I like to imagine what it would be like if I could time-machine myself back to myself in the 1960's. So there I am, in 1967, in Rockford, Ill., mourning the loss the *Land O' Corn*, our hometown streamliner, which has just made its last run. *"Hey Schafer. . . it's me—or I mean* you*—from 1991. Don't sweat it! In the 1970's, you'll not only have a streamliner still serving Rockford, but it will have domes and diners, and then later, brand-new equipment!"*

Or how about this one: It's 1968 and I'm madly typing away at my college English Composition term paper, which is on the impending demise of the *California Zephyr* (on which I received an "A" and actually convinced the professor and his family to take the *CZ* to *California*). . . *"Schaf, me again from 1991. Do you realize that you'll be riding the* California Zephyr *20 years from now?!*

Here's another: It's 1970 and four of us are riding a heavyweight ex-Pennsy P70 day coach on Penn Central's Cincinnati-Chicago train 65 making cracks about the dilapidated equipment. *"Schaf, would you believe you'll be riding a press run in 1979 debuting new sleepers, coaches and diners?!"*

O.K. One more. It's Friday afternoon, April 30, 1971, and I'm watching the last eastbound B&O *Capitol Limited* recede from Ash Street crossing in Chicago. The *"Cap"* was one of my favorite pre-Amtrak trains, and I just *had* to be on hand for its passing. *"Schafer. Skip the grieving. . . In 20 years almost to the day, you'll be taking the* Capitol Limited *to Washington, D.C., to meet with Amtrak folks. . . who will be helping you with a book you are writing on Amtrak's 20th anniversary."*

On with the show.

—Mike Schafer
Waukesha, Wis.
August 1991

1/Countdown to Amtrak

SETTING THE STAGE FOR A NEW ORDER

TOP: The special drumhead on the rear of the last westbound Union Pacific *City of Los Angeles* at Salt Lake City, Utah, on May 1, 1971, says it all for the traditional railroad-operated passenger train. **ABOVE**: The following day, crowds and media greeted the final *City of L.A.* as it pulled up to the bumping post of Los Angeles Union Passenger Terminal.—*Both photos, Jim Heuer*

Once upon a time in America, a traveler could reach nearly every metropolis, town or hamlet by passenger train. Railways helped build America, so it follows that for a long time they reigned as the chosen transportation mode of mobile Americans.

The first half of the 20th Century belonged to the passenger train, and the spotlight was on the passenger train particularly during World War II. In terms of moving supplies and people, the railroads were instrumental in war efforts. After its conclusion, American passenger trains were swept by postwar euphoria into yet another era—one of new trains . . . and then one of almost no trains.

What happened? Why did the U.S. go from a lifeblood of *20th Century Limiteds*, *Daylights*, *Fast Mails* and no-name locals to almost the unthinkable—a world-class industrialized nation devoid of intercity passenger trains? The subject could almost itself be a book. We'll capsulize.

Actually, rail passenger traffic reached its peak in the late 1920s and shortly after was pruned by the Great Depression. In the early part of the century, Americans were becoming increasingly enamored by the freedom of the auto; meanwhile, federal and state governments responded by constructing a network of numbered highways, from U.S. 1 to California 99. Backed by government support, the auto became a formidable foe for the passenger train.

But late in the 1930's railroads began a large-scale retaliation with a new weapon, the streamlined train. The streamliner era ushered in a galaxy of flashy landlocked liners that contrasted sharply from the steam-powered conveyances plying the land, and once again passenger trains captivated Americans.

Though World War II brought unprecedented business from civilians and troops alike, rail travel was often at the expense of comfort and convenience. Wartime travelers remembered this after V-Day, and more and more of them opted for the auto—despite a "baby boom" of new trains.

The success of the streamliner had been interrupted by the War, but railroads had every reason to believe that afterward the success would resume. To an extent, it did. . . until President Eisenhower signed what some consider to be the ultimate death warrant of the passenger train: the bill that spawned the Federal Defense Highway System—the Interstate.

The Interstate brought incredible ramifications—good and bad—to U.S. transportation. While other industrialized nations strengthened their commitment to rail, the U.S. government had clearly skewed its support to highways by setting up a permanent funding mechanism for their construction, the gas tax-funded "trust fund."

By the late-1950's, railroads could see the handwriting on the wall—and in the sky as commercial aviation gained a stronghold, benefitting from military-inspired commercial jet aircraft and the government-trained pilots to fly them. Train-offs increased sharply in the mid-1950's as railroads began bailing out of the passenger business, although several roads maintained a positive stance, even claiming their passenger services were relatively healthy. In 1956, for example, Great Northern bought new dome cars for its world-class *Empire Builder* while Chicago, Burlington & Quincy completely re-equipped the *Denver Zephyr.* As late as 1965, Kansas City Southern was taking delivery of new cars, and Illinois Central was buying secondhand cars to handle traffic.

Other railroads were downright adamant about getting out of the business, claiming that passengers had deserted them. Rail advocates, meanwhile, cried foul, stating that railroads had a lackluster record for passenger marketing, innovation and operation. *Trains* Magazine's David P. Morgan asked "Who Shot the Passenger Train?" in its April 1959 special passenger issue, which analyzed what had become an alarming situation. (The answer to the question, of course, was . . . everybody.)

In that final decade of old-school private-railroad passenger operation, the 1960's, came the final blows. The major one was dealt by the United States Postal Service, which in 1967 effected a wholesale termination of nearly all railway postal service, which had shifted most delivery to airlines and highways. With declining passenger revenue already making the trains unprofitable, the elimination of mail contracts provided both the catalyst and justification to ask the Interstate Commerce Commission (ICC) for discontinuance.

Then, on New Year's Eve 1968, the Pullman Company ended operation of sleeping cars throughout the U.S. It would now be up to individual railroads to staff and operate sleeping cars. The net result? Many roads saw it as an opportunity to drop sleeping-car service, and passenger service took another dive.

Discontinuances now escalated at an alarming rate, and it appeared that the

Streamliners and dome cars only prolonged the inevitable time when U.S. railroads would throw in the towel on passenger trains. Chicago, Burlington & Quincy's eastbound *Morning Zephyr* has just departed Oregon, Ill., on a crisp autumn day in 1967 and is slicing through topography not usually associated with the "Prairie State." The Minneapolis-Chicago run and its twin, the *Afternoon Zephyr*, were the first streamliners in the country to feature regularly assigned dome cars, in 1947.—*Mike Schafer*

ABOVE: The forfeiture of Railway Post Office contracts was one of the more-fatal blows for U.S. passenger service in the late 1960's. Mail business offset losses incurred on passenger operations.—*Mike Schafer* **BELOW:** This Pullman attendant serving on a sleeper on the joint PRR-L&N-SCL *South Wind* in December1968 faced a uncertain future. The demise of Pullman-operated sleeping-car service on New Year's Eve of that year was yet another setback in a continuing series of events that led to the formation of Amtrak.—*Phil Gosney*

1970's would bring with it an America without intercity passenger trains.

WHICH BRINGS US TO Amtrak. We know that Amtrak operations began on May 1, 1971—that's when Amtrak, the machine, began to function. But who built it, and where did the parts come from?

A lot of parts came from one Anthony Haswell, who in 1968 founded the National Association of Railroad Passengers (NARP), a Washington-based lobby group dedicated to saving the passenger train. Haswell and NARP faced a herculean task: convincing political leaders that preservation of a rail passenger system was up to the U.S. government.

Haswell's NARP and other rail advocates began lobbying congressional leaders and certain key areas of the railroad industry, in this case the Association of American Railroads. Though essentially powerless, AAR on Valentines Day 1969 did approve a concept of subsidized passenger-train operations and a government-owned equipment pool.

Passenger trains are as American as apple pie and all the rest, so convincing congressional leaders to save rail service was perhaps one of the easier aspects of the project, despite indifference in some congressional circles. In the late 1960's, America was a sea of train discontinuance notices, and the public—at least those aware that passenger trains still existed—was already up in arms about loss of service, to say little of the decline in quality of what was still around.

Two cases in point: First, Santa Fe's Oct. 4, 1967, announcement to discontinue 33 of its 39 passenger runs. If a carrier like Santa Fe—who arguably hosted the finest and most-well run passenger-train fleet in the U.S.—couldn't make a go of it, then who could? Second, and at the opposite end of the spectrum, was Penn Central and its long-sought petition to discontinue trains 66-67—a shabby Chicago-Logansport (Ind.)-Cincinnati run that advocates held as an example of railroad management gone hostile on the passenger.

The evidence and the lobbying worked. On June 11, 1969, several congressmen signed a resolution to save the passenger train. Then, on July 16, the ICC announced its support for rail passenger subsidies.

Now the momentum spread to the U.S. Department of Transportation and the Federal Railroad Administration, and the latter assembled a task force to study where the passenger train might be headed in America. Despite its long-standing reputation for lukewarm support of the passenger train, DOT at that time was headed by John Volpe who, unlike many DOT leaders since, championed the passenger train. The FRA task force concluded that, despite the widespread disintegration of U.S. rail passenger service, ridership remained strong on selected routes and that a new well-run, coordinated core system could capitalize on this. On Jan. 18, 1970, DOT announced plans for a quasi-public rail passenger network (historians may wryly note that on the following day the Nixon Administration denied the existence of any such plan).

We can thank Indiana for the next step, which was to develop a subsidy plan. This was accomplished by Hoosier Senator Vance Hartke, and on March 12, 1970, the Senate approved it. Next came the formal bill for the concept, the Railroad Passenger Service Act of 1970, which was introduced on May 1, 1970 (this is when the "Railpax" name began to take hold), exactly one year prior to The Big Day. The Senate approved the bill by a resounding 78-3 on May 6, after which it went to the House for approval. The House version was passed on Oct. 14, with both the House and Senate agreeing on this final version.

Then, it went to the White House, and Railpax supporters began an agonizing wait for the verdict. Nixon, his aides, including John Erlichman (of Watergate fame) and the Office of Management &

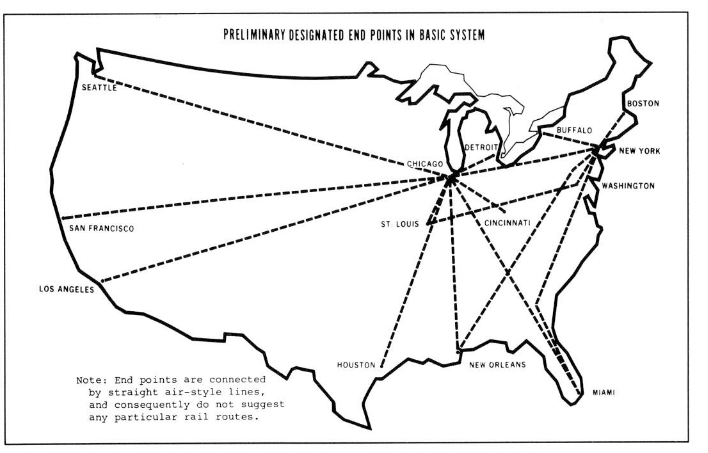

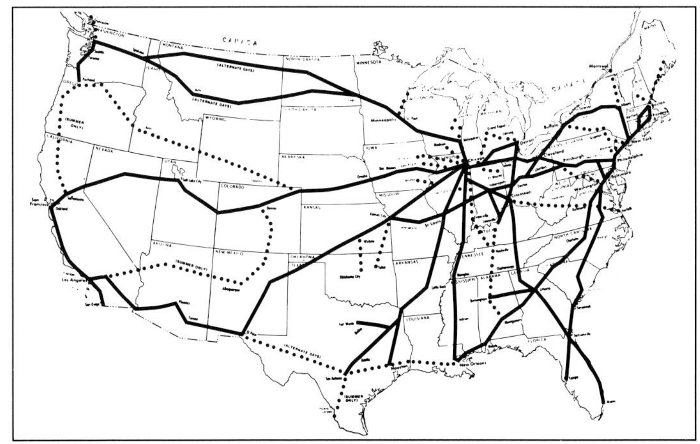

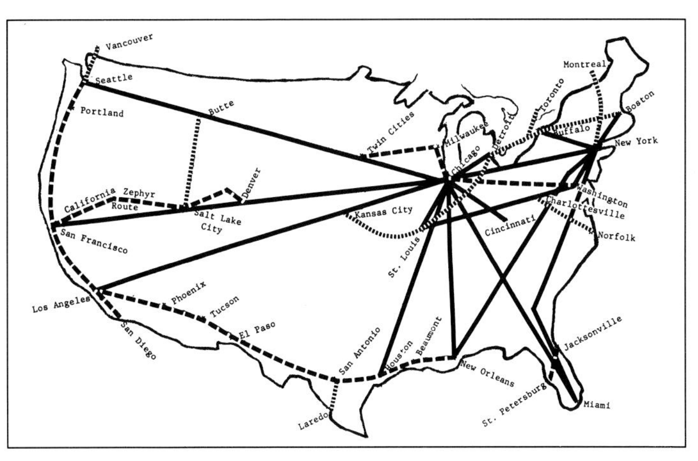

Budget headed by Caspar Weinberger were openly against the Railpax concept, and there were many battles between OMB and DOT on the subject. Perhaps not wanting to be pasted with the stigma of nationalization—a very potential scenario if railroads could not be relieved of deficit-ridden passenger operations—nor of being the bad guy for allowing the ICC to permit the death of the passenger train (an almost certain outcome should Railpax be vetoed), President Richard M. Nixon reluctantly signed the legislation on Oct. 30, 1970, and Public Law 91-518–the National Railroad Passenger Corporation–was born.

Now things became more public, and the news media began focusing attention on the state of the passenger train and the impending new order. Toward the end of 1970, newspapers throughout the land carried DOT's preliminary-report endpoint map released on Nov. 30—a map which disturbed passenger advocates account of its alarming simplicity (above left). Based on guidelines set by Congress, sixteen city pairs had been selected for service: New York-Washington, New York-Boston, New York-Buffalo, Chicago-New York, New York-Miami, New York-New Orleans, Washington-St. Louis, Chicago-St. Louis, Chicago-Detroit, Chicago-Cincinnati, Chicago-Miami, Chicago-New Orleans, Chicago-Houston, Chicago-Los Angeles, Chicago-Oakland/San Francisco and Chicago-Seattle.

Actually, this preliminary system was considerably larger than the Nixon administration wanted. In fact, OMB pressured DOT to accept the White House's barebones proposal—basically the Northeast Corridor, New York-Miami, New York-Chicago, a Chicago-West Coast service and not much else—so much so that Volpe threatened to resign. The White House backed down.

Interested parties, including the ICC, the railroads themselves, state public utility commissions, labor organizations and, of course, lobby groups had until the end of 1970 to provide input for DOT's final submission to Congress, due by the end of January 1971.

NARP rushed in with a far more logical proposal (top right), albeit at greater dollar cost but then also with a significantly higher potential success. NARP's system was more balanced and included a number of seasonal services and secondary feeder routes. Hard on NARP's "yellow block," the ICC submitted its proposal as well (above), which consisted of DOT's awkward map with dashed lines added to show ICC amendments.

Based on additional input, DOT on Jan. 28, 1971, announced a yet-larger route system which added New York-Kansas City, Cincinnati-Newport News, Los Angeles-New Orleans, Seattle-San Diego, Chicago-Washington, New York-St. Petersburg and Chicago-St. Petersburg. In the following weeks, the details of specific routing were finalized and an official map of the new

TOP LEFT: The original "system" map issued by DOT was a hasty affair that portrayed a bare bones network—but it wasn't nearly as skeletal as what the White House wanted. NARP's version (TOP RIGHT), which was in response to the first map, seemed much more well thought out, with some surprising parallels to what is being operated 20 years later. ABOVE: The ICC's counterproposal to the DOT map was in fact the DOT map with additional routes pasted in.

Railpax system was released, which is the map that appeared in the first system timetable. In determining final routes, the best of the intermediate routes were examined following a criteria of existing ridership, running times, population centers, track conditions, alternative transportation, track connections at crucial junction points and existing (or lack of) service.

In some cases a traditional pre-existing route worked best (e.g., Chicago-Pittsburgh-New York via the former Pennsylvania Railroad), but new combinations also appeared (e.g., the Amtrak *Empire Builder* would forsake East Dubuque, Ill., New Rockford, N.D., and Wenatchee, Wash., for Milwaukee, Wis., Grand Forks, N.D., and Yakima, Wash., respectively).

CORPORATELY, how would the new rail passenger company work? The act which created the NRPC on Oct. 30, 1970, emphasized that it was not to be a government institution (such as the U.S. Army), but a quasi-public, for-profit corporation—"public" because it would receive subsidies from taxpayers. So, although the media and many individuals to this day insist that U.S. passenger trains are "government run," such is technically not the case. Nonetheless, the subsidy factor did and does make Amtrak a sort of ward of the government—and a choice political football, particularly in the early days of high subsidies.

Passenger-carrying railroads had the option to "join" the NRPC, the membership price of which was an amount—in the form of cash and/or equipment and services to NRPC—roughly calculated to be half the road's losses for the last full year of passenger operation (1970), or they could buy common stock. The cash fee or the value of equipment and services could be balanced against shares of common stock in the new company or be used as write-offs on income tax. Only four railroads went the stock route: Milwaukee Road, Burlington Northern, Penn Central and Grand Trunk Western. Of course, the biggest benefit for member roads was that, overnight, they would be relieved of the financial burden of maintaining passenger service.

Under the new regime, individual railroads initially were still responsible for passenger operations, but the direct costs (labor, fuel, maintenance, etc.) would be compensated by NRPC. Each railroad was required to maintain its passenger routes to certain standards, and probably in nearly all cases this was a level higher than necessary for freight operations.

All railroads that were operating long-distance passenger trains at the time the Amtrak law was signed into being were eligible to join and had until May 1, 1971, to do so. Roads intending to join Amtrak were required to post discontinuance notices at least 30 days prior to May 1 for all passenger trains—commuter excluded—

Never a complainer about the burdens of passenger-train operation, Gulf, Mobile & Ohio did its best, with limited resources (read, heavyweight equipment), to maintain a reputable operation which included full dining and parlor services on its day runs. On the Chicago-Springfield (Ill.)-St. Louis corridor, "Gee-Mo" fielded three trains each way (*Abe Lincoln*, the *Limited* and the legendary *Midnight Special*) right up to May 1, 1971. Here's the *Abe* trekking out of Chicago a week before Amtrak. Operation of heavyweight diner-lounges—one of which is toward the rear of the train in this scene—was an anomaly even in 1971. Interestingly, these elderly diners, built for *Alton Limited* service in the 1920's, were briefly used in Amtrak service! In the Amtrak era, the Chicago-St. Louis route remains an important corridor, with four trains each way between Chicago and Springfield, and three beyond.—*Tom Nemeth*

subject to discontinuance. Thus by April 1, 1971, slews of train-off petitions papered the walls of depots across America. Railroads that elected to stay out were required to continue their passenger services for five years, after which the option to join Amtrak resurfaced.

The first casualty of Railpax was not a train, but the name. On April 19, 1971, the Railpax name was dropped in favor of Amtrak, an acronym for American Travel by Track. The new name was accompanied by a new corporate logo and the now-familiar Amtrak arrow and colors.

As the first timetable was being printed, not all major eligible roads had made their decision to join Amtrak and some assumptions had to be made. Thus, the map in the first Amtrak timetable shows an Amtrak-operated New York-New Orleans service, a Chicago-Oakland route through—not around—the Rockies, and no intercity services to the likes of Peoria, Ill., Augusta, Ga., and Asheville, N.C.

During the final countdown to Amtrak, Rock Island said "no thanks," probably because the financially destitute carrier simply did not have the wherewithal to join; its services to Peoria and Rock Island, Ill., continued past May 1. Amtrak had planned to continue operating Southern Railway's New York-New Orleans flagship *Southern Crescent*, but no other SR services; thus SR's holdout came as good news for the Southeast, since it would have to retain all existing services including the Washington-Atlanta *Piedmont*, a Washington-Lynchburg (Va.) local, the old *Asheville Special* between Salisbury and Asheville, N.C., and, of course, the celebrated *Southern Crescent*.

At nearly the final hour, Rio Grande washed its hands of the whole deal, throwing Amtrak into a bind since D&RGW was a crucial link right in the middle of the planned Chicago-Oakland service. Amtrak turned to member road Union Pacific for an alternate route, via Wyoming—a state that had been slated to be voided of passenger service on May 1. Meanwhile, D&RGW's little *Rio Grande Zephyr*—born on the ruins of the *California Zephyr* in March 1970—would continue to shine the rails of Grande's extraordinarily scenic main line between Denver and Salt Lake City.

There were some "almosts," too: Santa

TOP: Baltimore & Ohio's *Capitol Limited* was probably the most well-known Chicago-East Coast flagship to be discontinued on May 1, 1971. Here, the final eastbound *"Cap"* strikes west out of downtown Chicago on the Chicago & North Western. Just for the last run, B&O doubled the dome space.—*Harold Edmonson*
ABOVE: During the final westbound *City of Los Angeles*'s short layover at Cheyenne, Wyo., on May 1, UP conducted a special ceremony in the depot, presenting a complete UP place setting to the State of Wyoming. Then the *City* resumed its trip—behind UP 4-8-4 No. 8444.—*Jim Heuer*

TOP: Dearborn Station was the only major Chicago terminal to close altogether when Amtrak began (nearby Central Station would close almost a year later). Photographers are at hand at Dearborn on the morning of April 30, 1971, for the final departure of Santa Fe's westbound *San Francisco Chief*. ABOVE: Chicago & North Western train 209, formerly the *Peninsula 400*, made its last departure from Chicago later that afternoon behind a pair of F-units.—*Both photos, Harold Edmonson*

Fe wavered, and Seaboard Coast Line had second thoughts as well. Hindsight now suggests that, had they stayed out, they probably would have ultimately joined Amtrak in 1976 if not later anyway.

Among the lesser-known eligible bachelors in the Amtrak marriage were: Georgia Railroad, with its four mixed trains; Chicago South Shore & South Bend, whose 88-mile Chicago-South Bend runs were considered long-distance; Reading Company, which had two routes in the 90-mile range; and Long Island Rail Road with its far-reaching trips to Greenport and Montauk, N.Y. Principally commuter roads, CSS&SB, RDG and LIRR probably felt it wasn't worthwhile to join for the sake of unloading a cadre of "long-distance" services that were in reality commuter-oriented for at least a portion of their runs.

By now, it began to sink in that Amtrak really was going to start on May 1, when more than half of the existing intercity passenger trains in the U.S. would make their final runs, including such institutions as B&O's *Capitol Limited* and UP's *City of Los Angeles*. Two senators, Mike Mansfield of Montana and Warren Magnuson of Washington, unsuccessfully lobbied for a delay in Amtrak startup, while various entities filed suits to halt the impending bloodbath. All were overruled by the U.S. Circuit Court of Appeals.

WHAT HAPPENED on April 30 and May 1, 1971, made front-page newspaper headlines and televised news from coast to coast. Perhaps some readers are old enough to have been a part of the news, as railfans and the general public alike jammed depot platforms and the trains themselves for a last salute to the traditional American passenger train.

Short- and medium-haul trains made

their final departures and arrivals on April 30; overnighters arrived at their destinations for the last time on May 1, sometimes amid the launching of the first Amtrak trains. Last-run transcons did not arrive at their terminals until May 2.

April 30 was a day of sadness and apprehension. Perhaps had rail advocates known of the good that lay ahead—from revived *Capitol Limiteds* to new bilevel long-distance cars to grandly resuscitated Union Stations—the pill would not have been so bitter.

Chicago Tribune
Amtrak Signal: All Green

LEFT: Despite scattered lawsuits, Amtrak began on time, as attested by the May 1, 1971, *Chicago Tribune* being held up by two fans out recording the day's first Amtrak trains.—*Harold Edmonson* ABOVE LEFT: For ceremonies on the East Coast, at least one Penn Central E-unit received a surrogate Amtrak paint scheme.—*Roger Puta, collection of Mel Finzer* ABOVE: Among the first Amtrak trains to depart Chicago were the *City of New Orleans* and the *South Wind* (departing at 8 a.m. and 8:10 a.m. respectively), standing at Central Station on May 1, 1971. BELOW: Later in the morning, the first Amtrak *Empire Builder* hustles out of town on its new route to the Twin Cities, on the Milwaukee Road via Milwaukee, Wis.—*Two photos, Mike Schafer*

2/Infant Amtrak

1971-1976: A NEW BEGINNING

TOP: Early symbols of progess for Amtrak: Turboliners delivered from France in 1973 and 1975.—*Joe McMillan* ABOVE: Under the young Amtrak, observation cars made a comeback, and new trains were born such as the *North Coast Hiawatha*, shown at Milwaukee in 1972.—*Mike Schafer*

On May 1, 1971, some 20 persons stood in bright morning sun on a footbridge spanning Illinois Central's Chicago-Champaign (Ill.) main line just south of Chicago's Central Station. Under the trainshed sat two sparkling-clean streamliners; the one clad in brown and orange was a familiar sight at the lakefront station, which had been built by IC in 1893. The other train, with its mostly Seaboard Coast Line rolling stock led by a pair of Louisville & Nashville E8's, was the obvious newcomer. On this morning, however, both represented a single new company. As passengers boarded both consists, suited officials scurried about the trains with their notepads, making certain everything was set for the launching of the first Amtrak passenger trains from Chicago.

At precisely 8 a.m., the storied *City of New Orleans* rolled forth from the station complex, pretty much the way it had for the previous 24 years. Ten minutes behind it, the "new" *South Wind* blew out of town, belching a voluminous cloud of blue smoke which all but obscured the train for the photographers who had patiently gathered on the footbridge. (Also at 8 a.m., the Chicago-St. Louis *Limited* marched out of Union Station on the other side of the Loop.) Amtrak operations were underway at what was destined to become *the* hub city for the National Railway Passenger Corporation. Shortly after, the photographers turned their attention southward for the final arrival of IC's northbound *Panama Limited*—a poignant reminder of the sig-

RIGHT: Are we back in the 1960's or what? During the first few months, Amtrak in some places didn't look much different than the days of individual railroad operation. Witness the *City of San Francisco* at Oakland, Calif., on Oct. 23, 1971. The SP is still much in evidence.—*T. O. Repp* BELOW RIGHT: Red, white and blue stripes on the cars of the combined *Super Chief/El Capitan* winding through Apache Canyon on the Santa Fe near Lamy, N.M., in May 1973 indicate a growing Amtrak presence, although the train's makeup is much the same as it was in Santa Fe days.—*Mike Schafer*

nificance of the previous day.

Meanwhile, in an also-sunny Washington, D.C.—the nerve center of Amtrak—more-formal ceremonies welcomed in the nation's newest railroad. Amtrak President Roger Lewis and DOT Secretary John Volpe carried a giant ticket aboard a special six-car New York-bound *Metroliner* that would commemorate Amtrak's first day. At New York's Penn Station, a Penn Central E-unit and coach, both wearing a crude Amtrak scheme, awaited the bevy of VIP's and reporters that disembarked from the special.

Despite the significance of the occasion, these send-offs were modest compared to future celebrations that would usher in resurrected trains, new equipment and new or refurbished stations. But then, May 1, was a venture into the unknown. Amtrak had to operate between its designated endpoint routes until July 1, 1973, after which it could discontinue any service it felt did not meet certain performance criteria. There were already strong feelings that Amtrak was a ruse to convince the public there was no hope for the passenger train, and that it was created merely to oversee an orderly shutdown. Was this deadline really a loophole in the Rail Passenger Service Act that would allow Amtrak to be terminated? We may never know; fortunately, it all became moot.

AMTRAK BEGAN WITH $40 million cash in its pockets, $300 million in guaranteed loans, a president, an eight-member board of directors (originally Amtrak's incorporators), a team of DOT/FRA administrators and precious few employees. Amtrak's first president, Roger Lewis, came from General Dynamics Corp. and had no previous railroad experience. He was recognized for his ability to structure and manage large corporations. Could anyone have guessed that the infant carrier, left in ragged swaddling clothes on Congress' doorstep, was poised

TOP: We're deep in southern Illinois at Cobden on Nov. 13, 1971, watching the final southbound "traditional" (i.e., day schedule) *City of New Orleans*. Cars of Northern Pacific, Union Pacific, Illinois Central and Louisville & Nashville vintage comprise this day's dayliner. The UP sleeper is being deadheaded to New Orleans to serve on the first northbound *Panama Limited* on Nov. 14, 1971. ABOVE: On that same date, the "Great Wall of Chicago" fell as through Milwaukee-St. Louis service was introduced. The St. Louis-bound *Abe Lincoln* is at Joliet, Ill., on July 21, 1972, with Burlington Northern F-units leading a symphony of equipment that includes former Milwaukee Road, UP, Northern Pacific and Burlington rolling stock.—*Both photos, Don Crimmin*

High-windowed observation-lounge *Cathedral Mountain* on the *North Coast Hiawatha* leaving Chicago in the summer of 1972 looked much the same as when it was delivered new to Great Northern for *Empire Builder* service 21 years earlier. In the late 1960's, GN's classic green-and-orange livery gave way to Big Sky Blue—as illustrated by the diner ahead of *Cathedral Mountain*—then to green and white—as on the dome two cars ahead of the obs—following the 1970 Burlington Northern merger. *Cathedral Mountain* and its kin had been stored by GN/BN, but Amtrak put the celebrated cars back in service.—*Mike Blaszak*

at the start of a remarkable two decades in U.S. rail passenger service—a period in which the passenger train would again come of age?

For many months into the "experiment," passenger trains were in fact still being operated by the very railroads which as a group had paid $202.8 million *not* to run "varnish" anymore. Amtrak was essentially just a contractor, outlining the services it needed and compensating the individual carriers to maintain track and facilities and to provide crews, servicing, locomotives and rolling stock. Because Amtrak did not yet have an operations department fully in place, the companies that ran the trains still, by necessity, called many of the shots.

Because of this, Amtrak's presence was imperceptible in the early months. The first Amtrak-operated *Limited* on Gulf, Mobile & Ohio's Chicago-St. Louis route was still an all-maroon-and-red streamliner; *Metroliners* clad in Penn Central emblems still flashed back and forth between New York and Washington, as they had been doing since their celebrated inaugural in 1969; and "warbonnet"-scheme Santa Fe locomotives still skimmed Pacific Ocean beaches with *San Diegans*.

But clues of a new regime began to appear in short order, and nowhere was this more evident than in the realm of equipment, which Amtrak began to acquire in autumn 1971 from member railroads fol-

The Washington section of the combined ***Broadway Limited/National Limited*** is in the able command of a stately PC GG1 electric near Conowingo, Md., on July 3, 1971. During the early days of Amtrak, the ***National*** and ***Broadway*** both served New York and Washington and were combined east of Pittsburgh; the combined train itself was split into Washington and New York sections at Harrisburg, with the former shortcutting to D.C. by way of PC's ex-PRR Columbia & Port Deposit line along the Susquehanna River. Prior to Amtrak, this route was freight-only; Washington-bound trains operated out of Harrisburg on the more-populous but congested line through York, Pa. With no stops planned between Harrisburg and Baltimore for Amtrak's ***Broadway/National***, it was run via a path of lesser resistance, in this case the C&PD.—*Mark Nelson*

lowing a period of selection that began before Amtrak even started operations. With 20 member railroads*, Amtrak had a rainbow of rolling stock and motive power to choose from—some 3,000 passenger cars and hundreds of locomotives.

Of course, the newborn corporation hardly needed all 3,000 cars to protect the spindly network of services that survived past May 1, 1971, so it set about picking the best of the lot—narrowing it down to some 1,200 cars and 300 locomotives. The new pool resulted in what many Amtrak-watchers and passenger-train aficionados were anxiously awaiting: Amtrak's short-lived era as a rolling artist's palette. Well into the summer of '71, cars and locomotives were being re-deployed throughout the U.S. In particular, equipment of Western roads, which in general had a history of meticulous maintenance, migrated eastward. Shabby Penn Central cars that had tumbled along in *Broadway Limited* service were largely replaced by Union Pacific rolling stock, while former Burlington *Zephyr* cars began showing up on the Northeast Corridor. (Eventually Amtrak did buy some of PC's better cars after the terms of PC's 1970 bankruptcy had been sorted out.)

The shuffling worked better on paper than in practice. It didn't matter how well-maintained a Santa Fe sleeper had been: If it experienced an air-conditioner failure while on, say, the Seaboard Coast Line, it probably couldn't get fixed right away—to the SCL carman, steam-injection air-conditioning systems, somewhat unique to Santa Fe, were "foreign." As a result, equipment malfunctions became a sore point, ranking third (behind haphazard reservation procedures and often-indifferent personnel) in the list of customer complaints in the early months of Amtrak.

But overall—especially in terms of being a visual indicator that improvements were underway—the shuffling could be consid-

*Atchison, Topeka & Santa Fe; Baltimore & Ohio; Burlington Northern; Central of Georgia; Chesapeake & Ohio; Chicago & North Western; Delaware & Hudson; Gulf, Mobile & Ohio; Grand Trunk Western; Illinois Central; Louisville & Nashville; Milwaukee Road; Missouri Pacific; Norfolk & Western; Northwestern Pacific; Penn Central; Richmond, Fredericksburg & Potomac; Santa Fe; Seaboard Coast Line; Southern Pacific; Union Pacific

TOP: **During the first year-plus of Amtrak, the train that became the *Coast Starlight/Daylight* operated all the way through from Seattle to San Diego. On June 11, 1972, operation was cut back to Los Angeles, with connecting service to San Diego provided instead by *San Diegan* corridor trains. Because of this short-lived operation through the country's second-largest city and the train's tri-weekly schedule, the famous-to-be long-haul was rarely photographed south of L.A. But, here's one view showing then-nameless No. 12 near Del Mar, Calif., on a not-so-sunny July 4, 1971.**—*Bob Schmidt* **ABOVE:** **Amtrak co-operated with U.S. DOT in operating experimental United Aircraft TurboTrains on selected runs; here's the *Turbo Yankee Clipper* leaving Boston South Station on Oct. 22, 1972.**—*George W. Turnbull, collection of Bob Wilt*

ered at least a small victory for rail traveling mankind. Service improvements were the next hurdle.

AMTRAK ARRIVED SO QUICKLY that its small cadre of planners barely had time to deal with start-up operations, let alone the planning of service improvements. On May 1, 1971, the schedules of most Amtrak trains were merely those in effect the previous month under private-railroad proprietorship—never mind that trains often didn't connect with one another. Thus, the eastbound *James Whitcomb Riley* on the Chicago-Cincinnati route was not scheduled to arrive in Cincinnati until after the Cincinnati-Washington/Newport News *George Washington* had left, although the connection worked westward. A similar situation existed on the Northeast Corridor, where Boston-New York trains were basically in a world of their own in regard to New York-Washington timings. Indeed, there were but three through Boston-Washington trains as of May 1, 1971.

There were exceptions. One was the introduction of a new through New York-Kansas City service which borrowed the name of a former-Pennsy flyer, the *Spirit of St. Louis*. Another similar new through service was destined to become an Amtrak classic: Seattle-San Diego, created by combining pre-Amtrak BN "pool" trains 195-198 (Seattle-Portland), SP's *Cascade* (Portland-Oakland) and *Coast Daylight* (Oakland/San Francisco-Los Angeles) and a Santa Fe *San Diegan* (L.A.-San Diego).

Fine tuning continued throughout Amtrak's first summer, during which Amtrak people were lining up the ducks for what some consider to be the first of many turning points for the NRPC: the debut of the 1971 fall timetable. The May 1 and July 12 editions basically had been carryover timetables done through the publishers of the *Official Guide of the Railways*. The Nov. 14, 1971, folder was Amtrak's own; more importantly, it reflected vast changes in services which proved to be a significant step in Amtrak's emergence as an entity. Some of note:

- Six through trains each way Boston-Washington.
- Six coordinated Boston-Washington schedules through newly established connections at New York City's Penn Station.
- Through twice daily (in each direction) Milwaukee-St. Louis through service.
- Through service from Boston to Miami and St. Petersburg on the *Silver Meteor* and *Champion*.
- Through New York-Los Angeles (via New Orleans) sleeping-car service.
- Chicago-Cincinnati-Washington service (*James Whitcomb Riley/George Washington*) extended to New York and Boston
- New Orleans-Birmingham-New York service in cooperation with Southern Railway extended to Boston.
- Memory schedules on the Northeast Corridor
- Expanded Northeast-Florida services for winter season.
- A doubling of service on the Twin Cities-Chicago route.
- L.A.-San Diego upped to three daily trains in each direction.
- A new route: Washington-Parkersburg, W. Va.
- New experimental fares.

On a broader note, the new timetable unveiled an unprecedented array of new

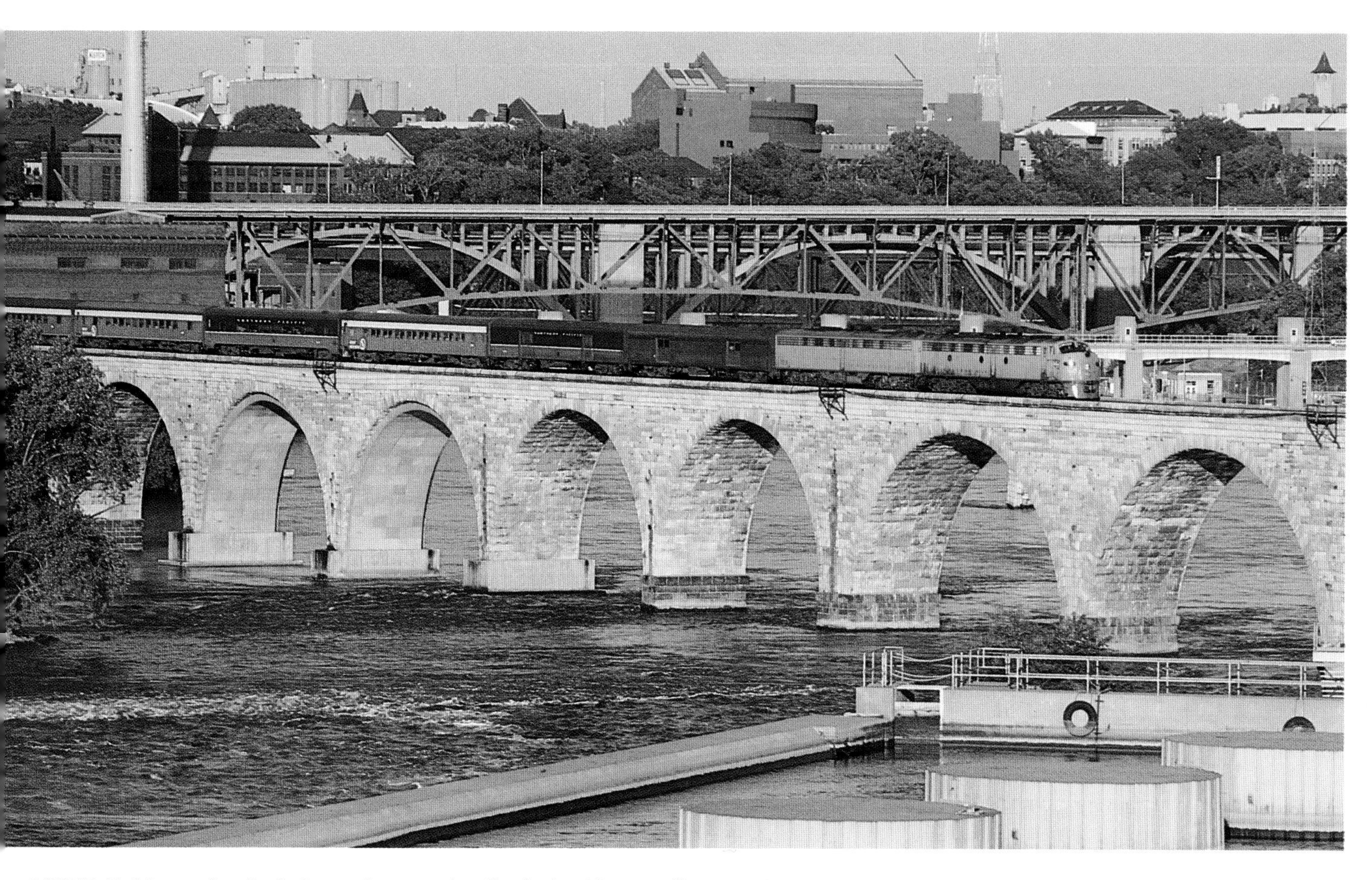

ABOVE: Not long after Amtrak was born and epitaphs had been written for more than half the nation's passenger trains, new trains began to appear. Added to the national system on June 5, 1971, was the *North Coast Hiawatha*, here easing over the Mississippi River on Stone Arch Bridge on the approach to Great Northern Station, Minneapolis, in June 1972. BELOW: The *Broadway Limited* was the first Amtrak train to be completely refurbished, on the carrier's first anniversary. The "new" *Broadway* for a time carried ex-Baltimore & Ohio sleeper-lounge-observation cars *Dana* and *Metcalf*. Unrefurbished cars have already crept back into the consist of this *Broadway* leaving Chicago in summer 1972, but one of the former-B&O cars, the *Dana*, provides a nice conclusion to the train. RIGHT: New images weren't all paint; some involved people. Passenger Service Representative Carol Byrd takes a break from her duties to have dinner in the *Broadway*'s twin-unit diner on New Year's Eve 1972.—*Three photos, Mike Schafer*

ABOVE: A quartet of F-units, all but one in Amtrak paint (the loner still clad in SP gray and red), wheel a detour westbound *Sunset Limited* through Klondike, Calif., on Santa Fe rails on May 26, 1974. Ex-Santa Fe Hi-Level coaches were regulars on Nos. 1 and 2 for a time, and were mixed with single-level cars (diner, lounge and sleepers) through use of a Hi-Level transition coach.

and revived train names, forever squashing the rumor that the new Amtrak—whose personnel included a fair number of former-airline people—was going to adopt the airline practice of simply numbering all services. Back again were such time-honored monikers as *National Limited* (New York-Kansas City), *Wolverine* (Chicago-Detroit), *Hiawatha* (Chicago-Twin Cities), *Prairie State* (Milwaukee-St. Louis), *Florida Special* (New York-Miami), *City of San Francisco* (Chicago-Oakland) and a whole host of former New Haven names for the Northeast Corridor: *Merchants Limited*, *Bay State*, *Colonial*, *Senator*, *Patriot* and *Yankee Clipper*. Elsewhere, brand-new names appeared: *North Coast Hiawatha* (for the new Chicago-Seattle service that had debuted on June 5 as nameless Nos. 9 and 10), *Coast Starlight/Daylight* (Seattle-San Diego), *Puget Sound* (Seattle-Portland), *Illinois Zephyr* (Chicago-West Quincy, Mo.) and *Saint Clair* (Chicago-Detroit).

The new timetable did introduce some

Stalwart GG1's, most of them built in the 1930's for (and by) the Pennsylvania Railroad, remained the mainstay locomotive for Northeast Corridor electric operations during most of Amtrak's first decade. By the time "G" 926 was photographed at Morrisville, Pa., in April 1973 on a corridor run made up of ex-New Haven "American Flyer" coaches, it had traded its somber Penn Central black-and-white livery for this unique red-snout scheme. W. C. Fields would have been happy.—*Bob Wilt*

airline-style formats, such as the "quick-reference" section between major cities and the use of symbols to denote on-board services. And because the new folders were entirely designed in-house, they carried much-more-detailed train information including schedules of non-Amtrak carriers, explanations of equipment accommodations, listing of all passenger stations and even a house ad introducing the slogan that probably best defined Amtrak's hoped-for destiny for the 1970's: "We're making the trains worth traveling again."

THE "RAINBOW ERA" was short-lived. By 1972, an official paint scheme had emerged. NRPC was now contracting with various shop facilities throughout the country to revamp equipment, at least cosmetically if not mechanically, and cars and locomotives were now appearing in the Lippincott & Marguiles image of red, white and blue against stainless steel (Platinum Mist or white on smooth-sided surfaces). By 1974, the color-chaos days of Amtrak were virtually at an end as the carrier assimilated its own image.

On May 1, 1972, another also-brief era emerged, marked by the launching of Amtrak's first all-refurbished train: the "new" *Broadway Limited*, complete with observation car, on-board movies, twin-unit diner and bright new interiors. The period of postwar-style streamliners had returned! Although the new Amtrak scheme was beginning to replace familiar colors like UP Armour Yellow, Pennsy Tuscan Red or Great Northern's orange and green, equipment was still right out of the postwar era: The 1970's were well underway, but throaty E- and F-unit locomotives from the late 1940's and the 1950's still rushed domes, diners and observation cars of the same era from coast to coast.

But even this epoch soon changed. Amtrak went shopping for brand-new equipment and by the end of 1972 had ordered new diesel-electric locomotives from Electro-Motive Division of General Motors and two off-the-shelf (they were actually part of an order placed by French National Railways) turbine-powered trainsets from France. In the early months of 1973, additional locomotives were ordered from General Electric—straight electrics for the Northeast Corridor.

TOP: This December 1973 duck-and-duckling scene at Charlottesville, Va., clearly illustrates that most passengers aboard the *George Washington* were destined to the nation's capital rather than to the Hampton Roads area, served by an elfin split-off train. The Washington and Newport News (Va.) sections have just been separated; on this day, a Chesapeake & Ohio GP9, dome coach and borrowed Western Maryland coach were sufficient to handle the few travelers heading to the Virginia coast. This section was dropped on June 14, 1976.—
Mike Schafer **ABOVE: A victim of track problems in Indiana, the *George/Riley* was subject to numerous delays and reroutes, so much so that timetables carried disclaimers! On Aug. 1, 1974, the train finally found a semi-permanent route through the Hoosier State on the C&O. Westbound 51 is at Richmond, Ind., on Aug. 25, 1974.—***Dave Oroszi*

TOP: The *South Wind* stands at Louisville Union Station in August 1971.—*Mike Schafer* ABOVE: The *Floridian* was another run beleaguered by track problems in Indiana until, on April 27, 1975, it found sanctuary on L&N's former Monon route. In this 1977 scene at Hohman Avenue in Hammond, Ind., southbound 57 has just entered the old Monon and is crossing the Indiana Harbor Belt main line.—*Lou Gerard*

It must be remembered that Amtrak's first two years were possibly its most critical. Recall the July 1, 1973, deadline after which Amtrak could discontinue any trains deemed unsuccessful. The critical date came and went, and though the carrier had made moves to discontinue the Chicago-Miami/St. Petersburg *Floridian*, the death warrant was rescinded. There were no discontinuances (although a state-supported Chicago-Cleveland-New York run had been terminated on Jan. 5, 1972). The last half of fiscal 1972 had shown ridership 12.6 percent higher than during the same period of 1971. Amtrak had reached another milestone: For the first time in more than a quarter century, the decline in rail ridership had finally reversed.

With its position thus solidified a little more, Amtrak could now confidently order its first built-new rolling stock. (Had Amtrak failed and been dismantled, ownership of its new locomotives could simply have been assumed by any number of freight railroads; passenger rolling stock was another matter.) That Amtrak ordered its first locomotive-drawn equipment—57 "Amfleet" cars from Budd—in October 1973 (as well as additional diesel and electric locomotives) was prophetic, as it was this month the U.S. entered its first widely publicized "energy crisis."

As we are beginning to see, Amtrak had many benchmarks during the 1970's, and this pair was particularly significant. The energy crisis, caused by an Arab oil embar-

RIGHT: With their imposing girth and wide red noses, the new EMD SDP40F's became a fixture on Amtrak trains in the mid-1970's. SDP's 610 and 640 head up the northbound *Champion* at Jacksonville, Fla., in December 1975. By this time, most trains were clad in the Amtrak "uniform" of stainless steel or platinum mist with the wide red-and-blue "cigar band" striping.—*David L. Hill* Many classic cars from the 1950's found renewed life on Amtrak, such as ex-Great Northern parlor-observation *Port of Seattle* (**BELOW RIGHT**), built in 1950 for GN's Seattle-Vancouver (B.C.) *International.* The car is shown on the first run of the "new" *Abraham Lincoln* at Chicago Union Station on Oct. 26, 1975. The *Abe* made a triumphant return on that date following a shifting of Turboliner assignments; Turbos had spelled the demise of full diners on the Chicago-St. Louis route, resulting in complaints from state politicians using that corridor.—*Bob Schmidt*

go, suddenly made Americans aware of the importance of alternatives to auto transportation. Soon the passenger train was in the spotlight again, and Amtrak found itself with more passengers than it could handle. The Amfleet order represented a step into the future (or at least into the present) for the American passenger train. New equipment has always been a very marketable commodity for any carrier, on the ground or in the air, and new rail passenger rolling stock was big news in those heady early years of Amtrak.

The energy crisis prompted Congress to provide Amtrak with capital for widescale equipment purchases, thus the early locomotive and equipment orders were expanded upon. For example, the initial order for 57 Amfleet cars grew to nearly 500 cars! New equipment was necessary not only for improved performance and reliability, but also to protect Amtrak's growing system. Throughout most of the 1970's, numerous new routes and trains were added to that skeletal foundation system unveiled at the beginning of the decade (see special section at the end of this chapter).

Along with new routes and equipment came more employees. By the end of Amtrak's first full year in business, 1972, it had but 1,500 employees, mostly clerical and administrative to handle the job of overseeing contract services. By the end of Amtrak's first five years, employment was at nearly 10,000 as Amtrak took a more-direct control on passenger-service operation by hiring its own car attendants, ticket agents, waiters/waitresses, station personnel and the like.

MARK MARCH 1, 1975, as another pivot

point for Amtrak. On that day, Paul Reistrup was named Amtrak's second president. A graduate of West Point Military Academy, Reistrup was a dynamic, youngish railroader who had left his mark in the pre-Amtrak passenger departments of Baltimore & Ohio, Illinois Central and the affiliated B&O/C&O system. Now that NRPC was headed up by a railroader, host railroads could better relate to Amtrak, itself a railroad in the throes of growth. "[Amtrak] is my Vietnam," said the former military man.

One month after Reistrup entered office, Amtrak took over, from Penn Central, the ownership and operation of the former-New York Central Beech Grove Shops near Indianapolis, Ind. It was a small step toward independence and self-sufficiency, and it gave Amtrak a little more control over its destiny (more on this front shortly). Then, on April 2, the day following the Beech Grove acquisition, Amtrak placed an order for 235 Superliners and 200 more Amfleet cars. A little more than a month later, on May 8, 1975, the first group of what was destined to become the standard motive power of Amtrak—the F40PH—was ordered. Clearly, Amtrak was taking steps to bring itself out of infancy.

Which brings us to April 1, 1976—a date that radically changed Amtrak and Northeastern railroading as Conrail (Consolidated Rail Corporation) was born. As a sort of freight version of Amtrak for bankrupt Northeast roads, Conrail faced a monumental task of streamlining and rationalizing a new rail freight system built upon the ashes of Penn Central, Erie Lackawanna, Lehigh Valley, Reading Company, Jersey Central and other bankrupt unfortunates.

For Amtrak, though, April 1, 1976, was truly a day of reckoning as ownership of PC's Northeast Corridor—from Washington to Boston, from New Haven, Conn., to Springfield, Mass., and from Philadelphia to Harrisburg—began to be transferred to Amtrak. (At the same time, Amtrak also acquired a portion of PC's Chicago-Detroit main line, between Porter, Ind., and Kalamazoo, Mich.) For the first time, Amtrak owned its own rights-of-way, track, bridges, tunnels and stations. It was at this point, notes Reistrup, that Amtrak finally began to be taken seriously by the freight railroad community.

Amtrak had entered adolescence, the road to adulthood.

Tracks are back!

In the cavernous waiting room of Great Northern Station in Minneapolis, Amtrak President Paul H. Reistrup welcomes Minnesota state officials, the public and media to the inaugural run of the Minneapolis-Superior (Wis.) *Arrowhead*, a state-supported train. Date: April 15, 1975. Knowing that public awareness is integral to an increasing acceptance of rail travel in general and on new routes and trains in particular, Amtrak makes the most of inaugurals.—*Mike Schafer*

Route expansion, May 1, 1971-May 1, 1976

If crystal balls were real, students of the passenger train during the 1960's probably wouldn't have believed them anyway. The *Montrealer*, lost in 1966, returning to the rails in 1972? No way. The *Capitol Limited*—whose last run on April 30, 1971, saddened veteran riders from Chicago to Washington—back again in 1981? Couldn't happen. A reinstatement of a descendant of UP's famed *City of Portland* across Wyoming in 1991? Uh-uh.

But, after the initial swath discontinuances that came with the start of Amtrak, new routes and trains indeed came back. Soon, an event that rail advocates of the 1960's thought they'd never see again became commonplace: the train inaugural.

Basically, there are four scenarios whereby trains and/or routes could or can be added to the basic Amtrak network. First and most common, a state can introduce new service through provision 403(b) in the Amtrak Act by picking up a percentage of the losses. Second, with the Amtrak Improvement Act of 1973, Congress began mandating NRPC to introduce one "experimental" route each year. Third, political pressure has on occasion motivated Amtrak to implement new services (sometimes the distinction between items 2 and 3 became blurred). Fourth, Amtrak can initiate a new route or train at its own discretion.

Other inducements prevail as well. For example, Congress in June 1972 simply appropriated $2 million for the startup of three international trains. And, operation-related situations occasionally have resulted in new routes, if not new trains.

Additions to the Amtrak system started almost right away, and most since then have been state-sponsored (403(b)). Illinois and New York top the list of states most active in the program, with Michigan, Califor-

One of Amtrak's most well-remembered but now dearly departed trains was the *North Coast Hiawatha*, added to the basic system on June 5, 1971. Initially a Minneapolis-Spokane operation that was combined with the *Empire Builder* east and west of those cities, the *North Coast* eventually became a completely separate entity. Its scenic trip along the routes of its predecessors, Northern Pacific's *North Coast Limited* and Milwaukee Road's *Morning Hiawatha*, made it a popular choice for travelers destined to the Pacific Northwest, many of whom felt the scenery was superior to that of the *Empire Builder* route. This view of westbound train 9 near Logan, Mont., on June 27, 1976, provides some convincing evidence of that point. Alas, the *NCH* met an untimely demise in 1979.—*Larry Zeutschel*

nia and Pennsylvania in hot pursuit. Other states that have or have had 403(b) trains include Missouri, Minnesota, North Carolina, Alabama, Wisconsin, Mississippi, Louisiana, Oregon, Florida and Massachusetts.

The Congressionally mandated "experimental" provision ended in 1977 since it became evident that it was not always in the best interests to force Amtrak to introduce a new train every year.

The political motivation to add new services remains, but politicans today are more aware of the financial restrictions and equipment constraints facing Amtrak with such endeavors.

Amtrak itself continues to examine potential new routes and trains, following self-imposed strict guidelines regarding cost recovery and targeted revenues. New trains and routes are expected to cover their fully allocated costs within a reasonable period

The "Tracks are Back" sections at the end of this and the following two chapters highlight some of the new routes introduced during the time frame of these three chapters.

The State of Massachusetts introduced Boston-New Haven service via Worcester and Springfield, Mass.—the Inland Route—on May 17, 1971. In this view from the cab of Penn Central freight NS-5 in June 1974, the westbound *Bay State* approaches the depot at Thompsonville, Conn. Former-New Haven *Roger Williams* Rail Diesel Car 27 leads a standard RDC. The *Bay State* was discontinued on March 1, 1975, but it runs again today as a regular (i.e., non-403(b)) Amtrak train.—*Scott Hartley*

Loping through Carondolet Park near St. Louis in the spring of 1976 is the *Inter-American*, the third train in the "international" series (after the *Pacific International* and *Montrealer*). As inaugurated on Jan. 28, 1973, it was entirely an intra-state Texas train, running between Fort Worth and Laredo by way of San Antonio over Santa Fe (Fort Worth-Milano) and Missouri Pacific (Milano-Laredo) tracks; later, Katy tracks were used between Taylor and Temple. Unlike the first two international trains, the *Inter-American* never crossed the border into Mexico, although through service to Mexico City was considered. Eventually the run was expanded to St. Louis and Chicago, then cut back from Laredo to San Antonio. Overall, *Inter-American* operations provided the base for what is today's *Texas Eagle*.—*Mike Schafer*

On Sept. 8, 1971, the *West Virginian* began service between Washington and Parkersburg, W.Va. This controversial train was inspired by powerful West Virginia Congressman Harley Staggers—who at the time happened to be chairman of the House Commerce Committee, which had budgetary control over the fledgling Amtrak. On Jan. 16, 1972, it became the *Potomac Special*, and on or about this date a United Aircraft TurboTrain was assigned to the route, which only added fuel to the controversy over the true necessity of the run. "Harley's Hornet," as it was informally known, is shown at Parkersburg in April 1973.—*Mike Schafer*

Tracks are back!

LEFT: Dawn is gaining a foothold on White River Junction, Vt., as the tardy northbound inaugural *Montrealer* halts for festivities on Sept. 30, 1972. The *Montrealer/Washingtonian* was the second of three Congressionally mandated international runs and was also the first Amtrak train staffed by Amtrak employees rather than contracted railroad personnel. ABOVE: Departure board at Montreal.—*Both photos, Mike Schafer*

Trains 347 and 348, the *Illinois Zephyr*, between Chicago and West Quincy, Mo., was the first and possibly most successful of many 403(b) operations for Illinois. The "Baby Zephyr," as it has become known locally (it shares part of its route with the *California Zephyr*), follows Burlington Northern's ex-Chicago, Burlington & Quincy Omaha and Kansas City mains across the state, hitting a number of college towns—hence the secret to its success.—*Joe McMillan*

On Oct. 31, 1974, the New York-Buffalo *Empire State Express* was extended west to Detroit via Penn Central's ex-NYC line through southern Ontario. Although the *Express* now crossed the border—twice—the train was "sealed" while passing through Canada and so technically was not an international train. This view on Oct. 30, 1974, shows the inaugural special at Buffalo, curiously with a name plate carrying a moniker the train would not actually gain until Oct. 29, 1978.—*Ken Kraemer*

Tracks are back!

EFFECTIVE FEBRUARY 14, 1974

Amtrak

NEW!

The Black Hawk

CHICAGO — ROCKFORD — DUBUQUE

Read Down (Central Daylight Time) Read Up

371		←Train Number→	370	372
Black Hawk		←Train Name→	Black Hawk	Black Hawk
Daily		←Frequency of Operation→	Mo thru Sa (except Holidays)	Su and Holidays
	Miles	←Type of Service→		
6 20 p	0	Dp.........CHICAGO, IL.........Ar	10 25 a	12 00 n
7 15 p	18	..............Elmhurst......⊕......	9 20 a	10 55 a
8 25 p	85	.............ROCKFORD............	8 10 a	9 45 a
8 55 p	113	..............Freeport......⊕......	7 40 a	9 15 a
10 07 p	164	...............Galena.......⊕......	6 27 a	8 02 a
10 36 p	180	..........East Dubuque, IL..⊕......	6 02 a	7 37 a
10 50 p	182	Ar.........DUBUQUE, IA........Dp	5 55 a	7 30 a

Holidays—Feb. 18, May 27, July 4 and Sept. 2.

ABOVE: The *Black Hawk* was a Valentine's Day (1974) present to northern Illinois and yet another entry in Illinois' growing fleet of 403(b) runs. The Chicago-Dubuque train, which initially was assigned Budd Rail Diesel Cars (RDC's), followed Illinois Central Gulf's western main line through the state's second-largest city, Rockford, on a schedule not unlike that of Illinois Central's pre-Amtrak streamliner *Land O'Corn* over the same route. The eastbound *Black Hawk* is at the former-IC depot in Rockford shortly after its debut.—*Mike Schafer*

A second Montreal train in the form of a day run from New York via Albany/Rensselaer, N.Y., came with the introduction of the *Adirondack* on Aug. 6, 1974. The 403(b) operation was jealously guarded by its host railroad, the fabled Delaware & Hudson, which for a while insisted on providing its own motive power and rolling stock, all rehabilitated by the State of New York, the train's sponsor. With its Alco PA locomotives and its blue-and-yellow cars, the *Adirondack* of the 1970's looked much like its pre-Amtrak predecessor, D&H's *Laurentian.* This vestibule view catches the *Adirondack* on Aug. 30, 1976, with an Amtrak dome (later, D&H supplied a borrowed Canadian Pacific dome) that ran north of Albany/Rensselaer.—*Scott Hartley*

<u>ABOVE:</u> The Oakland-Bakersfield *San Joaquin* was a California 403(b) proposition that began on March 5, 1974; the train is reminiscent of Southern Pacific's *San Joaquin Daylight* which in part plied the same route in pre-Amtrak days; in fact, ex-SP locomotives and cars were commonplace in the train's early years. Westbound No. 711 is at San Pablo Bay near Martinez, Calif., on July 9, 1975.—*Bob Wilt* <u>BELOW RIGHT:</u> Michigan's first 403(b) endeavor was the *Blue Water*, which began connecting Chicago and Port Huron, Mich. (shown) on Sept. 15, 1974, using Penn Central's line to Battle Creek, Mich., thence Grand Trunk Western to Port Huron. The *Blue Water* provided the foundation for today's Chicago-Toronto *International.*—*Mike Schafer* <u>BELOW LEFT:</u> One of the biggest success stories for new trains was the Oct. 31, 1975, unveiling of the new Chicago-New York/Boston *Lake Shore Limited.* Inaugural ceremonies drew huge crowds and the first train even rated a special menu.—*Collection of Mike Schafer*

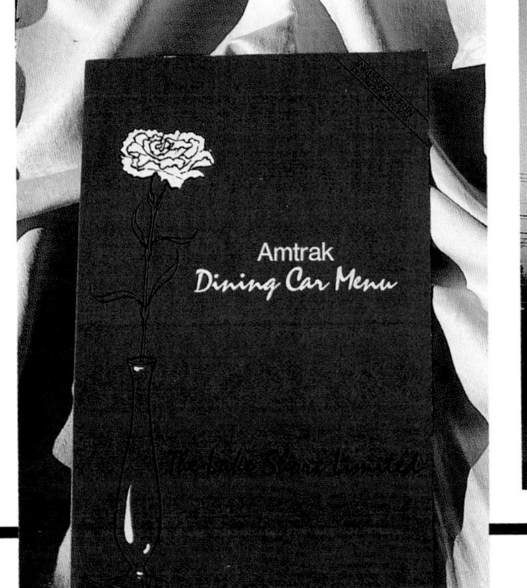

Two of the most-notable points regarding Amtrak's "adolescence"—its second five years—were (1) the acquisition and deployment of large quantities of new equipment, and (2) the purchase of the Northeast Corridor and other properties from Penn Central. ABOVE: New Amfleet rolling stock and F40 locomotives were ferried in large blocks to West Coast assignments; this assemblage—led by a soon-to-be-ill-fated SDP40F, no less—heads through Cajon Pass on the Santa Fe near Alray, Calif., on April 30, 1976, with equipment destined for *San Diegan* assignments.— *Steve Patterson* **Later in the decade came the Superliners (RIGHT).—***Ken Rattenne*

3/Autonomy and adolescence

1976-1981: AMTRAK COMES OF AGE

April 1, 1976, may have been the most important day in Amtrak's life. No foolin'.

With Amtrak's huge acquisition of property from Penn Central (621 miles) on that date, as PC and several other bankrupt Northeast carriers vanished into Conrail, the NRPC went from being a contract agency to a real railroad. Overnight.

As then-Amtrak President Paul Reistrup noted, it was at this point American railroads finally began to take Amtrak seriously. The purchase may have been the most-significant of Reistrup's many accomplishments during his relatively short term as NRPC's leader. At the time, DOT Secretary William Coleman (under then-U.S. President Gerald R. Ford) was against Amtrak owning anything, much less there being an Amtrak to begin with. But Amtrak's board of directors approved the NEC purchase as well as PC's Porter (Ind.)-Kalamazoo (Mich.) line, and Amtrak was on its way up the corporate ladder.

The purchase was made possible by the passage of the Regional Rail Reorganization ("Three-R") Act in 1973 and the Railroad Revitalization and Regulatory Reform Act ("Four-R") Act in 1976. Without those two bills, Amtrak would not have had the authority to make property acquisitions.

RIGHT: The purchase of the Northeast Corridor from Penn Central on April 1, 1976, signaled the beginning of a new era for Amtrak. Now, NRPC was a real railroad, with a considerable amount of property and a greatly expanded employee base. At the start of this period, the electrified portions of the NEC were still in the domain of 1960's-era *Metroliners* and the unforgettable GG1 electrics, the latter breed dating from the 1930's. Both types of equipment meet on a curve near Newark, N.J., in 1981.—*Don Jilson* **BELOW RIGHT:** Overshadowed by the purchase of NEC properties, a portion of PC's Chicago-Detroit route—nearly 100 miles, from Porter, Ind., to Kalamazoo, Mich.—also went to Amtrak on April 1, 1976. Amtrak subsequently upgraded the line with welded rail and improved signaling, and revamped the Michigan City "Drawbridge" interlocking tower and swing span, here being "load tested" by the Detroit-bound *Wolverine.*—*J. P. Baukus Jr.*

On the heels of the NEC purchase came the Northeast Corridor Improvement Project (NECIP), which began on March 31, 1977. In this nine-year program, Congress authorized the spending of $2.5 billion to upgrade track and signaling to permit 125 mph operation, and to rebuild and renovate terminal facilities.

Other stars were lining up for the company, which during its first five years had received mixed reviews from public and politicians alike. Unreliable equipment had undermined the upbeat promotions and new services Amtrak had bannered early in the 1970's, but in late 1975 new Budd Amfleet equipment—the first three groups of which were ordered during the Lewis administration—began to come on line. Although intended mainly for service in the Northeast Corridor, Amfleet soon found its way into other routes as well as Amtrak struggled to keep up with the demands brought on by unreliable equipment all over the system. (Not until 1990 would most of the Amfleet I cars finally congregate on the NEC as originally planned!)

Only a few days after the big purchase from Penn Central, Amtrak's first batch of new F40PH locomotives began entering service, and, by the end of 1976, Turboliners built by Rohr Corporation in Chula Vista, Calif., began augmenting the equipment roster. Meanwhile, additional orders for Superliner equipment boosted the original April 1975 order for 235 cars to 249 (on July 29, 1976) and then to 284 (on Nov. 24, 1976). The F40's, Rohr Turbos and Amfleet cars together with locomotives and French-built Turboliners acquired in the early 1970's provided a new level of reli-

Winters of the late 1970's were relentless on Amtrak, then mostly still a steam-heated operation. LEFT: The Chicago-bound *Illinois Zephyr* mushing through Hinsdale, Ill., on New Year's Eve day 1978 is lucky it isn't snowbound as well.—*Don Crimmin* **BELOW: Don't let the drumhead on this "obs-sicle"-lounge fool you; it's actually a nearly frozen *Inter-American* about to slog out of Chicago on Dec. 31, 1976. The car didn't warm up 'til Little Rock.**—*Bob Schmidt*

able, comfortable service for Amtrak of the late 1970's. (The final vehicles of the 492-car Amfleet I order were delivered on June 9, 1977.)

Amtrak would need the reliability more than expected. With the late 1970's came some of the most brutal winters of recent history. Amfleet-equipped trains fared well, but all long-distance services were still in the domain of steam-heated rolling stock—and were the primary victims of a particularly nasty winter lashing in January 1977. On the 19th of that month, most Amtrak service in the central U.S. was suspended and did not return to normal until March of that year. So bad was the cold, that whole trains of frozen cars were moved to New Orleans from Chicago for thawing and repair.

This harrowing winter experience probably played instrumental in another landmark program of the Reistrup era: the conversion of Amtrak's conventional passenger rolling stock to all-electric climate control. With minor exceptions, most of the cars Amtrak had inherited from other railroads were heated by a steam boiler in the train's diesel or electric locomotive(s), a vestige from propulsion of an earlier era. Though rudimentary train lighting was often provided by a low-voltage (30-volt d.c.) line from the locomotive, power-hun-

Alleged tracking problems with SDP40F locomotives compounded Amtrak woes when some railroads slapped speed restrictions on the big EMD's. One stopgap remedy was for Amtrak to lease five Southern F-units, assigning them to the Seattle-Portland Burlington Northern segment of the *Coast Starlight* so that schedules could be maintained. At Black River, Wash., on June 26, 1977, a BN Alco Century 425 assists two SR units and two Amtrak E9's on the northbound *Starlight*.—*T. O. Repp*

gry air-conditioning units relied on individual battery/generator systems on each car. Power for climate operation and lighting on Amfleet cars, on the other hand, was from a single source, a head-end power (HEP) generator located either in the locomotive or specially equipped power car (usually a converted baggage car).

Steam heating worked well during railroading's Age of Steam, but the superiority of HEP for diesel-era operations was a point driven home by the winter of 1976-77. The few trains that could operate during the crisis period were those that were HEP-equipped. With lessons so learned, Amtrak on May 26, 1977, initiated a massive program at Beech Grove Shops near Indianapolis to convert selected conventional rolling stock to HEP along with a complete rebuilding. Thus was born (or reborn, as the case may be) the "Heritage Fleet," and during the next five years, the phase-in of Heritage equipment became an ongoing operation. Consequently, Amtrak's rolling-stock reliability factor increased sharply; unfortunately, the down side of this was that the HEP program actually reduced the number of cars available for service, since budgetary constraints limited the number of cars to be converted.

More news on the equipment front during the Reistrup administration centered on the Northeast Corridor, where in October 1976 Amtrak initiated testing of a Swedish-design high-speed electric locomotive; nearly a year later, on Sept. 28, 1977, Amtrak ordered eight new electrics—designated AEM7's—based on the design of that Swedish unit, to be built in the U.S. under license by Electro-Motive and Budd Company. The Northeast Corridor was about to be revolutionized.

Other news on matters locomotive in 1977 was not so encouraging: A rash of derailments involving Amtrak's 150 SDP40F locomotives rendered them highly suspect. The evidence seemed ambiguous, but it was enough for some roads—notably Burlington Northern and Chessie System—to ban the units (or severely restrict their speed), which threw Amtrak on-time performance into turmoil. To this day, the problems remain only alleged, but Amtrak had little choice but to prematurely retire the SDP's and subsequently scrapped, sold (mostly to Santa Fe for freight service) or traded them into builder EMD, with many of the internal parts used in new F40's.

RIGHT: In 1974-75, Amtrak rebuilt five E-units with head end power. They were intended to work with the 1958-built long-distance bilevel coaches Amtrak had purchased from Chicago & North Western—pioneer HEP cars constructed by Pullman-Standard for *400* service (*Flambeau 400, Peninsula 400*, etc.). More often than not, they wound up powering new Amfleet consists out of Chicago. The five, renumbered 495-499 in 1977, spent their last years in Northeast Corridor service, mostly east of New Haven. The 498 is at Providence, R.I., with the westbound *Beacon Hill* on Oct. 22, 1980.—*David P. Oroszi* **BELOW: During the latter half of the 1970's, Amtrak relied on rebuilt Geeps leased from Precision National Corp. to assist in yard and shop assignments. It's a pleasant May afternoon in Chicago in 1977 as PNC Geep 1508 jockeys two Amfleet consists across South Branch lift bridge. Eventually, Amtrak purchased units from PNC.**—*Steve Smedley*

ABOVE: The *Floridian* vacated Louisville Union Station on Nov. 1, 1976, in favor of using Auto-Train's Louisville terminal when Amtrak and A-T began joint operation between Louisville and Sanford, Fla. The cost-saving measure became moot when A-T's Midwest-Florida service ended on Sept. 8, 1977. Amtrak continued to use the A-T facility until the *Floridian* itself succumbed, in October 1979.—*Mike Schafer* **ABOVE RIGHT:** Amtrak more than doubled its Turboliner fleet in 1976 when it took delivery of seven turbo trainsets from Rohr Corp. of Chula Vista (San Diego), Calif. Upstate New York routes have been home to the Rohr turbos since delivery, so this view of one of the trains being ferried eastward on Cajon Pass in Southern California shows an uncommon environment for the speedsters.—*Joe McMillan*

Reistrup's career at Amtrak was itself about to hit some bad track after President James Earl Carter was sworn into office in January 1977. Carter's hard-line stance on Amtrak's appropriation for fiscal 1978 was a flat $500 million; Amtrak had requested $534.1 million. An unsympathetic Congress came in with only $488.5 million. Reistrup's eternal optimism was probably bruised, for he had just unveiled a five-year (1978-1982) corporate development planned that called for $4.5 billion in federal monies. The plan called for new equipment and facilities, including stations, and—given the advantage of hindsight—it's interesting to note some of the other points in the plan, among them:

- Development of an a.c. traction motor applicable for diesels or electric locomotives. [Experimental a.c. traction-motor diesels entered service on Amtrak in 1987.]
- Development of non-NEC corridors, particularly Los Angeles-San Diego and Chicago-Detroit [both corridors today are highly successful], but also the likes of Pittsburgh-Cleveland and Chicago-Madison (Wis.). [Interestingly, non-corridor service began between Pittsburgh and Cleveland in 1990, and in spring 1991 a test train operated on a portion of a Chicago-Madison route.]
- Examination of "potential" longer-haul

Though always trying to emphasize a modern image, Amtrak is not ashamed of its heritage. In 1977, the carrier cooperated with a group called "Friends of the GG1" in restoring one of its G's, No. 4935, to the classic Brunswick green pinstripe scheme of the late, great Pennsylvania Railroad. The freshly painted motor glides through Morrisville, Pa., on its inaugural run on May 15, 1977. The Raymond Loewy-styled electric is now on permanent display under the trainshed of the restored (ex-PRR) Harrisburg Amtrak depot.—*Bob Wilt*

routes including Mobile-New Orleans and Atlanta-Montgomery, Ala. [Successful though short-lived Mobile-New Orleans service began in 1984, and resumption is now being studied using idle *City of New Orleans* equipment; also, today there is direct service between Atlanta and Montgomery.]

Many advocates saw Reistrup's departure from Amtrak on May 31, 1978, as a premature conclusion to a successful career directing passenger operations. The following day, Alan S. Boyd became NRPC's third president.

While Reistrup brought sorely needed railroad expertise to Amtrak, Alan Boyd balanced the Reistrup years with a good dose of politician—another very necessary qualification for any president of Amtrak during the first two decades. Boyd did have railroad experience, though, having served as president of Illinois Central (during Amtrak's birth, no less) and the country's first Secretary of Transportation. But mainly he was well tied in with political circles, and Amtrak was going to need the help of a skilled politician to survive into the 1980's.

During the early months of Boyd's presidency, the first Superliners—perhaps Reistrup's best legacy—arrived on the property, on Oct. 27, 1978, following a long and painful gestation period. (Initial planning for the cars actually began during the Lewis years; delivery probably would have been during Reistrup's waning months had it not been for delays relating to design changes and a strike at Pullman-Standard).

The importance of the Superliner purchase can not be underestimated, and it represents yet another benchmark in Amtrak's development. The new bilevels ushered in an unprecedented new high level (pun intended) of cost-effectiveness and reliability in long-distance operations. The

Text continued on page 38

Superliners changed the face of Amtrak long-distance trains. TOP: The first Superliner *Empire Builder* at the then-new Midway Station in St. Paul on Oct. 28, 1979, shows a whole new look to passenger railroading in America. ABOVE: Earlier in the month at Chicago Union Station, Amtrak President Alan Boyd addressed media and guests about to board a special Superliner press run.—*Both photos, Mike Schafer*

Casualties of the battlefield

The only major visible losses Amtrak has sustained in its multitude of confrontations in the political arena were the swath of train-offs that occurred in October 1979. The bloodbath was the result of a hostile Department of Transportation, under the James Earl Carter administration, pushing for Amtrak curtailment; a somewhat unsympathetic Congress at the time applied an evalutation criteria to all routes. The unfortunate results were the loss of five well-remembered major long-haul trains, illustrated here.

TOP: Always in trouble for something—usually extreme lateness, detours and equipment failures (and consequently, a history of dwindling patronage)—the New York/Washington-Kansas City *National Limited* was an easy target. On Feb. 20, 1978, the westbound *National* rolls past the skyline of Dayton, Ohio. The *National*'s irony? Not long before the end, its performance was improving account of newly assigned HEP equipment and upgraded track.—*R. D. Acton*
RIGHT: One of the most-painful losses of all was the *North Coast Hiawatha*, a train which had many devotees. A glistening *NCH* is ready to highball Seattle on Jan. 17, 1975.—*T. O. Repp*

The demise of the Chicago-Fort Worth/Dallas-Houston *Lone Star* embittered Oklahomans, whose state on Oct. 8, 1979, became bereft of rail passenger service. The train, shown southbound at Oklahoma City on March 5, 1978, was in fact Amtrak's version of Santa Fe's pre-Amtrak *Texas Chief*. When the regular *Lone Star* ended on Oct. 1, 1979, a court order kept a surrogate service going for an additional week in the form of a Newton (Kan.)-Fort Worth train connecting to and from the *Southwest Limited* at Newton. Since then, there have been several unsuccessful grass-roots efforts to restore service to Oklahoma, although Amtrak of late has hinted about doing so.—*Mike Blaszak*

ABOVE: The southbound *Floridian* trundles down the street toward its station stop at Clearwater, Fla., on Jan 28, 1978. The loss of this train left a critical gap in the Amtrak network, the Midwest-Florida travel market being one of the strongest in the U.S. for any travel mode. A resumption by the mid-1990's looks promising, however.—*Denis Connell* RIGHT: Another Florida-liner lost in the shuffle was the New York-St. Pete *Champion*, shown northbound at Callahan, Fla., in the mid-1970's.—*Dave Hill*

TOP: The close of Amtrak's first decade also meant the end of some of the traditional trappings of U.S passenger-train operations of the 1940's, 1950's and 1960's. The E-unit, for example, was in its twilight, both literally and figuratively in this view of the westbound *Lake Shore Limited* at Oscawanna, N.Y., on the evening of July 25, 1979. Shortly, the *Lake Shore* would become the first major single-level long-distance train to be converted to rebuilt Heritage equipment.—*Alan Tillotson* ABOVE: A Heritage *Lake Shore* behind F40s swoops in on Hammond, Ind. Consist also includes new Amfleet II cars.—*Mike Schafer*

Superliners proved to be extremely popular with the traveling public (if not rail aficionados who mourned the subsequent loss of the Vista-Dome experience), and they gave Amtrak a new tool for marketing. Even W. Graham Claytor, Amtrak's president as of its 20th birthday, stated that Western long-haul service would not have survived to the extent it had in 1991 without Superliners, crowning the statement with an order for 140 more, slated for a 1993 delivery.

The *Empire Builder* was the first long-distance train to go Superliner, on Oct. 28, 1979. That upbeat event helped offset one of Amtrak's major setbacks which occurred earlier that month—the wholesale discontinuance of five long-distance trains: the *National Limited* (New York/Washington-Kansas City), the *North Coast Hiawatha* (Chicago-Seattle via Butte, Mont.), the *Lone Star* (Chicago-Oklahoma City-Houston), the *Champion* (New York-St. Petersburg) and, arguably the most controversial, the *Floridian* (Chicago-Miami/St. Pete). Also cut was the *Hilltopper*, a medium-haul day train on a New York-Catlettsburg, Ky., run.

Reistrup had been busy beefing up Amtrak's physical plant during his term; now, Boyd was busy saving Reistrup's work from wanton destruction by a hostile DOT, lead by President Carter-appointed Brock Adams. As the nation entered its second major energy crisis in 1979 and Amtrak ridership was at an all-time high (21-plus million), DOT blithely presented a plan to slash Amtrak by 43 percent. Congressional support for the carrier at the time was also weak, and under pressure from Congress, Amtrak was required to apply a route-evaluation criteria to all routes as a means of controlling costs and losses. The trains so named had failed to meet the criteria and were discontinued on or shortly after Oct. 1, 1979. The good news (besides the arrival of those Superliners) was that most of the Amtrak system did meet specifications and remained intact. In fact, by the end of the month there was actually a bit of re-expansion with the inauguration of the Ogden-Los Angeles *Desert Wind*. Also, the *Inter-American* gained a Temple (Texas)-Houston leg to offset the loss of the *Lone*

Star, while Missouri funded an extension of the Chicago-St. Louis *Ann Rutledge* to Kansas City to cover the St. Louis-K.C. portion of the *National*'s route.

Events during 1980 also tempered the losses of October 1979; in particular, a number of new services appeared, most of them through state cooperation (see special section at the end of this chapter on new routes and trains 1976-1981). In February 1980 came the most-significant equipment order placed during the Boyd years, that of 150 "second-generation" Amfleet cars—Amfleet II—primarily for service on Eastern long-hauls. Amfleet II would be the only major rolling stock purchase during the Boyd years, which were more associated with the introduction of all-electric (HEP) Heritage Fleet trains—in reality a product of Reistrup's leadership. On May 9, 1980, the first new AEM7 electric entered revenue service on *Metroliner* train 108 out of Washington.

Boyd had his hands full just with the political end of things, and the situation did not necessarily get better with President Carter's exit from office in January 1981. In the 1950's, Hollywood actor Ronald Reagan had touted train travel in Union Pacific ads that showed him feasting in a dome diner; but as U.S. president, Reagan felt passenger trains were simply not a priority. Actually, it was his budget director, David Stockman, who seemed preoccupied with feasting on Amtrak, singling it out as a sort of fatted calf that had reaped the benefits of the taxpayer feed trough. Ax figuratively in hand, Stockman led Amtrak out behind the barn with intentions of solving the budget deficit problem. Fortunately, Congress was in the mood for chicken that night.

The new administration also included a new DOT secretary, Drew Lewis. The Reagan appointee favored a very substantial reduction in Amtrak, stating that it "had grown like Topsy," and that it was "an economic disaster." At the same time, Budget Director David Stockman pushed a plan to change Amtrak's ground rules for achieving a satisfactory cost/revenue ratio. He proposed that Amtrak reach an 80 percent ratio by 1985; i.e., 80 percent of NRPC's total operating expenses were to covered by revenues. That Amtrak reached this figure in 1991 shows that the goal itself was not unreasonable—only the time in which it could be accomplished. Fortunately, nothing came of Stockman's proposal, and throughout Amtrak's second decade, Congress was usually pretty guarded of its rail passenger system.

In February 1981, Amtrak President Alan Boyd presented a budget for FY82 of $716 million in operating funds and $254 million in capital spending; total: $970 million, a slight reduction from what Amtrak received the previous year. Such a reduction would not come without some bitter medicine: Boyd said the Chicago-Washington *Cardinal* and the Cincinnati-Washington *Shenandoah* would probably have to go, and that the *Inter-American* would have to be cut to triweekly south of St. Louis, with the Houston and Laredo legs dropped altogether. Further, local services such as Chicago-Valparaiso (Ind.) and New York-Philadelphia would be cut unless support came from local agencies.

Reagan was on a crusade—rightfully so, many will maintain—to cut spending and deficits in general, and the national

Two trains of the late 1970's whose lives intertwined. . . TOP: The *Mountaineer* lopes through coal-mining country at Glen Lyn, Va., in April 1975; in the background above the New River is the abandoned Virginian Railway main line.—*Mike Schafer* **The *Mountaineer* was another failed DOT experiment which on June 1, 1977, was restructured into a Washington-Catlettsburg (Ky.) run, the *Hilltopper* (ABOVE). That train operated on the Richmond, Fredericksburg & Potomac from D.C. to Richmond, Va., where it was wyed and hauled backward over the Seaboard Coast Line to Petersburg, Va., so as to be properly positioned for the track connection there to enter the Norfolk & Western. On an October afternoon in 1977, the westbound '*Topper* scoots through Centralia, Va., behind an RF&P GP7; the Amtrak GE P30 on the rear will head the train west of Petersburg.**—*Dale Jacobson*

debt in particular. The White House countered Boyd's funding request with a $613 million budget, to which Amtrak responded it would probably have to shut down everything outside the Northeast Corridor, and that large amounts would have to be spent simply on labor protection.

Boyd countered with a compromise budget of $853 million and later with a proposal for a multi-year contract with Congress so as to end the energy-draining year-to-year funding crisis—energy better spent maintaining, building and improving a national rail passenger system. The multi-year contract idea fell by the right-of-way when Boyd followed up with another eye-opening overture: No subsidies for sort-term avoidable costs by 1985, with the government supplying only capital and overhead monies after that date.

Despite lurking shadows, a resolute Amtrak—under the tenacious, unfaltering leadership of Alan S. Boyd—celebrated its tenth anniversary on May 1, 1981. The company had achieved a remarkable position in its first ten years: It had become a recognized name in U.S. transportation; it deployed a youthful (or heavily rebuilt) fleet of locomotives and rolling stock; it owned more than 600 miles of track and rights-of-way as well as numerous other properties; and its trains were full and popular. More than 20 million people rode U.S. intercity trains in 1981, some 4 million more than in Amtrak's first year.

Amtrak stood at the brink of a new decade, one fraught with ongoing budget battles, but with a silver lining of new achievements and improved stability. During its tenth year, Amtrak revenue-to-expense ratio was 48 percent. In ten more years, this would rise to 80 percent—a remarkable achievement that serves as the heart of the next chapter.

Ticket counter at Chicago Union Station in the mid-1970's.—*Mike Schafer*

Tracks are back!

Route expansion, May 1, 1976-May 1, 1981

Despite the increasing controversy over Amtrak among federal officials during the late 1970's, as well as a significant loss of selected trains and routes in 1977 and 1979 due to funding and budgetary constraints, new trains and services continued to go into action during the corporation's second five years. Some of the new runs became steadfast performers that would be an integral part of Amtrak's second decade, while a few others experienced a nova-like lifespan, dying out after only a short time in the limelight. Some of the notables of the period are illustrated herein.

The Washington-Cincinnati *Shenandoah* was the abbreviated result of a Washington-Cincinnati-St. Louis-Kansas City-Denver experimental route so designated by U.S. DOT in 1974. Track problems and freight traffic congestions doomed the wandering run—dubbed "Week of Wheels" by some, playing on an Amtrak car-rental promotion of the period—before it was ever launched. Instead, the *Shenandoah* was born, on Oct. 31, 1976, operating over the B&O and connecting to and from the *Cardinal* at Cincinnati, where it is shown in July 1978.—*R. D. Acton*

ABOVE LEFT: The New York-Toronto *Maple Leaf* added another international connection on April 26, 1981. Private car Lehigh Valley 353 brought style to ceremonies at Toronto Union Station.—*Don Jilson* ABOVE: Through cooperation with the Toledo, Peoria & Western, Amtrak found an unusual path to Peoria for its *Prairie Marksman*, which made its first run out of Chicago on Aug. 9, 1980. Illinois's fifth 403(b) train followed a through passenger routing that hadn't been used since 1927: Chicago-Chenoa on Illinois Central Gulf (ex-Alton) and Chenoa-East Peoria on TP&W.—*Mike Schafer* LEFT: Oregon got into the 403(b) act with its double-daily *Willamette Valley* runs on SP between Portland and Eugene. The first northbound train is near Canby on Aug. 3, 1980.—*Keith Wilhite* BELOW: Among the most important of the new guard were the *Pioneer* (Salt Lake City-Seattle), starting on June 7, 1977, and its soon-to-be companion train, the Ogden-L.A. *Desert Wind*, (shown at Cajon Pass in March 1980) which began on Oct. 28, 1979.—*Ken Rattenne*

For the United States, the 1980's spelled record prosperity and growth, for people as well as industries and cities. Amtrak, too, flourished as it struggled to become a respectable, modern force in American transportation. Even in car-concious California, rail travel became "in." Los Angeles looms above a departing *San Diegan* in May 1991.—*David C. Crammer*

4/The struggle for stability

1981-1991: A DECADE OF FINE TUNING

The Amtrak of May 1, 1981, was radically different than that of newborn NRPC ten years earlier. The carrier had its own distinctive image, character and modus operandi: Superliner transcons were the hallmark of Western rail travel; for most long-distance travelers east and south of Chicago, Heritage Fleet trains—where tradition and state-of-the-art had been melded into one—were the mainstay. On corridors and medium-haul routes, clientele were delivered to their destinations in comfortable Turboliners or in Amfleet equipment powered by speedy electric locomotives or the ever-familiar F40. Computer reservations were the norm, and Amtrak's red/white/blue motif and logo had become well-recognized symbols of a once-forgotten travel mode.

Now, fast-forward ten years to May 1, 1991. Outwardly and overall, Amtrak pretty much looks the same. Did anything really happen in the last decade? You bet! But much of the change was internal.

If Amtrak's first decade was about developing, rebuilding and buying new infrastructure (cars, locomotives, right-of-way, stations), its second decade was about using those resources to its best advantage. It was a decade bent on erasing the image of passenger trains being a leprous money-losing operation (read, tax burden), improving financial security and illustrating that rail was a solution to a problem—not a problem in itself.

Has it worked? Apparently so. Ridership in 1991 was headed for an all-time high of over 22 million, and even that crucial U.S. institution most skeptical about passenger trains—the White House—has fielded a kinder, gentler attitude about rail passenger service. More importantly, Amtrak revenues in 1991 covered nearly 80 percent of

TOP: For more than half of Amtrak's life, Superliners have been the norm for Western long-hauls, such as ***California Zephyr*** detouring through Green River, Wyo., in April 1983.—*Bob Johnston* **RIGHT:** For Eastern long-distance runners like the ***Crescent,*** eastbound at Cook Springs, Ala., in 1983, Heritage equipment has been the backbone of train consists for over a decade.—*John Gieske* **ABOVE:** Virtually unknown in 1971, the Amtrak logo today is a familiar transportation symbol.—*Steve Glischinski*

costs, up from 48.6 percent in 1981. A 20 percent subsidy reduces Amtrak's vulnerability to budget-cutters and the political system. Of course, then, zero subsidy nearly eliminates the vulnerability, and zero subsidy—not including capital costs—is the goal for the year 2000.

U.S. PRESIDENT RONALD REAGAN, whose term spanned most of Amtrak's second decade, may have been one of the best things to happen to Amtrak. His impenetrable *laisse fare* stance helped toughen the carrier in the 1980's, perhaps providing the additional impetus it needed to weather violent political storms and to emphasize the importance of self-sufficiency. Never mind the fairness aspect; i.e., that the White House seemed to condone public support of air and highway passenger transport but not

TOP: The Chicago-Houston *Lone Star* was dropped on Oct. 1, 1979, but a semblance of through Chicago-Houston service was restored on Oct. 28, 1979, in the form of a new Houston section for the *Inter-American,* splitting off at Temple, Texas. But that train, shown at Brenham in February 1980, also vanished, on Oct. 1, 1981. Not until the *Eagle* gained a Dallas-Houston leg on Nov. 15, 1988, did direct Midwest-Houston service return.—*Joe McMillan* **ABOVE:** Steam-heat equipment was in its twilight when the *Silver Star* crossed Neabsco Creek, Va., on the RF&P on a fall day in 1981. Amtrak's head-end power conversion program more or less concluded on March 9, 1982, when the *Star* was completely converted to all-electric HEP rolling stock. Isolated HEP projects followed, such as the rebuilding of Vista-Dome cars for the new *Capitol Limited.*—*Mike Schafer*

rail. In the long run, it worked to Amtrak's advantage. The corporation has captured the spotlight as a rare example of a government-spawned industry that has made good, and it also proved that the American form of government—in its weird and sometimes schizophrenic way—works. After all, the public wanted its passenger trains, and, so informed by their constituents, Congressional leaders thus helped preserve a national system.

Amtrak's Reagan years did not start out so well, though, as we saw in the previous chapter. Almost immediately following Reagan's sweep into Washington early in 1981, the popular President and his entourage took aim at Amtrak. After all, passenger-train subsidy to this day remains an easy target: NRPC's subsidy is an out-in-front line item on the national budget, whereas other forms of transportation receive their monies through convoluted and indirect paths. The result? Starting in 1985, the White House usually simply put a "0" in the line-item entry for Amtrak when budgets came due.

The crisis at hand as we left chapter 3 and Amtrak's 10th birthday was indeed a Perils of Pauline situation, with Amtrak tied to its own track. NRPC's request for $970 million was countered by a White House budget for $613 million, to which Amtrak proffered a $853 million compromise. The House and Senate came in with $735 million, the figure ultimately adopted for Amtrak's FY82 budget, which began on Oct. 1, 1981. That figure also included some tax advantages and interest-payment relief, so its worth was closer to $830 million—close to Amtrak's $853 million compromise figure. However, by the time the budget went into effect, the Reagan administration reneged on its $613 million offer and its $735 million agreement with a new downsized FY82 budget of $47 million! The $735 million amount prevailed.

The FY82 budget battle ultimately turned out to be one of Amtrak's bloodiest, with several casualties: the Cincinnati-Washington *Shenandoah*, the Chicago-Cincinnati-New York *Cardinal*, the Seattle-Vancouver *Pacific International*, portions of the *Inter-American*, the Boston-New Haven *Beacon Hill*, the Chicago-Dubuque *Black Hawk*, the Chicago-Peoria *Prairie Marksman*, one train in each direction between Boston and New York, three trains in each direction between New York and Washington, five trains each way between New Haven and Springfield, Mass., and two trains each way between Chicago and Milwaukee.

This budget battle also spawned the 1981 Amtrak Bill, which had several significant clauses. First, it called for a new nine-member board of directors whose members included Amtrak's president, a governor from a pro-rail state, and a representative from a business having a general interest in rail transportation. Second, the bill called for an increase from $20 million to $24 million for 403(b) services, with the states underwriting 45 percent of the costs in the first year, and 65 percent in subsequent years. Third was the mandate that Amtrak cover 50 percent of its long-term avoidable costs by the end of September 1982. The fourth item—which would end up having some distasteful side effects—directed that food and beverage losses had to be eliminated by October 1982.

Amtrak responded to this last item by introducing a bare-bones, limited-entree, pre-prepared food service on all long-distance trains, at the same time eliminating amenities like crockery and linens, even on the elegant new Superliner diners, which came with their own china. Fortunately, the experiment was relatively short-lived, although as of 1991, most long-distance trains were still bereft of dining-car china.

Amidst the wisps of smoke rising from the battlefield, there was some bright news. As several trains were axed on Oct. 1, several new services came on line including a new long-distance run—one slated to become one of Amtrak's finest trains, the Chicago-Washington *Capitol Limited.* A month later, the new Amtrak reservation computer, ARROW, went into service, and ten days after that, the first of the new Amfleet II cars was unveiled at Budd Company's Red Lion (Pa.) plant. Amtrak was soldiering on.

SLEEPY-EYED is how one might describe the start of 1982. There were no major winter snarl-ups, the budget controversy had cooled (for the interim, anyway) and trains were running more or less on time and staying on the tracks. The biggest news had been the Jan. 8 reinstatement of the *Cardinal*, the result of a provision of Congress' funding bill for FY82.

About the time of the spring timetable release (April 25), though, there came a wake-up call. . . for a new NRPC president. A war-weary Alan Boyd announced his resignation, to take effect July 2, 1982. To the delight of rail advocates, former Southern Railway Chairman W. Graham Claytor Jr. was, at a young 70 years, selected as Amtrak's fourth president.

Roger Lewis' forte was business management; Paul Reistrup's expertise was railroad operation, and Alan Boyd's was in political choreography. Claytor's unique talent is that he is skilled in all three areas. He is a man who knows, understands and—perhaps most importantly—loves railroading. Under his successful leadership, Southern Railway emerged as one of the country's leading railroads and operated one of the nation's premier passenger trains, the *Southern Crescent.* Following his term at SR, Claytor served as Secretary of the Navy under President Carter as well as Acting DOT Secretary of Transportation. Claytor was a statesman all the way and well tied into the political arena.

Claytor made it clear that he was going to concentrate on improving Amtrak's bottom line and its service standards, and not necessarily push for expansion except where costs would be covered. Continuing certain programs that had been initiated by Boyd, Claytor and his management team began systematic search and experimentation for ways in which Amtrak could become more self-sufficient. Several key areas emerged during the 1980's:

Real estate. Until the NEC acquisition in 1976, Amtrak owned scant property. Now, the carrier holds title to well over 600 miles of rights-of-way as well as several significant parcels of land and buildings, among them the shop complex at Beech Grove (Indianapolis); all of Chicago Union Station and its ancillary properties and trackage; 30th Street Station, Philadelphia; Penn Station, N.Y.; and Sunnyside Yard in Queens, N.Y., just outside of Manhattan.

Amtrak's corporate development arm began marketing its non-essential properties by leasing them to other corporations. Many depots have been leased to commuter authorities or developers or outright sold. Some stations still serve their as-built intended purpose—i.e., as a place to catch trains—but contain retail developments and other tenants that help offset the costs of operating a depot. Even active rights-of-way have been generating income other than through their main purpose of supporting track that carries revenue-producing trains: Amtrak has leased linear rights to fibre optic communication and telecommunication companies.

The impact real-estate resources has had on the company's bottom line is dramatic—there was no real-estate income to

ABOVE: Amtrak's acquisition of the Northeast Corridor included tributaries from Harrisburg and Springfield, Mass. A portion of the latter branch is shown near Pecowsic, Mass., in September 1990, as the Boston-Springfield-New York *Charter Oak* heads southward after passing a northbound Conrail freight; CR exercises trackage rights on portions of the NEC. BELOW: Amtrak has put its rights-of-way to double use: The work train at right is for a fiber-optic cable-laying project along the Shore Line in 1990; meanwhile, a pair of ex-Santa Fe locomotives work a westbound ballast train.—*Both photos, David Patch*

RIGHT: Amtrak on April 1, 1975, took over Penn Central's Beech Grove Shops near Indianapolis, Ind. The former Big Four/New York Central complex—which dates from the 19th century and has for its entire life span been used as a railcar repair facility—today is an integral part of a behind-the-scenes Amtrak. In the 1980's, the shop further boosted Amtrak's bottom line by offering contract work. Here, shop forces at "the Grove" assemble subway cars for the Washington (D.C.) Metro in 1988. Work has also been done for New York's Metropolitan Transportation Authority.—*Mike Schafer*

The Amtrak crew of a Shore Line East commuter train wearing the celebrated colors of the late, great New Haven Railroad, takes on orders at Clinton, Conn., on the morning of Aug. 15, 1990, just prior to heading into Old Saybrook to pick up passengers for the trip to New Haven. Although SLE trains between Old Saybrook and New Haven are sponsored by the Connecticut Department of Transportation, ConnDOT contracts with Amtrak to supply crews and compensates Amtrak for the use of its Shore Line main in southeastern Connecticut—yet another example of how Amtrak has improved its revenue picture. —*David Patch*

speak of before 1976, $9 million per year by 1981 and $31 million by 1991; some $100 million per year is expected by the end of the 1990's.

Travel agents have been selling Amtrak transportation almost as long as the company has been around, but not until the 1980's did Amtrak began an aggressive program of getting more agents involved in sales and ticketing. With its limited resources, Amtrak has hardly been in a position to hire the sales agents it needs, but with thousands of travel agencies blanketing North America, the company had a ready-made sales staff who could be paid through commissions.

The key was to tie in more directly with the airline reservation computers most agents already had; Amtrak's new (as of 1981) ARROW system permitted this. In addition, Amtrak in 1985 joined the Airline Reporting Corporation (ARC), which issues common ticket stock and a single revenue collection system. These steps plus an ambitious program of familiarizing agents with the peculiarities of rail travel has paid off. Whereas some 12,000 travel agents were authorized to sell Amtrak tickets early in the 1980's, there were 32,000 by Amtrak's 20th anniversary providing more than 40 percent of all ticket sales—but at a fraction of the expense of direct sales.

Service contracts. During the budget battle of 1981, Congress mandated that Amtrak maximize all its resources—real estate, facilities and employees—to reduce federal support. In the case of employee skills, Amtrak took two different approaches. Labor skills allow Amtrak to contract shop work to outside concerns. For example, Beech Grove shop forces assembled new orders of rolling stock for Washington, D.C.'s, Metro subway system, and Amtrak has performed track maintenance for commuter agencies.

The skills of Amtrak's white-collar workers have taken another route. In 1986, Amtrak won a bid to manage Boston's MBTA (Massachusetts Bay Transportation Authority) 18-million passenger-per-year commuter-rail system in a cost-plus-profit arrangement that provided still more new revenues. On a related basis, Amtrak supplies crews to operate certain MARC (Maryland Rail Commuter) and Connecticut DOT suburban trains and, as this book goes to press, is studying the potentials of managing and operating impending or planned new commuter services in northern Virginia, Dallas/Forth Worth and the San Francisco Bay Area.

Yield management. Amtrak in the late 1980's initiated this program as a means of maximizing revenues with its finite equipment roster. The problem is not that Amtrak can't fill coach seats, roomettes and bedrooms; the challenge is to sell each of those spaces at the highest price the market would bear—i.e., when demand outstrips supply, then the price goes up. The solution has been used by airlines for years: Offer a widely varied ticket price structure that is sensitive to travel peaks and valleys and the idiosyncrasies of individual routes. In little over a year after yield management had been established, Amtrak realized an additional $1 million in revenues as a result of the program.

Employee acquisition. Amtrak has been adding its own employees since almost the beginning, with a big jump occurring in 1973 as the company began taking over those directly associated with onboard passenger services (versus train operation); elsewhere, Amtrak simply contracted with individual railroads for the services of their respective employees. Another big increase came with the purchase of the Northeast Corridor in 1976, but in 1983 another important step was achieved when Amtrak first began hiring its own engineers, conductors and trainmen. Initially this involved the Northeast Corridor only, but eventually the transition from contract services to direct hire of employees spread throughout the system.

Improved labor service contracts. As the NRPC implemented direct employment of train crews, it also improved productivity and cost-effectiveness through new labor contracts. Through a multitude of negotiations, Amtrak and the various labor unions were able to establish landmark precedents in the area of work rules—rules that had been in force since early in the century (and carved on stone tablets, some would say). Formerly, for example, a train and engine (T&E) crew working a Washington-New York *Metroliner* received 4½ days' wages for two round trips per week (about 12 hours of work) since the run was based on mileage and not time. Under new arrangements, a train crew's on-duty time is based on a standard eight-hour work day rather than by mileage, which means that one crew can make one New York-Washington round trip during an eight-hour pay period. Further, the number of crew members required in the cab has been reduced to one on many runs.

Mail and express. A few rail historians wryly note that some of today's Amtrak trains are beginning to resemble those of the 1950's and 1960's what with their rakes of head-end express and baggage cars. Mail and express was a key to pre-Amtrak passenger trains surviving as long as they did, and in the 1980's NRPC figured that what worked then could work again now. Although the RPO (Railway Post Office) car—once a familiar institution with its bevy of on-board employees sorting mail en route—is probably forever committed to

ABOVE: Amtrak's takeover of train and engine crews from host freight railroads began following a prototype procedure established with the new *Auto Train* service in 1983. As of 1991, CSX Transportation was the only railroad with which Amtrak was still contracting for crewing, for a portion of the *Cardinal*'s route. Here, CSX crews do ticket accounting in the dinette of No. 50 in 1986.—*Bob Johnston* **BELOW:** While Amtrak may have been created to move passengers, its movement of mail and express has seen substantial growth. The westbound *Fast Mail* is at Bridgeport, Conn, on New Year's Day 1991.—*Scott Hartley*

ABOVE: It was a lucky catch for the photographer standing at Dale Junction, Wyo., on April 15, 1983, as east- and westbound *San Francisco Zephyrs* met within camera range. The reroute of Amtrak's second decade that generated considerable controversy—as well as impressive passenger loads—was that of moving the *San Francisco Zephyr/Desert Wind/Pioneer* off Union Pacific's Overland Route through Wyoming. What the Cowboy State lost, colorful Colorado gained, and on April 24, 1983, the *California Zephyr* was reborn—but with a twist of irony: mudslides had closed the train's new Rio Grande route through the Rockies. **ABOVE RIGHT:** On July 15, 1983, the mud was gone and the *CZ* headed for the hills, in this case James Peak, under which the *CZ* passes via the 6.8-mile-long Moffat Tunnel. Date: May 21, 1987.—*Both photos, Steve Patterson*

history, moving sealed mail by rail has been making a comeback.

Early evidence of this came in 1981 when the *Empire Builder* permanently returned to daily (from triweekly) operation—a prerequisite to winning a contract from the U.S. Postal Service to move mail along the Chicago-Twin Cities-Seattle route. Then, Amtrak even inaugurated dedicated mail trains on the NEC in 1984. The importance of moving sealed and priority mail as well as express shipments was underscored with the 1986 delivery of 62 of what Amtrak calls material handling cars (MHC's)—vehicles which look not unlike the classic express boxcar of the 1930's and 1940's.

THE ABOVE-MENTIONED PROGRAMS did not happen all at one time, nor were all of them necessarily a product of the Claytor administration, but they continued to be developed and nurtured throughout the Claytor years. Overall, Amtrak operations remained stable throughout the 1980's, but, as in the 1970's, there were several noteworthy events.

It was early during Graham Claytor's years as Amtrak's CEO that the corporation implemented what is perhaps one of the most-significant train reroutes (and there have been many) in NRPC history: that of moving the *San Francisco Zephyr, Pioneer* and *Desert Wind* to the Denver & Rio Grande Western between Denver and Salt Lake City. Amtrak had long realized the tremendous marketing potential of a route through the Rockies, and so on July 16, 1983, the first Amtrak trains headed over Rio Grande's Moffat Tunnel Route.

It was Claytor himself who provided the impetus for Amtrak to make good on its 1971 "promise" to revive the *California Zephyr*. As outlined in the first chapter, Rio Grande nixed the deal five days before Amtrak began operation, indicating that the $1.6 million cash payment to join NRPC was just too much; as well, D&RGW was uncomfortable with the open-ended Amtrak contract which theoretically did not limit the number of trains NRPC could operate over the line.

By the time Claytor proposed the re-

Pounding the concrete piers that take the Richmond, Fredericksburg & Potomac main line over Powells Creek, Va., is southbound Amtrak train 53, *Auto Train*. The unqualified success of the Northeast-to-Florida operation has resulted in trains of rather enormous proportions, sometimes well over thirty cars long. Because of *Auto Train*'s length, equipment assigned to the run has freight-type braking systems and thus tends not to stray from trains 52 and 53 (although braking systems can be changed over with relative ease when cars have to be reassigned). For most of *Auto Train*'s existence, General Electric P30CH locomotives—such as the three heading up this day's train on Sept. 12, 1987—have been the mainstay power, but in 1991 the ubiquitous Electro-Motive F40 began infiltrating *Auto Train* consists.—*Alex Mayes*

route, the situation for both Rio Grande and Amtrak had changed considerably. Rio Grande's losses on its famed *Rio Grande Zephyr* had tripled since 1971, despite significant ridership increases. Meanwhile, Amtrak had acquired a stature as a stable, respectable operation—an operation that Rio Grande could now view as a revenue-generating customer, since that was, in essence, what Amtrak would be on its line.

April 24, 1983, was set as the changeover date, but the reroute was delayed by a mudslide at Thistle, Utah, which blocked the Rio Grande main line for several weeks. The fact that Amtrak and Rio Grande solidified the reroute details so fast became a sore point with Wyoming, which stood to lose all Amtrak service (a point that thankfully became moot eight years later). The state filed an injunction to stop the reroute, but to no avail.

The revival of the *CZ*—at least to the extent such a famous flagship could be recreated—ushered in the expected results. Patronage on the *CZ* and its companion trains boomed. It's tempting to say Amtrak hasn't looked back since the shift, but it has. As a result of the reroute, the combined *CZ/Pioneer/Desert Wind* became a victim of its own success. Summer train consists were up to the maximum limit for operation over the mountains; two diners were required between Salt Lake City and Denver. Services began to suffer because of overcrowding, and timekeeping became erratic. That and other problems regarding operation of the *Pioneer* in particular led to a "re-reroute" of that train on June 16, 1991, splitting it from the *CZ* and *Desert Wind* at Denver instead of Salt Lake City and sending it northwest back through Wyoming.

The year 1983 also heralded another significant revival: the phoenix-like reinstitution of *Auto Train* service between Washington, D.C. (actually, Lorton, Va.) and Sanford, Fla., on Oct. 30. The take-your-auto-with-you-on-the-train concept was hardly new; B&O/C&O had experimented with it in the 1960's, and Canadian National had likewise dabbled in the service. But these operations were paled by the 1970 introduction of Auto-Train Corporation's *Auto-Train* between Lorton and Sanford, and later between Louisville, K.Y., and Sanford as well (with that run eventually being combined with Amtrak's *Floridian*). Initially a huge success, *Auto-Train* was often bannered as an example of what innovation could do for U.S. rail passenger travel. Unfortunately, a series of derailments and management problems split Auto-Train Corp. asunder, and its trains went out of

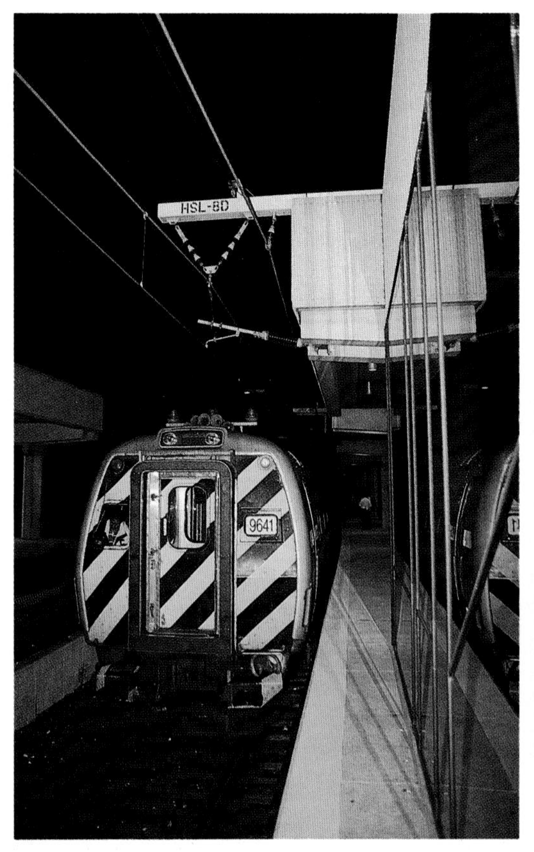

ABOVE: The Atlantic County Improvement Authority built the new Atlantic City terminal for the joint Amtrak/New Jersey Transit service. Amtrak's Atlantic City endeavor had several firsts. Whereas other new corridors have started with but a single train, with additional trains introduced at later dates (with Oakland-Bakersfield, Calif., as a prime example), the Atlantic City route right from the start featured multi-frequency service. In addition, for the first time in this country, direct-link air-rail service—with through ticketing and baggage handling—was marketed through a cooperative effort with Midway Airlines at Philadelphia International Airport; unfortunately, the service ended with Midway's retrenchment in 1991.—*Mike Schafer* **RIGHT:** One of the *Atlantic City Expresses* at the airport in summer 1990; Amtrak operated over SEPTA (Southeastern Pennsylvania Transportation Authority) trackage to reach the new SEPTA station at the air terminal. All *Atlantic City Expresses* utilize push-pull equipment, with cab-control cars such as this rebuilt from Metroliner m.u.'s.—*Bob Johnston*

business the day before Amtrak's 10th birthday in 1981.

Graham Claytor knew a good thing when he saw it, and made the revival of the concept a priority. Amtrak acquired Auto-Train Corporation's assets—mainly the Lorton and Sanford terminal facilities and selected A-T rolling stock—and on Oct. 30, 1983, Amtrak's version rose from the ashes of the original operation. Amtrak's *Auto Train* has since enjoyed such popularity that there are plans to expand to other markets should capital funding of equipment become available.

Tapping new markets is what prompted Amtrak to implement its largest single expansion project to date: the Philadelphia-Atlantic City route, which debuted on May 23, 1989. Amtrak didn't introduce just one train, but a whole new corridor (68 miles long) of trains, the *Atlantic City Expresses*.

The project was a joint effort between: New Jersey Transit, which owns the right-of-way and contributed $56 million to re-

During the 1980's Americans acquired an increased awareness of buildings of historical significance, a trend that manifested itself with hundreds of renovation projects throughout the land. The focus did not escape Amtrak, which undertook or at least sponsored numerous station renovation projects—of which Washington Union Station deserves special mention. Following a thorough facelift and an infusion of new life in the form of dozens of retail outlets, the "new" Union Station was unveiled on Sept. 30, 1988. A shabby cavern during the 1970's, WUS is now considered the crown jewel of Amtrak stations.—*Mike Schafer*

"Dear Bombardier Corp.: We are woefully short of passenger cars and need something quick. We think the basic design you and predecessor Pullman-Standard have used for the hundreds of commuter cars built since the 1970's will work fine, but with reclining seats and carpeting. Enclosed please find a check for $104 million for 104 vehicles. Thanks!—Amtrak." The actual acquisition of Horizon Fleet equipment probably wasn't quite that simple, but the million-dollar cars have performed just fine since their delivery in 1989-90. Most of the flat-sided fleet hovers about the Chicago hub, but several Horizonliners are assigned to Oakland-Bakersfield service in California. Five of the cars comprise this *San Joaquin* at Pinole, Calif., on April 8, 1991. Amtrak was using a CalTrain F40 in trade for an Amtrak F40 CalTrain was using on its Los Angeles-San Juan Capistrano commuter train.—*Phil Gosney*

building; the Atlantic County Improvement Authority, which put in $20 million for the new Atlantic City depot; and Amtrak, which contributed $30 million toward rebuild. With gambling made legal, Atlantic City in the 1980's regained its title as a principal tourist destination, and Amtrak (and NJT) were betting they could capitalize on the constant stream of fun-seekers heading for the Boardwalk.

Despite the fanfare, the new service got off to a bumpy start since projected ridership did not materialize for Amtrak nor NJT, which later began commuter runs on the route. Amtrak had underestimated the almost-monopolylike grip the charter bus industry had on moving people to the gambling mecca, and it was also hampered by the out-in-the-swamps depot location and the unwillingness of casinos to offer the same perks provided to bus groups.

A heavily advertised extension of Atlantic City trains to Philadelphia Airport in 1990 for coordinated rail-air service with Midway Airlines died prematurely with that airline's 1991 retrenchment from Philadelphia, but Amtrak finally seems to have found its niche in the Atlantic City market—as a travel option for those traveling medium-to-long distances to Atlantic City. Thus, Amtrak's through *Atlantic City Express*es from the likes of Richmond, Va., and Springfield, Mass., have fared better than the short Philly-Atlantic City trips and even the New York City runs.

THERE WERE OTHER TRIALS and tribulations in Amtrak's second decade. Certainly the low point came on Jan. 4, 1987, when the Washington-Boston *Colonial* collided with a set of Conrail locomotives at Gunpow interlocking near Chase, Md.—with tragic consequences. Sixteen people died in the aftermath, which brought new awareness to the problem of drug and alcohol use by railroad crews—the crew of the Conrail locomotives was convicted of substance abuse in relation to the wreck.

On a more-upbeat note, there were three milestones in the area of rolling stock. First was the in-house development of a new generation of single-level long-distance passenger cars, the Viewliners, which began in 1981 during the last months of the Boyd administration. Second was the completion of the Heritage Fleet program, which occurred when all sets of the *Silver Star* went all-electric on March 10, 1982. Third was the ordering of additional cars to bolster corridor operations in the Midwest and West; Bombardier Corporation began delivery of 104 Horizon Fleet

EMD's F40PH's have proven to be a hardy locomotive, but locomotive failures increased with alarming frequency in the late 1980s. RIGHT: GP40TC's were acquired from GO Transit in 1988 to supplement the F40 fleet; two GP40TC's, one at each end of a consist, head out of Milwaukee for Chicago in 1989.—*Mike Schafer* BELOW: A Milwaukee Road GP40 assists ailing units on the *Empire Builder* at Red Wing, Minn., in 1986.—*John Gieske*

cars in the spring of 1989.

Locomotives, too, were in the news, but not always in a kind light. Amtrak's mainstay in motive power—EMD's venerable F40PH's, the oldest of which dated from 1976—were beginning to feel the effects of years of intense, rigorous service. New batches of F40's arrived during the 1980's, but by mid-decade the motive-power situation was becoming critical, with shortages and increasing down-time of older units resulting in an inordinately high number of train delays. Amtrak, meanwhile, went shopping for secondhand as well as new power and in 1989 began experimenting with what it (and the railroad

The *Montrealer* is hardly a new service for Amtrak; it made its first run under the red, white and blue in September '72. But when the train resumed service on July 18, 1989, following a two-plus-year hiatus that resulted from deteriorated track conditions on the Guilford Industries' Boston & Maine line used by the *Montrealer*, the reinstated streamliner received accolades worthy of an all-new train. Amtrak brought suit against GI, and the litigation was still ongoing in 1991. Amtrak instead uses an all-Central Vermont routing north of New London, Conn. ABOVE: A re-inaugural *Montrealer* special made its way through Vermont in daylight on July 17, 1989; officials and guests wave from Amtrak business car 10000 at Roxbury, Vt.—*Gary Knapp* RIGHT: The classic depot at White River Junction, Vt. , was suitably attired for the festivities.—*Ken Houghton*

industry in general) hoped would be a new generation of diesel-electric technology—locomotives with a.c. traction motors.

As Amtrak neared its 20th anniversary, it undertook another major reroute scenario, one that was perhaps as controversial (possibly more so) than the *Zephyr* change of 1983. Conrail's long-time insistence of downgrading the former Pennsylvania main line between Chicago and Pittsburgh, which would require Amtrak to either vacate the route or totally finance its maintenance, finally came to a head as the decade drew to a close. In deference to maintaining peace and harmony with one of its largest host railroads—and because it didn't have the wherewithal to assume maintenance costs—Amtrak instead opted to seize the demotion of the old Pittsburgh, Fort Wayne & Chicago as an opportunity to open new markets. This was accomplished in November 1990 by rerouting the *Capitol Limited* between Chicago and Pittsburgh via Conrail's ex-New York Central main line between Chicago and Cleveland and a former-PRR secondary main between Cleveland and Pittsburgh. This shift gave populous northern Ohio a direct tie-in with Washington, D.C., and the Southeast. The *Broadway Limited* may not have fared as well, since its transfer to the parallel former-B&O main line of CSX between Chicago and Pittsburgh meant the loss of two important on-line cities, Fort Wayne, Ind. (still served by connecting buses, though) and Lima, Ohio, although it did gain Akron and Youngstown, Ohio, in the process.

Most of the 1980's brought continuing budget battles not unlike The Big One described earlier in this chapter. Zero funding for Amtrak (and public transportation in general) became a way of life in Reagan budgets. Amtrak weathered the conflicts with aplomb and deftness, all the while continuing with its strategies for improving operations and finances and reducing its dependence on federal monies. With Claytor's dignified leadership during budget confrontations and Congress' increasing willingness to shield Amtrak from its foes, even the popular Reagan was unable to derail the corporation, which continued to report increased revenues and growing or at least stable ridership while marching

The reroute news of 1990 was the moving of the ***Broadway Limited*** and ***Capitol Limited*** off Conrail's ex-Pennsylvania Railroad route between Chicago and Pittsburgh on Nov. 11. **LEFT:** The name of the grain elevator at Valparaiso, Ind., confirms the heritage of the nearby line, on which the westbound ***Capitol Limited*** draws a bead on its depot stop on Aug. 25, 1990.—*Rob McGonigal* **ABOVE:** To put the controversial reroute into better light, Amtrak dispatched a special train over all the new trackage to be used by the ***Cap*** and the ***Broadway***. Nappanee, Ind., on the CSX route, welcomed the special on Nov. 7.—*Bob Johnston*. **TOP:** The following day, children danced in celebration as the special left Alliance, Ohio.—*Mike Schafer*

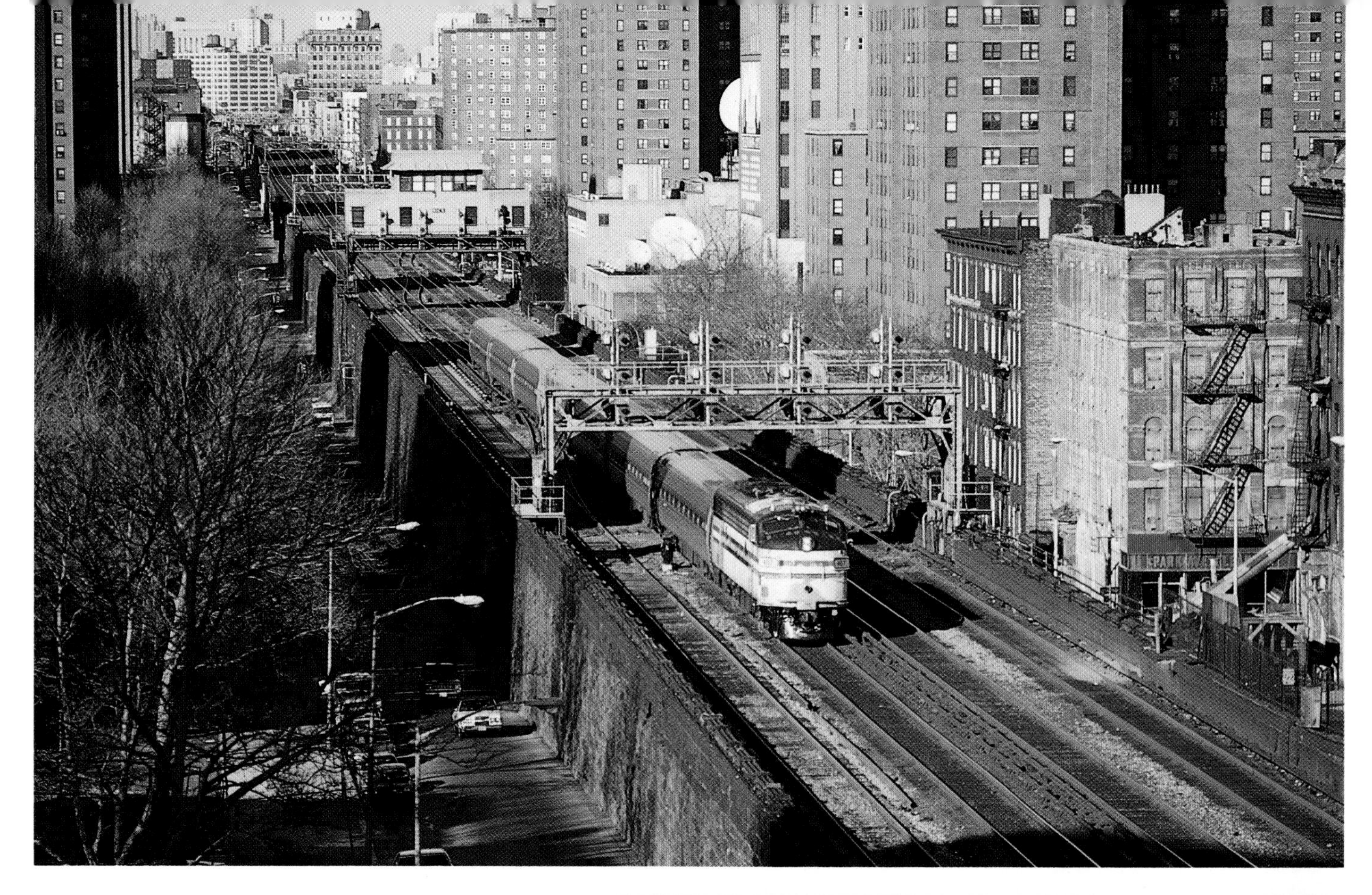

ABOVE: Highballing through Harlem in New York City, Amtrak train 284, the *Niagara Rainbow*, is on the home stretch to Grand Central Terminal on a brisk March day in 1991; in moments, the FL9 locomotive will lead 284 into the Park Avenue Tunnel leading to the legendary station. An era closed the following month on April 6 when the last intercity trains departed Grand Central Terminal, leaving the 1908-built structure to serve only suburban runs. The following day, Amtrak trains off the Hudson River line began terminating in Manhattan at Penn Station.—*Bill McBride* **RIGHT:** To reach Penn Station from the Hudson line, Amtrak acquired and revamped a former-NYC freight line on the west side of Manhattan Island and built a new tunnel into the station. The new route and its control point locations of Inwood (Spuyten Duyvil drawbridge), Martha (under the George Washington Bridge, of course) and Empire are controlled from this CTC panel in the depths of Penn Station.—*Mike Schafer*

LEFT: With the Washington-New York end of the Northeast Corridor shaping up nicely by the end of the 1980's, Amtrak turned its attention to the Boston extremity. East of New Haven, electrification and new alignments are on the horizon, but in the interim the carrier has improved New York-Boston running times with its new (in October 1990) limited-stop *New England Expresses*. One of the westbound speedsters, train 153, bolts through Bridgeport, Conn., in February 1991.—*Scott Hartley*

Strange bedfellows

With the 1980's came many colorful twists and turns in U.S. railroading. In 1971, would anyone have believed this 1985 scene (ABOVE) of a *California Zephyr*, at Sacramento, Calif., sitting next to a Southern Pacific E9 clad in SP's classic *Daylight* color scheme of the late 1930's?—*Roger Puta, collection of Mel Finzer* Or (LEFT), how about a *Capitol Limited* in the company of an all-first-class Chicago-New York luxury liner, the *American-European Express* (and a Metra commuter train) in the spring of 1991?—*Rob McGonigal* BELOW: Mainline steam in the U.S. vanished years before Amtrak, but imagine a modern passenger train, in this case the eastbound *Cardinal* at Mount Carbon, W. Va., shouldering transportation duties with a live, thundering Chesapeake & Ohio 4-8-4. . . in 1985!—*Don Jilson*

down the (rail)road to self-sufficiency.

The closing of Amtrak's second decade was marked with much optimism and more benchmarks. In 1990, Congress appropriated $125 million for the development of high-speed service, including electrification, east of New Haven, Conn., to Boston. Early in 1991, Amtrak ordered 52 new locomotives of three varying types (see locomotive chapter for details). Even bigger news rode the heels of the locomotive order: Amtrak's signing of a $340 million contract with Bombardier for 140 new Superliners—a certain sign of continued growth. Another reroute, on April 7, 1991, consolidated all New York City operations at Pennsylvania Station with the shift of Empire Corridor runs from Grand Central Terminal to a revamped freight line on the west side of Manhattan. This change is expected to have significant positive impact on ridership, revenues and costs. Finally, the almost unheard of happened: The White House's budget for fiscal 1992 actu-

ally recommended money for Amtrak!

While you're putting on your Amtak birthday hats, consider the following:

- ●Ridership in 1971 was 16.6 million; in 1990 it was 22.2 million.
- ●1972 revenues amounted to $162.6 million; 1990 revenues were $1.3 billion, nearly a 100 percent increase.
- ●As of May 1, 1971, Amtrak operated some 200 trains daily; in 1991 the figure was about 250.
- ●Today these trains operate over 24,000 route-miles, serving nearly 575 cities; in 1971, it was 23,000 route-miles and 380 cities and towns.
- ●Amtrak in 1990 carried more passengers than all U.S. railroads combined carried on a considerably larger route system during the last full year (1970) before Amtrak startup.

These momentums need to be increased or at least maintained for the foreseeable future, but to do so will require a continued source of funding, both to cover the losses still being sustained and to provide capital for new equipment and physical plant development. If that can happen, then the party will only be starting for U.S. rail passenger transportation in general and Amtrak in particular.

ABOVE: Amtrak and the Electro-Motive Division of General Motors (EMD) began testing a.c. traction motor propulsion in 1989 with two experimental locomotives, designated F69's. The pair, Nos. 450 and 451, began operating on regular Amtrak runs in 1990; ice-encrusted 450 is humming out of Milwaukee with the midday *Hiawatha Service* train to Chicago in January 1991. RIGHT: Nearly ten years earlier in the Beer City, F40'S are about to slip away into the Wisconsin night with the Minnesota-bound *North Star*.—*Both photos, Mike Schafer*

Tracks are back!

Route expansion, May 1, 1981-May 1, 1991

The beauty of the Amtrak law signed in 1970 is that it allows the carrier to add or discontinue trains without the burden of interstate regulatory red tape that was necessary in pre-Amtrak days. This flexibility has encouraged Amtrak and states active in the 403(b) program to experiment with new services—which is precisely what has happened during Amtrak's first two decades.

Despite continued budget squeezing in the '1980's, which in several cases resulted in the demise of routes and trains established during Amtrak's first decade, many new services were welcomed in during the last ten years. Too, there were a couple of new stars that didn't quite make it, such as the Miami-St. Petersburg *Silver Palm*, but there is at least one service—North Carolina's *Carolinian*—which has had not one, but two incarnations during the 1980's!

And, there are encouraging indications that the introduction of new routes and services will continue. Perhaps in a future edition of another Amtrak book, you'll be able to read about a new Chicago-Florida train, an extension of the *Sunset Limited* route east to Florida, an additional central corridor route for Western trains through northern Illinois and Iowa, a closing of the gap between Bakersfield and Los Angeles, a Chicago-Madison (Wis.) run, a service restoration to Oklahoma, and trains to Maine. These are not off-the-wall dreams; these are indeed proposals being studied as this volume goes to press.

Meanwhile, let's celebrate some of the new trains of the second decade.

Throughout Amtrak's second decade, new routes and services continued to draw great press. ABOVE: On Oct. 26, 1981, the *Empire Builder* gained a Spokane (Wash.)-Portland (Ore.) leg, just as it had in pre-Amtrak days. The "Baby *Builder*" operates between those two points mostly on Burlington Northern's former-Spokane, Portland & Seattle main line. Eastbound No. 28 is shown at John Day Dam, Wash., in May 1988.—*Scott O'Dell* **BELOW: They said it couldn't be done, but it happened: Wisconsin, a state that hitherto had been considered "no-rail" became decidedly "pro-rail" with the 1989 introduction of two new Chicago-Milwaukee round trips in cooperation with 403(b) veteran State of Illinois. Musicians strike up the band in recognition of the accomplishment on the first Milwaukee-Chicago *Hiawatha Service* train of the day on Oct. 30, 1989. The expansion was at the behest of Milwaukee's then-new agressive Mayor John Norquist; Wisconsin Governor "Tommy" Thompson subsequently joined Amtrak's board of directors.**—*Mike Schafer*

ABOVE: Unquestionably one of the most successful new trains of Amtrak's second decade was the *Capitol Limited*, which rolled onto the scene on Oct. 1, 1981. Since May 1, 1971, Amtrak's Chicago-Washington endpoints had been served by through cars split from the *Broadway Limited* at Harrisburg and later Philadelphia, Pa. Eventually Amtrak concluded a more-direct route would be better, and ten years after Baltimore & Ohio's *Capitol* had departed for the big Union Station in the sky, Amtrak's version began burnishing B&O rails again between Pittsburgh and D.C. Eastbound 440 greets a PATrain suburban (Pittsburgh) run at McKeesport, Pa., on May 17, 1982. Since that time, the *Cap* has grown to a full-size train, complete with full diner and Vista-Domes.—*H. E. Brouse*

Two trains added in conjunction with the 1984 Louisiana Purchase Exposition (World's Fair) at New Orleans were the *Gulf Coast Limited* (ABOVE LEFT, crossing Canal Street in New Orleans), born on April 29, 1984, and the *River Cities* (ABOVE RIGHT, entering St. Louis off the MacArthur Bridge in August 1987), which began through Kansas City-New Orleans service on April 29, 1984, by piggybacking through cars on the Kansas City-St. Louis *Mules* and on the *City of New Orleans* (it runs as an entity only between St. Louis and Carbondale, Ill.). The *Gulf Coast* survived until Jan. 6, 1985; the *River Cities,* though minus its through sleeper, continued into the 1990's.—*Mel Fiveash, R. Frascella*

LEFT: An overnight 403(b) denizen on the L.A.-Oakland-Sacramento route, the *Spirit of California* was a good idea whose time had not yet come. It began on Oct. 25, 1981, and made its last run on Sept. 30, 1983.—*Ken Rattenne* RIGHT: Other California 403(b)'s have had much better luck. During the 1980's, several new *San Diegans* were added, including a through Santa Barbara-San Diego run. A push-pull *San Diegan* coasts into San Juan Capistrano in June 1990.—*David C. Crammer*

Tracks are back!

RIGHT: Reviving a service made famous by Grand Trunk Western and Canadian National in pre-Amtrak years, Amtrak on Oct. 31, 1982,combined the Michigan 403(b) Chicago-Port Huron *Blue Water* with an existing VIA Rail Sarnia-Toronto run. The result: a through train between Chicago and Toronto, the *International.* As a joint Amtrak-VIA operation, equipment of both companies protects schedules: Witness the *International* on March 12, 1983, departing Chicago with a VIA consist.—*Joe McMillan*

ABOVE: The first revenue *Atlantic City Expresses* from Washington and New York arrive at the East Coast gambling capital on May 23, 1989. In terms of train frequency, the Atlantic City route was Amtrak's largest startup to date.—*David C. Warner* RIGHT: Introduced on June 29, 1986, the seasonal New York-Hyannis, Mass., *Cape Codder,* at Buzzards Bay in 1987, helps ease the incredible traffic congestion on Cape Cod, Mass.—*George A. Forero Jr.*

ABOVE: **The many faces of Amtrak are represented in this portrait at Boston South Station in 1979 during one of carrier's early Family Days exhibitions.**—*Glenn Mallow*
RIGHT: **The face of most North American passenger trains today is that of the F40, two of which approach a milling crowd at Joliet, Ill., with the *Southwest Chief* in spring 1989.**—*Mike Schafer*

5/Power for the people

FROM E-UNITS TO AMD'S: THE LOCOMOTIVES OF AMTRAK

As of its 20th anniversary, Amtrak had at its disposal, on any given day, approximately 1,235,000 horsepower with which to move some 60,000 passengers—the average number of customers Amtrak transports every 24 hours.

That horsepower is divided among 247 diesel-electric locomotives of four basic types, a rare breed of 6 diesel-electric/electrics, 65 straight electrics of two principal types and 26 turbine-powered vehicles—in all a fairly straightforward mix of motive power for a railroad the size and breadth of Amtrak.

These totals do not include the numerous types of locomotives used for switching, nor are they particularly constant, for as 1991 got underway, Amtrak placed an order for 52 new units and, as birthday time passed, began taking delivery of 15 lease locomotives.

ALTHOUGH A FEW of the locomotives Amtrak had as of its 20th anniversary were around at the time of NRPC's debut on May 1, 1971—mainly its GP40 and FL9 fleet and all of its switchers—they were owned by and at work on other railroads. Most of the rest of current fleet has been purchased new by Amtrak.

With some exceptions, most locomotives Amtrak had at its disposal in 1971 were those that were being used by NRPC member railroads prior to Amtrak startup. For the most part, these were E8's and

BELOW: As Amtrak purchased E's, it contracted with various shops throughout the country to overhaul them; they emerged in this rather pedestrian red-nose scheme—illustrated by the 291 at Rensselaer, N.Y., in 1975—and often included a variety of modifications, such as the removal of side portal windows, a trademark of stock E8's and E9's.—*Bill Chaplik*
RIGHT: Five E-units, Nos. 495-499, were rebuilt with HEP generators so they could work with Amfleet cars and the ex-C&NW bilevels. The 498, wearing the "cigar band" locomotive scheme ushered in by the F40's, wheels out of Chicago in 1977 with the ***Illinois Zephyr***.—*Mike Schafer*

The E-unit was the mainstay passenger power for pre-Amtrak railroads, and it would be the mainstay for Amtrak during its first five years as well. Illustrating the variety of former owners of Amtrak's E-unit fleet is this view of the northbound ***Abraham Lincoln***, led by Penn Central, Gulf, Mobile & Ohio and Union Pacific units, at Milwaukee in 1973.—*Mike Schafer*

E9's—the timeless classics of GM's Electro-Motive Division. E-units had been hauling passenger trains since 1937 and would continue to help Amtrak move passengers into the 1980's—albeit in greatly reduced numbers by then. Shouldering the work was another EMD classic: the F-unit. Although designed primarily for freight service, many pre-Amtrak roads had selected the F to head up "varnish" as well as tonnage. On the electric side, another product of the 1930's would be of prime importance to Amtrak—Pennsylvania Railroad's GG1. These were accompanied by a small stable of Penn Central former-Cleveland Union Terminal P2 electrics working out of Grand Central Terminal.

Even in 1971, there actually were some "new" passenger locomotives in service on U.S. roads, of note EMD's FP45—owned by Santa Fe and Milwaukee Road—and General Electric's U30CG, owned by Santa Fe. Also, a few roads had relatively new dual-purpose (freight and passenger) diesels. However, when Amtrak began, these railroads withdrew their newer passenger power from Amtrak's reach, reassigned them to freight duties and left the fledgling new company to carry on by leasing and/or purchasing the time-proven—and time-worn—E's, F's and G's.

As Amtrak acquired the best of the used units, it subcontracted with various shops around the country to rebuild them. Eventually Amtrak amassed some 200 E-units and about 30 F's—and meanwhile went shopping for brand-new motive power. Why did NRPC seek new locomotives before it went for new rolling stock? In the early 1970's, Amtrak was still very much a questionable proposition, and if it shut down, new locomotives could easily be peddled to power-hungry freight roads that could, with relative ease, regear them, repaint them and send them out on a string of piggybacks. Back then, the demand for passenger cars, even new ones, was negligible.

Amtrak's chosen new locomotive was $68 million worth of an EMD product called the SDP40F (for Special Duty/ Passenger; Full-width carbody). It was a direct descendant of the FP45's, but with a more tried-and-true V-16 power plant; the FP45's featured then-radical V-20's which

BOTTOM: Few things in U.S. railroading of the 1970's were quite as impressive as a passenger train stretched out behind a pair of thundering SDP40F's. Two of the hulking units roar out of Minneapolis in July 1975 with the westbound *North Coast Hiawatha*.—*Steve Glischinski* BELOW: Like the E-unit clan, some SDP's traded in their red-nose "Rudolph" livery for the banded scheme. Both are represented in this view at Chicago in 1977.—*Joe McMillan*

never quite caught on in the railroad industry. Since Amtrak trains were still nearly all steam-heated, the SDP's each came with not one but two steam generators, with the idea that one of the two would be replaced by head-end power (HEP) electric generators at a later date. Amtrak ordered 150 SDP's in 1972, and the first one entered passenger service (several first did a brief stint in freight duty) on the westbound *Super Chief/El Capitan* out of Chicago on June 22, 1973. (The SDP's permitted Amtrak to end the lease on 74 Santa Fe F-units, most of which were assigned to Amtrak trains plying Santa Fe routes.) Delivery of the burly units continued into 1974, and they were deployed throughout the Amtrak system, outside electrified routes.

Amtrak's next new "motive power" was in fact two whole trainsets, Turboliners built in France by ANF-Frangeco. This was an off-the-shelf purchase of equipment common in France and in fact was part of an order that had been placed by French National Railways. The arrangement permitted Amtrak to introduce all-new trains—flashy ones at that—relatively quickly. In the early 1970's, there were few domestic railcar builders that could swiftly produce new intercity passenger cars. The five-car Turbos were double-ended; that is, equipped with a control cab at each end to alleviate the need for turning at endpoints. However, only one cab-control car on each trainset had a power plant. Relatively satisfied with the "grounded airliners," Amtrak purchased four more sets from France in 1975; all six sets worked out of Chicago.

The ANF Turbos were not Amtrak's first experience with turbine-powered trains. On May 1, 1971, NRPC had inherited a United Aircraft TurboTrain, cousin to several UA Turbos that had been placed in service on Canadian National in 1967. Amtrak's three-car set had been owned by the U.S. Department of Transportation, which put them in service between Boston and New York in 1969 as a demonstration project. In 1973, Amtrak bolstered its UA set by purchasing two CN sets, although four

cars burned during an Amtrak acceptance run in Canada. The UA Turbos were retired in 1976 and eventually scrapped. The French Turbos fared better: After being "retired" on Sept. 8, 1981, three were revived in the late 1980's through a rebuild program at Beech Grove which gave them new, more-efficient turbines, new noses that matched the rakish style of the Rohr Turbos (more about those later), and upgraded interiors. They migrated to the Empire Corridor to work with their American-built Rohr cousins.

The next locomotive purchase was through General Electric for 26 E60's (for Electric, 6000 h.p.) and 25 P30CH diesels (for Passenger, 3000 h.p., C truck, Head-end auxiliary power for train lighting and climate control). Delivered in 1974-76, most of these units were intended for use with Amtrak's first batch (outside of the Turboliner equipment) of new all-electric passenger cars, Amfleet, delivery of which began in 1975. All of the P30's thus were equipped with HEP generators; the E60's were delivered mixed, with most equipped for steam-heating and a few with HEP. Unfortunately, E60 No. 950, the first one delivered, derailed at nearly 100 mph with its test train on the Corridor on Feb. 24, 1975. National Transportation Safety Board findings blamed truck design, thus both the E60's and P30's entrance into revenue service was delayed until November 1975 pending modifications.

The delivery of Amfleet equipment signaled the start of a technology long overdue the U.S. intercity passenger train: all-electric climate control and lighting for passenger cars, powered by a diesel-powered (electric on straight-electric locomotives) generating station in the train's motive power. The technology itself was hardly new. HEP was first used in the U.S. on some of the early streamliners of the 1930's and had been used in U.S. commuter-train applications since the 1950's. In 1958 Chicago & North Western had taken delivery of long-distance, all-electric bilevel equipment powered by F7's rebuilt with HEP generators. This same equipment was already in service on Amtrak.

For the ex-C&NW bilevels, Amtrak in 1974-75 rebuilt five E8's with HEP capability. As it turned out, these E's also went to work pulling the new Amfleet cars, since their intended motive power—the GE's—could not be put into service until truck modifications had been made.

It appears that Amtrak by this time was becoming disenchanted with six-axle motive power, which—aside from the problems relating to the GE units—Amtrak had deemed unsuitable

BELOW: One of the ANF-Frangeco Turbos working the *Blue Water Limited* snakes its way through the puzzle switches south of Chicago Union Station in August 1977. After the Turbos arrived on the boat from France in 1973, they ran under their own power from the East Coast to Chicago via Penn Central's ex-PRR main line, with the first trainset arriving Chicago on Aug. 11. Their initial assignment was to the Chicago-St. Louis corridor, but later were transferred to Michigan and Milwaukee corridors following numerous grade-crossing mishaps on the St. Louis line—purportedly because motorists on roads intersecting Illinois Central Gulf's ex-GM&O main line were confusing the Turbos' twin headlights with that of vehicles on Route 66, which paralleled the tracks.—*Steve Smedley*

LEFT: Amtrak's United Aircraft TurboTrains met with limited success. Its first set, a three-car version which came from the U.S. Department of Transportation, was used briefly in Washington-Parkersburg (W.Va.) service as the *Potomac Turbo*. Later, Amtrak acquired surplus Canadian National UA TurboTrains to make two five-car sets, primarily used on the curving Shore Line Route between New Haven and Boston, where a set is shown near South Station in 1974. The unusual trains were put out to pasture in 1976.—*Dale Jacobson*

RIGHT: Most Amtrak GG1's retained the all-black livery of previous owner Penn Central. The famous fleet was instrumental in maintaining high-speed service on the Northeast Corridor until the arrival of the smaller, but more-powerful and energy-efficient AEM7's. This G is not quite in its usual high-speed mode as it lumbers along the old Camden & Amboy on June 23, 1977, with a detour move resulting from the derailment of a Conrail freight on the NEC main. Trains detoured between Rahway and Monmouth Junction, N.J., via South Amboy.—*Bill Chaplik*

E60 972 strikes a classic pose at Elizabeth, N.J., with a westbound *Clocker Service* run in July 1982. Although the boxy GE's proved unsuitable for demanding *Metroliner* schedules, they continue to hold down numerous assignments on secondary Corridor runs and long-distance trains.—*Alan Tillotson*

for excessively curving routes, including the SDP's. The carrier approached EMD for a "sport model" version of the SDP40F, a unit which would employ the SDP's basic power plant, but on a four-axle chassis. And so was born the F40PH (for Full-width cowl, 40-series engine, Passenger, Head-end power), a locomotive destined to become a classic in its own right. What the E-unit was for the 1940's, '50's and '60's, the F40 would be to the late 1970's, '80's and beyond, not only on Amtrak, but on other passenger carriers as well.

The first batch of the 3,000-h.p., HEP-equipped units—30 of them—were delivered in March, April and May 1976 and were dispersed to the winding Shore Line route between New Haven and Boston,

LEFT: **If there is any doubt about the brawny proportions of GE's P30CH's, just check out the clearances between the 703 and the tunnel portal in this 1985 scene at 1st Street in Washington, D.C.; the units were heading light from Ivy City engine terminal to Lorton, Va., to pick up *Auto Train*. The "P-boats," as they were sometimes known (in reference to the "U-boat" nickname applied to their Universal-series ancestors, the U25B, U30C, etc.), tended to stay on routes where the host railroad had or has some familiarity with GE motive power.**—*George A. Forero Jr.* BELOW: **One train the P30's were relatively common on was the *Panama Limited* (later, *City of New Orleans*). It was somewhat uncommon for Amtrak to mix the P30's with other power, but this 1976 view of the *Panama* southbound on the ICG near 27th Street in Chicago shows it did happen. Behind the two P30's are an SDP40F and E8B.**—*Phil Gosney*

the Chicago hub, Seattle and to the *San Diegan* route. The next batch, 70 units delivered in 1977, were designated F40PHR's as the result of a strange twist of fate involving the big SDP40F's. Several other batches would be so designated as well.

A series of derailments involving the SDP's caused them to be banished altogether from some host railroads while being severely restricted speedwise on others. As a result, members of Amtrak's E- and F-unit fleet that had been stored when the big SDP's moved in made an encore, joining five leased Southern FP7's to fill voids left by SDP's that had suddenly moved back out. Despite extensive testing, there were no proven conclusions of faulty design on the part of EMD, but Amtrak, wishing to maintain peace with its sometimes cantankerous host roads, took no chances. The SDP's would be disposed of: Santa Fe took 18 of them in return for switchers Amtrak desperately needed and placed them in freight service; Amtrak traded most of its SDP's on various batches of F40's—the F40PHR's, the "R" standing for rebuild—which incorporated selected SDP internal components. A few SDP's were for a time retained for work-train duties, a sad demotion from their brief reign heading the likes of the *Empire Builder* and *Lake Shore Limited*.

For Amtrak, the mid-1970's continued to be active on the locomotive front. Not only did the purchase of the NEC from Penn Central include right-of-way, track and ancillary buildings, but locomotives, of note the FL9, which as a dual-power locomotive

ABOVE: **A momentous occasion—the first run of the first F40PH, Amtrak 200, piloting the eastbound *Lake Shore Limited* out of Chicago on April 4, 1976. You can almost smell the paint. Teammates that day included an E8A and an SDP40F.**—*Joe McMillan* LEFT: **By the 1990's, F40's would be a common sight in Chicago, just as E-units were at this same location—16th Street Shops, on the former site of Pennsylvania Railroad's passenger engine terminal. What will we see here in 2001?**—*Doug Koontz*

remains one of Amtrak's more-unusual breeds—and at 34-plus years currently its oldest over-the-road motive power. The FL9 can operate as a regular diesel-electric locomotive or as a straight electric, picking up power through third-rail shoes. EMD built them in 1956-57 and 1960 for the New Haven Railroad as a means of eliminating the diesel-to-electric locomotive change at New Haven for Boston-New York runs.

Amtrak got 12 FL9's, of which half were extensively rebuilt including (except one) a change to HEP capability; the remainder were disposed of. The NEC sale also included switchers: Electro-Motive SW1's and Alco RS3's. Also in 1976, Amtrak expanded its Turboliner fleet with seven five-car trainsets based on the French Turbo design, but built under license in the U.S. by Rohr Corporation of Chula Vista, Calif. These Turbos are unique in that each power car contains a small 600-h.p. traction motor that draws current from a third-rail pick-up shoe. City ordinances prohibit combustion locomotives (steam, diesel and turbine) from operating in Manhattan; the small traction motor enables Turbos to legally enter Grand Central Terminal (and now Penn Station) at a moderate maximum speed by using third-rail electric power.

And speaking of electric power, that subject became hot again in 1976-77 when Amtrak tested both a French and Swedish electric locomotive in high-speed service on the Northeast Corridor. Faced with permanent speed restrictions on the E60's,

RIGHT: Since most of the F40's preceded the Superliners, their assignments often included steam-heated trains. The new locomotives were HEP only, so steam-generator cars assisted in keeping passengers toasty. This pair of F40's leading the westbound *North Coast Hiawatha* out of the Windy City in December 1978 tote not one, but two steam-generator cars, both built from E-unit carbodies and chassis. The *North Coast* never did get HEP equipment; it was discontinued less than a year after this chilly scene was recorded.—*Mike Blaszak*

slipping performance on its self-propelled *Metroliners* and a roster of GG1's nearing the end of their service life (a situation hastened by PCB chemical leaks from the G's transformers as well as impending changes to the overhead electrical distribution system), Amtrak was on a quest for suitable straight-electric motive power that could play instrumental in transforming the NEC into a showcase high-speed rail route. The Swedish unit, a four-axle 7,000-h.p electric little brute of a locomotive, was chosen, and Amtrak put in three orders for 47 units, to be built by EMD in La Grange, Ill., under license from Sweden's ASEA.

Until delivery of the AEM7's began, GG1's sometimes held down *Metroliner Service* assignments while some Metroliner m.u. cars went through a rebuilding program intended to solve an overheating problem. In *Metroliner* service, the G's worked with power cars pulling Amfleet consists and successfully maintained the demanding schedules. Meanwhile, E60's worked secondary corridor runs as well as long-distance trains that traversed the NEC for a portion of their trips.

The first AEM7 arrived on the property in November 1979, and the rest slowly

Two motive-power acquisitions of note in 1976, beside that of the F40, were for seven new domestic Turbo power cars (and a like number of trainsets) and a dozen used FL9's. ABOVE: Two Rohr Turbos pose at the Rensselaer (N.Y.) maintenance facility in 1988; the third Turbo at far left is actually one of the French-built power cars, rebuilt with the Rohr-style nose.—*Jim Shaughnessy* LEFT: The FL9's are distinctive with their four- and six-axle trucks. The 491 is drifting along the Hudson River near Peekskill, N.Y., with the *Lake Shore Limited* in 1990.—*A. Bill McBride*

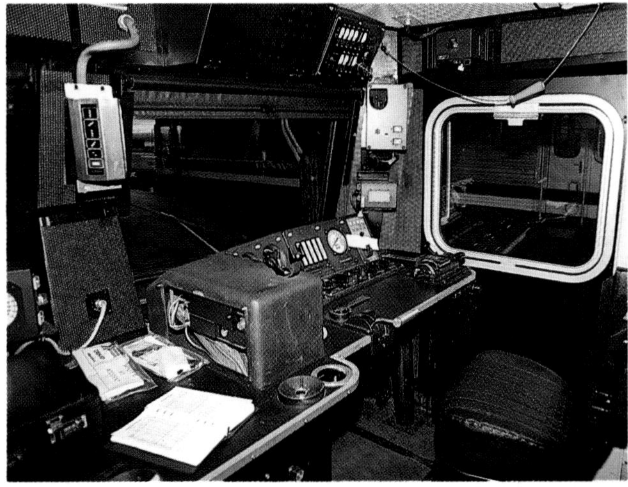

ABOVE: The 900 was the first AEM7 delivered, in November 1979, and spent several months testing with its blue-and-white EMD test-car companion (slightly visible in this shot).—*Bill Chaplik* **ABOVE: RIGHT: Cab interior of AEM7 No. 950 shows its console format.**—*Mike Del Vecchio*

BELOW: An F40 and an LRC unit make for a "Mutt 'n Jeff" combination on the *Shoreliner* at New Haven in April 1982. The LRC's were leased for purposes of testing the low-slung speedster and its tilt-body cars. An Amcafe serves as the food-service car on this day.—*Bill Chaplik* **BOTTOM: The SDP's met an untimely demotion—in the case of the 631, into work-train service, as shown at Michigan City, Ind., in October 1982.**—*Dan Munson*

began filing in in April 1980. Delivery was completed in spring 1982, and the rest, as they say, is history—and so was the famous GG1, Amtrak's last of which operated on May 1, 1981. Some of the E60's became history as well: Two were sold to freight roads in 1982, and in 1983 ten more were sold to NEC neighbor (and in some cases tenant) New Jersey Transit. Eventually, 11 of the remaining 14 E60's were refurbished, renumbered and eventually redesignated as E60MA to indicate rehab and HEP capability. Meanwhile, two boiler-equipped units remained on the active list, designated as E60CP's, and as of May 1, 1991, one damaged unit was in storage with an uncertain future.

The AEM7 lot was fortified in 1988 with seven additional units, two of which replaced the 900 and 903 which were dashed to pieces in the tragic *Colonial*/Conrail accident of Jan. 4, 1987.

Possibly one of the more unorthodox examples of passenger motive power to grace—briefly—Amtrak's roster were two LRC (for Light/Rapid/Comfortable) units built by Montreal Locomotive Works. The pair and their five-car low-slung trainsets were leased from 1980 to 1982 for service in the New York-Boston corridor, mainly to see if they could indeed cut travel times on the serpentine Shore Line route. The knife-nosed units and their trains were returned to Canada following mixed reviews, but nine cars were rebuilt and now operate on joint VIA-Amtrak Chicago-Toronto service.

THE ARRIVAL OF F40'S, all of which are HEP, throughout the late 1970's outpaced the delivery of all-electric equipment, be they new Amfleet cars or the older steam-heated equipment being rotated through Beech Grove Shops for transformation into the Heritage Fleet. To bridge this gap, steam-generator cars, built using baggage cars or E-unit or F-unit carbodies, were pressed into service with F40's so the new breed could haul steam-heated trains.

The F40 has one particular advantage over the E-unit. The four-axle locomotive is as at home on twisting mountain-climbing trackage as it is on the range. Proof of this grew ample as Amtrak's F40 fleet grew by leaps and bounds, and suddenly the F40 was everywhere—occasionally even on portions of electrified stretches of the Northeast Corridor! By 1988, as of press time the last year Amtrak received a batch of F40's, the carrier had amassed 216 of them (including three now off the roster).

By Amtrak's 20th anniversary on May 1, 1991, F40's were the rule in non-electrified territory, with few exceptions: (1) on the *Sunset Limited* and—until the summer of

ABOVE: **F69 451 leads the EMD test car, F69 450 and two F40s on the southbound *Coast Starlight* at Oakland, Calif., on Oct. 13, 1990. After exhaustive testing at DOT's Pueblo (Colo.) test track, the slope-faced F69's entered revenue service, at first in tandem with the test car, then independent. No major conclusions had been reached by the time of Amtrak's 20th anniversary, nor had Amtrak learned enough about a.c. traction to specify same on the locomotive order placed with GE early in 1991.**—*Mark Jones* BELOW: **Still under construction as the first edition of this book went to press were the first group of 20 new GE's, illustrated here as a carboard mock-up at Amtrak's Engineering Design offices in Philadelphia. Renderings show new paint schemes under consideration for the new units—and possibly for all motive power in the future.**—*Bob Johnston*

1991—*Auto Train*; where P30's had become *de rigueur*; (2) on the Empire Corridor (New York-Albany-Niagara Falls) where most extended corridor schedules are protected by Turbos and the through trains to and from Chicago and Toronto get FL9's south of Albany/Rensselaer, as do some New York-Rensselaer corridor runs; and (3) on selected trains operating out of Chicago that may be assigned GP40TC's, either singly or in tandem with an F40.

Amtrak's eight GP40TC's are five years older than the corporation itself. They were built in 1966 by General Motors Diesel, Ltd., London, Ont., for Toronto's then-new GO Transit commuter-rail system. As built, each unit contained a diesel-driven 500-kilowatt generator for train climate control and lighting. Power-starved Amtrak purchased all eight units in 1988 and quickly put them into mostly local service out of Chicago; some were assigned to the *City of New Orleans*, essentially working as booster units and, under normal circumstances, never leading. Nevertheless, they at least help augment the fleet of F40's, which Amtrak never seems to have enough of, and why in 1989 it made another run for the border. This time Amtrak

ABOVE: The former New York Central Alco RS3's were acquired at the time of the 1976 purchase of the Northeast Corridor. Amtrak's shop forces at New Haven, Conn., replaced the units' 244-series engines with that of standard EMD 567's. The 106 is shown at its long-time hangout, Boston, where it is pulling the *Lake Shore Limited*'s equipment out of South Station to head for the yards on May 8, 1982.—*Bill Chaplik*

BELOW: Many of Amtrak's GP7/9's got the "pumpkin orange" scheme, a bright color appropriate for work-train service. But the 763 (now retired), shown in Los Angeles in July 1979, received the traditional red-nose scheme—itself a common Amtrak livery, but not on too many Geeps.—*Alan Miller, collection of Joseph Oates* BOTTOM: Electro-Motive's SW1 switcher was once relatively common throughout the U.S. (660 were built), but a rarity by the 1990's. The 742 is helping split the *Lake Shore Limited* into its New York and Boston sections at Albany/Rensselaer in the summer of 1982. Amtrak still has a half dozen of the diminutive units.—*Jim Conroy*

found more-compatible units, six F40's deemed surplus by GO Transit.

In yet another move to improve locomotive availability and to allocate more time for proper maintenance to the F40 fleet, Amtrak in 1991 began leasing 15 EMD GP40/GP40-2 locomotives from Helm Financial Services. Having served on Boston & Maine, Conrail, Illinois Central Gulf and Soo/Milwaukee Road, the purely freight units were rebuilt with high-speed gearing and pass-through HEP cabling, enabling them to work as booster units for F40's.

In the late 1980's, Amtrak ventured into territory uncharted by most U.S. roads when in 1987 it exchanged the standard EMD d.c. traction motors for new a.c. equipment from Brown-Boveri on one of its F40PH's, No. 202, which has since been redesignated as an F40AC. Since the beginning of dieseldom stateside, d.c. propulsion has been the norm, but in recent years, advances in a.c. technology indicate that a.c. propulsion will reduce a diesel's maintenance costs, enhance its operating performance and improve reliability. A.c. traction is nearly universal in European diesel operation, but nearly unheard here. Expanding upon a.c. experimentation, Amtrak in 1989 took delivery of two special EMD locomotives built new with a.c. traction motors, F69PH's 450 and 451.

OUT OF THE LIMELIGHT, Amtrak maintains an eclectic array of motive power that provides backstage support to the stars. These are locomotives, all secondhand, used for switching and work trains. Most are former-Santa Fe units, model CF7 rebuilt by AT&SF from old F-units (some of which early on hauled Amtrak trains, no less) and model SSB1200 upgraded by Santa Fe from older switchers. Also alive and mostly well on Amtrak are 20 EMD GP7's and GP9's, once the ubiquitous road freight (and sometimes passenger) locomotive of the 1950's and 1960's. The "Geeps" are of various heritages and were acquired from Precision National, a locomotive-rebuilding and brokering company.

Ancient are Amtrak's EMD SW1 switchers, dating from the 1940's and formerly owned by New York Central and Pennsylvania; not much younger are a cache of SW8's, originally Lehigh Valley and NYC, and three ex-NYC Alco RS3C's, the latter rebuilt with EMD innards. Almost unknown, because Amtrak never used them, are eight former-PRR electric freight motors. They were intended for work-train service, and some even received the Amtrak silver scheme. However, the same fate that in part befell the mighty GG1 also did in the E44's—the PCB discharge from their transformers. As of May 1, 1991, most remained stored at Wilmington, Del.

FOR OVER A DECADE, General Motors' F40 has reigned over nearly the entire Amtrak system, at home on two-car locals as well as 18-car Superliners. It has become the standard passenger locomotive of North America. But, an order placed by Amtrak early in 1991 with GE for 52 locomotives, to be delivered in three batches (because it involves three different types of locomotives), is destined to change what has become a familiar face to many of those who have watched an Amtrak train rumble into a station or slash past a grade crossing.

The first 20 will be 3,200-h.p. units equipped with so-called "wide-nose" safety cabs that are rapidly becoming standard in U.S. freight application. The second group—22 units of 4,000 h.p each—are designated AMD103's and, if you believe the artist's renderings, are to resemble Germany's super-streamlined (and some say super homely) *Inter-City Express* (ICE) locomotives, although a new profile may be in the offing for the look of this group. The final batch of ten units will also be AMD103's but with dual-power; that is, they'll be a modern version of the FL9.

For a railroad said to be greatly homogenized, Amtrak has had a most-interesting motive-power history. And the story isn't over yet.

AMTRAK LOCOMOTIVE ROSTER

Current as of May 1, 1991

TYPE	CURRENT NUMBERS	PRIOR OWNER(S) (IF ANY)	H.P.	ORIGINAL BUILDER	DATE BUILT	DATE ACQ'D (IF SECOND-HAND)	NOTES
Turbo	58-69		1,600	ANF	1973-75		
RS3	104, 106-107	NYC, PC	1,200	Alco-GE	1951	1976	1
Turbo	150-163		1,600	Rohr	1976		
GP40TC	192-199	GO Transit	3,000	GMD	1966	1988	
F40PH	200-201, 203-229		3,000	EMD	1976		
F40AC	202		3,000	EMD	1976		2
F40PHR	230-269		3,000	EMD	1977		3, 4
F40PH	270-279		3,000	EMD	1977		
F40PHR	280-299		3,000	EMD	1978-79		3
F40PH	300-328		3,000	EMD	1979		
F40PHR	329-331		3,000	EMD	1980		3
F40PH	332-359		3,000	EMD	1980		
F40PHR	360-409		3,000	EMD	1980-88		3, 5
F40PH	410-415	GO Transit	3,000	EMD	1987	1990	6
F69PH	450-451		3,000	GMD	1988		7
FL9	485-489, 491	NH, PC	1,750	EMD	1957		8
SSB1200	550-567	AT&SF	1,200	EMD	1939-59		9
CF7	575-599	AT&SF	1,500	EMD	1949-56		10
E60MA	600-610		6,000	GE	1974-76		11
E60CP	620		6,000	GE	1974	1976	12
E60CP	621		6,000	GE	1975	1984	12
GP40/ GP40-2	650-664	B&M, CR,IC, SOO (MILW)	3,000	EMD	Various	1984 1991	13
P30CH	700-724		3,000	GE	1975-76		
SW1	732, 734, 736, 738, 742-743	NYC, PRR, PC	600	EMD	1941-50	1976	
SW8	747-750	NOUPT,	800	EMD	1953	1983	
GP7	766-767, 769-783	UP, C&NW, L&N, NC&StL, QNS&L, N&W, C&EI, CRI&P	1,500	EMD	1950-57	1978	14
GP9	764-765, 768, 770	UP, C&NW	1,750	EMD	1954-57	1978	14
AEM7	900-953		7,000	EMD	1979-88		15

1. Repowered with 1,200-h.p. EMD power plant in 1984, 1981 and 1983 respectively.
2. Built as F40PH; rebuilt with a.c. traction motors by Brown-Boveri in 1987.
3. Built using selected internal SDP40F components.
4. Units 236 and 246 stricken from roster.
5. Unit 366 stricken from roster.
6. Ex-GO Transit 510-515.
7. These are considered experimental (not prototype) units, equipped with a.c. traction motors.
8. Rebuilt by Morrison-Knudsen in 1979-80 using parts from other FL9's since stricken from roster.
9. Rebuilt by Santa Fe from its F-unit fleet during the 1970's.
10. Rebuilt from NW2's, SW9's and SW1200's.
11. Originally numbered in the 900-series; some originally came with boilers, some with HEP, but all now have HEP capability; they received their current numbers in 1985-86.
12. Contain steam generators.
13. Rebuilt with high-speed gearing and pass-through HEP cabling.
14. Acquired through Precision National Corporation.
15. Nos. 900 and 903 destroyed in Chase, Md., wreck, Jan. 4, 1987, and stricken from roster; replaced by second 900 and 903 delivered in 1988

CODES

Alco-GE = American Locomotive Works/General ELectric
ANF = ANF-Frangeco
AT&SF = Atchison, Topeka & Santa Fe
B&M = Boston & Maine
C&EI = Chicago & Eastern Illinois
C&NW = Chicago & North Western
CR = Conrail
CRI&P = Chicago, Rock Island & Pacific
EMD = Electro-Motive Division, General Motors
GE = General Electric
GMD = General Motors Diesel, Ltd.
GO Transit = Government of Ontario Transit
IC = Illinois Central
L&N = Louisville & Nashville
MILW = Milwaukee Road
N&W = Norfolk & Western
NC&StL = Nashville, Chattanooga & St. Louis
NH = New Haven
NOUPT = New Orleans Union Passenger Terminal
NYC = New York Central
PC = Penn Central
PRR = Pennsylvania
QNS&L = Quebec, North Shore & Labrador
Rohr = Rohr Corp.
SOO = Soo Line
UP = Union Pacific

6/Places on wheels

AN OVERVIEW OF AMTRAK'S DIVERSE ROLLING-STOCK ROSTER

Amtrak backbones: Amfleet (TOP) and Superliners (ABOVE). These two major car groups work together with the Heritage Fleet, Turboliners, Horizon Fleet and other members of Amtrak's varied rolling-stock roster to move thousands of passengers every day.—*Both photos, Mike Schafer*

When Amtrak was young, it was old. Until the arrival of brand-new French-built Turboliners in 1973, the entire fleet of rolling stock available to the carrier was secondhand. . . and thirdhand, and fourthhand. Some streamlined cars dated from the late 1930's, and at least one heavyweight diner-lounge used in early Amtrak Chicago-St. Louis service went back to the 1920's! It was like starting a new airline with DC3's.

The good news was that many of the cars were less than seven years old (the Metroliners and a block of UP coaches), and that even a large percentage of those built in the 1950's—which constituted most of the rest of the cars—still had a few years left on them if someone could give them a good home and a thorough rebuild.

One could write a book just covering Amtrak's early, eclectic and most-interesting car fleet. Suffice it to say here that most NRPC member roads were duly represented on early Amtrak trains, in billboard fashion until the red, white, blue and silver began to be applied.

Of course, to students of transportation, things like old TWA DC3's and Seaboard Sun Lounge sleepers may be exotic, but for the traveling public that wasn't necessarily what they wanted or needed. Passengers desired clean, comfortable, reliable equipment, and if it were new, so much the better. Things like new DC10's and Concordes were embraced by the contemporary traveling public, and up-to-date equipment is always quite a marketable item.

When Amtrak began, it had some 3,000 cars at its disposal belonging to member roads. (As a note of comparison, the company had close to 2,000 as of Jan. 1, 1991.) Early on, and with the assistance of subcontractors whose specialty was railcar equipment, it systematically began an examination of these cars to determine which were best suited for purchase.

The criteria for selecting cars was, basically, that they be of all-stainless-steel construction, which immediately narrowed it down to mostly cars built by the Budd Company (most "stainless steel" cars of other manufacturers—Pullman-Standard, American Car & Foundry, St. Louis Car—were in fact Cor-Ten steel cars sheathed in stainless steel, a deadly combination in railcar construction which expedited cancerous body rust), with a few exceptions, such as later-model P-S cars and numerous aluminum-body ex-UP cars.

The variety of car mechanical and electrical apparatus (air-conditioning units, alternators, lighting systems, etc.) was also an issue. Unfortunately, this aspect would backfire: Although the "new" federation of equipment comprised mostly Budd and Pullman-Standard cars, the fraternity reflected the customized whims and practices of 20 (or more) railroads, particularly where air-conditioners were concerned; e.g., use of propane-fired Waukesha air-conditioners was restricted in the East because of tunnels. As a result, equipment problems during the first year or so were rampant, not necessarily because of defects, but because shop forces weren't always familiar with all the varying mechanical aspects of cars being serviced.

The variety had its good side, though, especially for students of the American passenger train. When NRPC member railroads lay open their coach-yard doors for the purchasing agents, Amtrak unearthed many exotic cars that had been sidelined by the roads in the late 1960's. Though stored, many of these vehicles remained in good condition, met the above criteria and wound up on the new carrier's roster. Suddenly, observation cars were in vogue again, Vista-Domes began appearing on routes that had never seen them and twin-unit diners were again feeding *Broadway Limited* passengers.

The cars Amtrak selected were rotated through a refurbishment program done at various shop facilities—some railroad-owned, some independent. Externally, the stainless-steel cars received the official Amtrak paint scheme of wide red and blues stripes against a white window band, with the Amtrak logo at the car ends; the bulk of the body on smooth-sided cars were painted Platinum Mist to better match the stainless equipment.

Image-concious Amtrak was decidedly more creative with car interiors. Some may look back at the early interior designs with horror, but we must remember that this was the hippie era of the 1970's, when purple-paisley was the chosen art of women's blouses and men wore slacks that looked like they were made from living-room drapes. Rail passengers accustomed to the monotonous pastels of car interiors of the 1950's went into color shock, but the nouveau look probably helped drive home the message that said rail travel was moving directly from the 1950's into the 1970's.

THE REFURBISHED OLD EQUIPMENT had to make do until Amtrak could began buying all-new rolling stock, and its first venture in that direction was late in 1972 when it ordered two five-car (two cab/power cars, two coaches and a dinette coach) French-built Turboliners which immigrated to the U.S. in 1973; four more trainsets followed in 1975. Domestic passenger-car development and construction was virtually non-existent in the U.S. then, so these acquisitions allowed Amtrak to quickly usher in all-new equipment. Despite their faults (they were intolerant of harsh Midwestern winters; consist size was relatively fixed; the stock was incompatible with existing cars), the Turboliners had—thanks to huge windows—bright interiors, rode well, looked sleek and contemporary and generated lots of good press for Amtrak.

Amtrak capitalized on its program of car selection in its early marketing campaigns, producing this memorable ad that appeared from coast to coast in newspapers and magazines.—*Courtesy of Amtrak*

As Amtrak purchased cars from member railroads, they headed for the shops. Cars emerged with interiors redone to reflect styles of the period, which in the early 1970's often meant vivid colors. TOP: Interior of diner-lounge 8320 (an ex-SP car built in 1950 for the *Sunset Limited*) working the *Abraham Lincoln* in October 1975.—*Bob Schmidt* ABOVE RIGHT: One of the more-unique car series in early Amtrak days were SP's home-built "three-quarter" dome lounges, such as this on the *Starlight* in 1977.—*Brad Joseph* ABOVE: This ex-Santa Fe car on the *Arrowhead* in 1975 represents what was then a very common interior for coaches: blue seats with paisley slipcovers, blue ceiling and off-white luggage racks.—*Mike Schafer*

In fact, Amtrak was satisfied enough to also order an American version of the Turboliner in 1974. Seven five-car sets were delivered from the Rohr Corporation of Chula Vista, Calif., in 1975. They were built under license from ANF-Frangeco and thus were similar to the French sets except for an updated cab nose design, standard North American couplers, improved turbines, "Americanized" seating, first-class seating and small electric traction motors with third-rail pickup for operation into New York's Grand Central Terminal.

The new Turboliners joined two United Aircraft TurboTrains which had been built in the 1960's. The articulated format of the UA trains (adjacent cars shared a common wheelset) and other radical features, such as domed power cabs, and unreliability made them short-lived celebrities of Amtrak's ever-changing equipment roster.

The next new equipment order for Amtrak, placed in October 1973, was one of the most important. It was a domestic order placed with Budd Company, the dean of American passenger car builders, and in part based upon a car format that had been developed in the mid-1960's for a joint Federal/Pennsylvania Railroad (Penn Central as of Feb. 1, 1968) high-speed corridor project: self-powered, high-speed m.u.* cars known as Metroliners.

By utilizing the existing tooling and dies used in the manufacture of the shells of the 61 Metroliner cars of 1967, Amtrak could introduce a whole new fleet of conventional (i.e., single-level, locomotive-hauled) cars relatively quickly and inexpensively. This was the genesis of the Amfleet car.

The initial order for 57 Amfleet cars burgeoned into 492, ordered in three batches in 1973, 1974 and 1975 and delivered in 1975, 1976 and 1977 at a cost of $266 mil-

*M.u. stands for "multiple unit." Generally, in U.S. practice, m.u. cars are self-powered electric vehicles; that is, each car is equipped with its own traction motors. These cars usually can operate singly, or in "multiple" with other like cars, with all being controlled from a control-cab-equipped car leading the group.

lion (about a half million per car average). They came in five basic configurations: (1) Amcoach, most with 84 reclining seats of close pitch; (2) long-distance Amcoach, seating 60; (3) Amcafes, each with 53 coach seats and snack bar; (4) Amclub, with 23 coach seats, 18 club seats and snack bar; and (5) Amdinette, with 23 coach seats, table seating for 32 and snack bar. All cars feature all-electric heating, air-conditioning and lighting, retention toilets, disc brakes and carpeting throughout.

Since delivery, many cars have been modified, including two that in 1978 were rebuilt—briefly—into what Amtrak called Mini-Sleepers, featuring 48 coach seats, two twin-bed economy sleeping rooms and two dressing rooms. They worked the *Shenandoah* and the *Night Owl*. Some Amdinettes have been rebuilt into grill-lounges featuring 32 dining seats and 19 lounge seats, while other cars have been upgraded with improved seating for *Metroliner Service* operation.

Amtrak's next major order for rolling stock—the Superliners—revolutionized long-distance rail travel in Western U.S., although these cars, too, had roots that pre-dated Amtrak by more than 15 years. The Superliner order of 1975-76—$241 million worth—was built by Pullman-Standard, another well-known name in railcar construction, but Superliners are direct descendants of a line of double-deck cars known as Hi-Levels, built for Santa Fe by Budd in 1956 and 1964. The Superliners are basically updated versions of the Hi-Levels, incorporating improvements such as all-electric climate control/lighting and increased headroom. Assembly even incorporated Budd patents acquired by P-S.

In intercity practice, the bilevel concept calls for two completely separate floor levels with passage between the cars usually at the upper level (versus most commuter-rail bilevels, which have upper level "galleries" and lower-level car-to-car passage). Some ex-Santa Fe Hi-Levels have a transition stairway to bring the aisle to standard floor level, thus permitting Superliners/Hi-Levels to mix with single-level equipment—and why on almost every long-distance Superliner train you will usually see a Hi-Level at the front next to the baggage cars. The double-decking allows air-conditioning equipment and other car appliances to be fully enclosed, on the lower level, versus hanging out in the open underneath conventional cars. This plus the fact that an ample supply of restrooms can also be located on the lower level permits more passenger space elsewhere on both levels. In essence, one Superliner or Hi-Level replaces two single-level cars, so their use has great impact on the cost-effectiveness of train operation.

The first Superliner order was placed on April 2, 1975, for 235 cars, but this was increased by 14 cars on July 29, 1976, and again on Nov. 24 of the same year for 35 more. Total: 284 cars in five basic configurations: (1) coach, with 75 long-distance (legrest) seats; (2) coach-baggage with 78 seats of closer pitch; (3) sleeper, with 15

Amfleet marked a new dawn U.S. rail passenger transportation. The cars brought badly needed reliability and modernity to the struggling carrier, and ushered in widespread use of HEP equipment. The cars were not without their shortcomings: The tubular design coupled with slender windows and high-back seating (on the 84-seat cars) made them somewhat confining, although Amfleet cars are actually wider at the seat level than conventional cars. Amfleet II improved on some of these items.—*Mike Schafer*

ABOVE LEFT: Amfleet pioneered handicap accessibility in railcar design. For this youthful traveler boarding the *Gulf Coast Limited* at Mobile, Ala., in 1984, such accessibility means greater freedom.—*Don Jilson* **ABOVE RIGHT:** Many Amfleet cars have been modified in some way over the years. Not long after their delivery, three Amclub cars were reconfigured for *Montrealer* service as cafe-lounge "Pub" cars with lounge seats in one half, and dinette tables in the other. This view aboard the *Montrealer* in 1978 shows the lounge section.—*Mike Schafer*

Ex-Santa Fe Hi-Levels on the *Southwest Limited* get a scrubbing at Albuquerque in 1975. Superliner design has its roots in the Hi-Level car fleet built for Santa Fe in the 1950's and 1960's.—*Don Crimmin*

economy rooms for one or two each, five deluxe bedrooms for two each, a family room for two adults and two children and a handicap room for two for a capacity of 46; (4) diner seating 72; and (5) cafe-lounge with snack bar and 70 seats. With their floor-to-ceiling windows, the cafe-lounges are also known as "Sightseer" lounges.

As with the Amfleet armada, several Superliners have been modified. Some coaches were rebuilt into snack-coaches, while sleepers have had restrooms added to upper-level areas, and showers to lower.

Ongoing design modifications and a strike at the P-S plant in Hammond, Ind., delayed the Superliners' debut many months. The first car was accepted on Oct. 27, 1978, but none entered revenue service until Feb. 26, 1979. The order was completed in 1981, after which Pullman-Standard exited the passenger-car market. Amtrak people then speculated this to be the only Superliner order the company would need.

Although criticized (understandably) by some passenger-train aficionados because the new cars spelled the demise of the dome car on Western trains, the Superliners were a sensation with the public, who liked their spaciousness and quiet, smooth-riding (on good track, at least) characteristics. Ridership on long-distance trains surged throughout the 1980's, one major reason for the order for more bilevels in 1991 (another being the significant improvement in operating economics).

CONCURRENT WITH THE introduction of Superliners was another breakthrough on Amtrak's rolling-stock front—an advancement whereby "old" became "new" as a sizeable chunk of Amtrak's fleet of older conventional cars emerged from a radical reshopping as the "Heritage Fleet."

The Amfleet order of the mid-1970's together with a couple of particularly brutal winters solidified Amtrak's stance on train climate control and lighting; i.e., all operable rolling stock should be all-electric, with power for heating, cooling and lighting originating at a single source. Amtrak's ex-C&NW bilevels of 1958, the Turbos and all Amfleet equipment already were of this format, using power supplied by a generator in the train's locomotive or in some cases a custom-built power car if an HEP (head-end power)-equipped locomotive was not available.

In May 1977, following one of its worst winters ever, Amtrak embarked on a program to convert a group of cars to HEP, greatly improving their reliability and comfort while making them fully compatible

ABOVE: Superliner coaches provide passengers with roomy legrest seating, curtained windows and plenty of carpeting (right up the walls). Interior design reflects the change in decorative tastes from earlier in the decade; garish was "out"—earth colors were "in."—*Tom Nemeth* **RIGHT**: Superliner deluxe bedrooms used time-proven designs of post-World War II sleepers, with fold-out beds, enclosed lavatory and folding partitions to allow four to travel *en suite*, as shown. The Superliners brought a boom in sleeper travel in the West, which led Amtrak to include a high proportion of sleepers in its 1991 Superliner order.—*Mike Schafer* **BELOW**: The *Empire Builder,* shown westbound in June 1980, was the first long-distance train to go Superliner, on Oct. 28, 1979. As this scene near Minot, N.D., illustrates, the train for a time operated sans Sightseer Lounge, since those cars were among the last delivered. Note the Hi-Level transition coach-dorm behind the baggage car.—*Terry Chicwak*

ABOVE: The Superliner diners have an understated elegance about them, despite the perceived casualness of booth seating (now standard on all Amtrak diners). The all-electric kitchen is on the lower level, with food dispatched via dumbwaiters to the central serving area of the upper level. The Superdiners were delivered with their own crockery, used but for a short time before budgetary cutbacks in 1981 forced Amtrak to switch to plasticware. TOP RIGHT: Although nothing can quite replace the classic dome car, the Superliner lounges, with their floor-to-ceiling windows, offer a viewing sensation that's enjoyable in its own right.—*Two photos, Tom Nemeth* **ABOVE RIGHT: The lower levels of the Superlounges feature a snack/beverage serving bar and booth-table seating. As delivered, the cars sported electric pianos, but these have since been removed.**—*Mike Schafer*

with Amfleet (and, to an extent, Superliner) equipment. The guinea pigs were 25 ex-Union Pacific 10-roomette 6-double-bedroom sleepers; they were assigned to selected Amfleet trains, some of which under emergency conditions had been converted to Amfleet during the winter strife, including the *National Limited, City of New Orleans* and *James Whitcomb Riley*.

Deemed successful, the program was accelerated to include the best of Amtrak's conventional fleet, and one-by-one other single-level long-distance trains became all-electric: the *Lake Shore Limited* late in 1979, the *Broadway* in 1980 and the *Crescent* and *Silver Meteor* in 1981. With the *Silver Star's* changeover on March 10, 1982, Amtrak's active rolling-stock fleet was all-electric. Somewhat of a drawback to the program was that Amtrak, out of practicality, stuck largely with cars of a standard type—i.e., baggage, diner-lounges, 10-6 sleepers, Slumbercoaches and straight coaches. This spelled the demise for many oddballs Amtrak had been operating, such as ex-New York Central observations, former-Burlington and Wabash Vista-Dome parlor-observations, old Seaboard and Atlantic Coast Line sleeper-lounges, ex-Pennsy twin-unit diners and other "exotics" that had made Amtrak's roster of the 1970's a rolling history of the streamliner era. One notable exception: Nine ex-UP and CB&Q 11-bedroom sleepers assigned to *Auto Train*—as of press time the only standard all-double-bedroom sleepers on Amtrak.

Nevertheless, the floor plans of several other cars were drastically modified during the HEP program. Seven Santa Fe lunch-counter diners emerged as straight lounges as did ten former-PRR parlor cars. A whole series of ambulance cars purchased from the U.S. Army early in the 1970's metamorphosized into straight baggage cars, baggage-dormitories and pub lounges. Equipment for the Northeast-Florida runs took on special characteristics as Amtrak sought ways to accommodate especially heavy ridership on this route. Thus in the early-to-mid 1980's, several ex-CB&Q coaches, ex-SP lounges and ex-PRR parlors became cafeteria cars; three diners of Southeastern heritage became kitchen cars; and four coaches became "table cars." Some of these had already gone through the HEP program in the late 1970's.

Fortunately, Amtrak had second thoughts about the once-popular Vista-Dome coach, whose quantities were ample enough to render them as a "standard" car type in their own right. So in 1983 and

RIGHT: A bit of New York Central's world-renowned *20th Century Limited* survived into Amtrak in the form of ex-NYC sleeper-buffet-lounge-observation *Wingate Brook* (a protection car for the *Century* and other trains, built by Budd in 1949), here working the eastbound *San Francisco Zephyr* awaiting highball from Denver on July 20, 1976. In another year, Amtrak would embark on its massive HEP program for its pre-Amtrak single-level rolling stock, dooming such exotic, one- or few-of-kind cars like this.—*Don Crimmin*

ABOVE: Number 4602 was a 1979 graduate of the HEP school. The ex-UP coach and its sister cars are unusual in that they are aluminum. **BELOW:** Amfleet II equipment began arriving about the time the HEP program was winding down. It is often teamed up with Heritage Fleet cars on long-distance Eastern trains.—*Both photos, Bill Chaplik*

ABOVE: One antiquated practice vanquished by the HEP program was that of servicing ice-cooled kitchen facilities, as in this scene of the *Sunset Limited* at New Orleans in December 1978. As one worker tosses chunks of ice up to the roof of the train's diner, the other crewman places it into the car's food bunkers via rooftop hatches. —*Mike Blaszak*

1984, a dozen former-Northern Pacific, Great Northern and Spokane, Portland & Seattle dome coaches went through the HEP program, reviving the dome experience for the *Capitol Limited, City of New Orleans/River Cities, Auto Train* and (for a time) *Ann Rutledge*. In a like manner, six ex-GN, Milwaukee and CB&Q full-dome lounges have been HEP'ed for *Auto Train*.

If the Amfleet story of the mid-1970's had been made into a movie, and that movie had a sequel, it would probably be called "Amfleet II—Jason Reclines in Comfort." Anyway, Amtrak in 1980 placed a $115 million order with Budd for 150 more Amfleet cars, to be called . . . Amfleet II. (Note the dramatic per-car increase in price—over 50 percent—over the first Amfleet order.) The new batch included 25 Amlounge II's featuring 17 lounge and 32 table seats and a snack bar, and 125 long-distance coaches, most with 59 reclining seats but a few with 55 seats and an enlarged baggage area. The most-obvious differences from earlier Amfleet equipment? Larger win-

RIGHT: A consortium of Northeastern governmental officials spearheaded by Massachusetts Governor (and 1988 presidential candidate) Michael Dukakis have been working with Amtrak to further develop high-speed Boston-New York service. Studies included testing of low-slung, tilt-body rolling stock which would allow higher speeds on existing track. Spanish Talgo equipment was among that evaluated, with Turbo power-coaches as motive power. That odd combo is shown near Attleboro, Mass., on May 9, 1988.—*George A. Forero Jr.* **BELOW:** Bombardier's LRC (Light/Rapid/Comfortable) equipment was also extensively tested by Amtrak. Although Amtrak returned ten borrowed LRC cars and two locomotives to owner VIA Rail, nine of those cars now operate in joint Amtrak-VIA Chicago-Toronto service.—*Bill Chaplik*

All three Viewliner prototypes stand at Beech Grove Shops in various stages of assembly early in 1988. The Viewliners began as carbody shells manufactured to Amtrak specifications by Budd in 1987; "The Grove" completed assembly with some of their own components and the "finished" cars were ready for testing in revenue service beginning in 1988. Fine tuning continued into the 1990's, and an order was expected to be placed in 1991 or 1992.—*Mike Schafer*

dows and single vestibule. These cars went to work on various long-distance trains, including the *Lake Shore*, *Broadway*, *Star*, *Meteor* and *Auto Train*.

Amfleet II underscored the ongoing need for more brand-new single-level rolling stock, despite the recent Heritage Fleet program. With this in mind, and because until now there had not been time and resources to develop a totally new, true state-of-the-art car from scratch, Amtrak in 1983 ventured into its Viewliner project. The Viewliner was—and is—to be the single-level passenger car of the future, its every detail of design, construction and operation, researched by the company that best understands the long-distance rail-travel market in America—Amtrak.

At a cost of $12.2 million, Budd delivered three fluted stainless-steel Viewliner bodies in 1987 to Amtrak, which did the final assembly into two sleepers and a diner. In a crowd of Amtrak cars, the rakish Viewliners, with their upper row of windows (to add to the openness of the cars' interiors) and a tapered cross section, are unmistakable. The trio entered revenue test service in 1988 variously on the *Night Owl*, *Cardinal* and *Capitol Limited*.

The most-recent car order prior to Amtrak's 20th birthday fulfilled a need for additional short-distance cars. For this, Amtrak made a $104 million purchase of 104 cars from Montreal-based Bombardier Corp., which had acquired Pullman-Standard and Budd's carbuilding patents when they abandoned the railcar market. The Horizon Fleet, assembled in Bombardier's Barre, Vt., complex, comprises 86 coaches and 18 food-service cars based on a P-S car design that has been fundamental to the commuter-rail world since 1970. Once again, by utilizing tried-and-proven designs and existing tooling, Amtrak was able to quickly fill a need and save money, albeit at the expense of having a uniform style to its cavalcade of single-level cars.

Most of the utilitarian cars entered service in 1989 on Midwestern corridors and on the Oakland-Bakersfield (Calif.) *San Joaquin* route, freeing Amfleet equipment to return to the Northeast Corridor.

SPEAKING OF THE NEC, the new order of *Metroliner Service* that came with the 1980's—that of AEM7 electrics toting Amfleet cars refurbished specifically for the high-speed, premium-fare runs—resulted in an interesting domino effect involving the 1960's-era Metroliner m.u. cars.

Thirty-four of these cars were revamped in 1979-80 (those that were can be identified by a rooftop hump of cooling apparatus), but bumped from New York-Washington service shortly thereafter. Many of the demoted speedsters went to work on the Philadelphia-Harrisburg leg of the Corridor, where they became known as Capitoliners. Often, in this service, they were (in a twist of irony) hauled by AEM7's instead of operating under their own power.

Several Metroliner m.u.'s have made another interesting incarnation, as cab-control cars for diesel-powered trains operating in "push-pull" mode. Denuded of their traction motors, the m.u.'s-turned-cab-coaches are equipped with train lines that enable a locomotive to be remotely controlled from the cab of the car. The push-pull concept, which came of age in the U.S. on commuter lines in the 1960's, finally saw widespread use on Amtrak late in the 1980's (early Amtrak push-pull operations utilized the ex-C&NW bilevels, some of which had been rebuilt into cab-control cars) thanks to the rebuilding of ex-Metroliner m.u.'s into cab-coaches. Push-pull is now the norm on several corridors, including Chicago-Milwaukee, Los Angeles-San Diego and Chicago-Detroit.

AT THE HEAD-END (or hind end) of many an

ABOVE RIGHT: **A cab-control coach teams up with Horizon Fleet coaches and an F40 on a Milwaukee-Chicago *Hiawatha Service* train arriving Chicago in September 1990. Conversion of Metroliner m.u. cars into cab cars has enabled Amtrak to operate corridors more efficiently by reducing the number of locomotives necessary to protect a route and to eliminate the time necessary to turn a whole train or its locomotive at the end of a run.**—*Mike Abalos* **RIGHT:** **Some Metroliner cars have been demotored and operate as locomotive-hauled trains on the Philadelphia-Harrisburg line. This set is being pulled by an F40 at Overbrook, Pa., on March 1988. Car pantographs are up only for train lighting and climate control.**—*Rob Palmer*

on passenger, mail and express trains of the pre-Amtrak era: the express boxcar, which in the Amtrak era is known as the material handling car.

Amtrak's auto carriers are, of course, the key to the *Auto Train* operation. There are two basic groups: 43 bilevel carriers built in 1956 for Canadian National, acquired by Auto-Train Corporation circa 1970 and then Amtrak early in the 1980's; and 21 trilevel carriers built for Santa Fe in 1976 and acquired by Amtrak in 1983. Since the trilevels were built as your basic auto-rack freight car, Amtrak had to modify them with high-speed trucks, Tightlock couplers and improved sheathing.

ABOVE: ***Connecticut Valley Service*** **train 473, the Springfield connection to the Boston-Washington** ***Yankee Clipper*** **at New Haven, grinds into Berlin, Conn., on Jan. 12, 1986. This was the last day Amtrak made regular use of a now-generation of Rail Diesel Cars called the SPV2000 (for Self-Powered Vehicle for service into the year 2000). Amtrak returned the mechanically disinclined cars back to owner Connecticut DOT and went back to F40's and Amfleet (or regular RDC's) for Valley service.**—*Scott Hartley*

BELOW: The cab end of this ex-Metroliner m.u. wears a design unlike any other Amtrak vehicle because, inside, it ***is*** **unlike any other Amtrak vehicle. Number 9800 is the experimental conference-club cab car, which features 18 club seats, four conference booths, and (BELOW RIGHT) a conference table .**—*Bob Johnston*

Amtrak train are cars of an unassuming nature, equipment that passengers and even on-board crews have limited contact with. Nonetheless, baggage cars, material handling cars (MHC's) and *Auto Train*'s auto carriers generate important revenue.

The growth in mail and express business sent Amtrak looking for baggage and mail cars beyond what it had inherited in 1971. It came up with a large group of former-U.S. Army troop kitchen cars, which were rebuilt into baggage cars in 1976. Likewise, several former U.S. Army ambulance cars that had already been rebuilt by Amtrak into lounges and baggage-dorms, were rebuilt again. . . into straight baggage cars during the first half of the 1980's. Also joining the fray later in the decade were seven cars purchased from VIA.

To handle a glut of new contracts involving sealed mail and periodicals as well as its own express business, Amtrak returned to using a type of vehicle once prominent

AS BIRTHDAY TIME drew near on May 1, 1991, an important new passenger-car order for Amtrak drew considerable attention from the press—$340 million worth of new Superliners to be built by Bombardier for delivery by the mid-1990's. The 140 cars are to include transition-dorms, coaches, diners, lounges and sleepers.

They will bring the bilevel format to such trains as the *Capitol Limited, Auto Train* and *City of New Orleans* and allow the expansion of other trains that are already operating with Superliner equipment. Single-level equipment bumped from the above-mentioned trains will permit tri-weekly trains to go daily, and possibly to add new services.

Who would have guessed, in those lean days of 1971, that the then-new wobbling carrier would, by 1991, have given over 500 cars new life through total rebuild and placed well over 1,200 brand-new passenger cars into service?

CONDENSED AMTRAK PASSENGER-CAR ROSTER

Current as of Jan. 1, 1991

CAR TYPE	CURRENT NUMBER SERIES	CAPACITY	ACTIVE	DELIVERY SPAN	BUILDER(S)
Heritage Fleet					
Baggage	1000-1006, 1127-1379	N/A	152	1946-1957	ACF, Budd, P-S, SLC
Baggage-dorm	1610-1630	N/A	23	1947-1953	Budd, SLC
Slumbercoach	2050-2056	36	7	1949	Budd-NYC
Slumbercoach	2080-2097	40	16	1956-1959	Budd
11-bedroom sleeper	2220-2235	22	9	1952-1956	Budd, P-S
10-6 sleeper	2430-2997	22	82	1949-1952	Budd
Lounge	3100-3127	(34)	26	1948-1954	Budd, SLC
Handicap coach	4000-4020	44	21	1950-1954	Budd
Coach	4600-4742	44 or 48	78	1948-1964	Budd, SLC
Handicap NEC coach	7000-7007	85	8	1951	Budd
NEC coach	7600-7629	88	29	1951-1953	Budd
Diner	8500-8530	(48)	18	1948-1957	Budd
Diner-grill	8550-8559	(48)	10	1948-1957	Budd
Table car	8600-8603	(80)	4	1960-1964	SLC
Buffet-diner	8700-8716	(36)	12	1949-1951	Budd
Kitchen-buffet	8750-8752	(48)	3	1949	Budd
Full-dome lounge	9300-9302	(56)	3	1955	Budd
Dome diner-lounge	9310-9312	(84)	3	1950	P-S
Vista-Dome coach	9400-9411	46 and (20)	12	1954-1955	Budd
Hi-Level coach-dorm	33900-39938	40	36	1956-1964	Budd
Hi-Level coach	39940-39964	72	21	1956-1964	Budd
Hi-Level lounge	39970-39975	(86)	6	1956	Budd
Hi-Level diner-lounge	39980-39985	(80)	6	1956	Budd
Amfleet					
Amcafe	20000-20053 | 43000-43053	53	42	1975-1977	Budd
Amclub	20118-20146 | 48122-48145	23 and (18)	20	1975-1977	Budd
Club-dinette	48150-48158	19 and (32)	6		Budd
Amdinette	20217-20242 | 48221-48241	23 and (32)	22	1976-1977	Budd
Metroliner Service club	20970-20982 | 48970-48982	32	15	1975-1976	Budd
Metroliner Service dinette	20905-20928 | 48913-48942	23 and (32)	16	1976-1977	Budd
Amcoach	21000-21272 | 44000-44279	84	278	1975-1977	Budd
Long-distance Amcoach	21803-21886 | 44803-44886	60	13	1976-1977	Budd
Metroliner Service coach	21900-21989 | 44900-44989	60 or 68	63	1976-1977	Budd
Grill-lounge	28300-28304 | 43300-43304	(51)	5	1976	Budd
Cafe-lounge	28305-28307 | 43305-43307	(46)	3	1975	Budd
Amfleet II					
Amcoach	25000-25124	59	119	1981-1982	Budd
Amcoach w/bag. area	26002-26064	55	5	1981-1982	Budd
Amlounge	28000-28024	(49)	25	1981-1983	Budd
Superliner					
Coach-baggage	31000-31047	62 or 78	48	1980	P-S
Sleeper	32000-32069	44	68	1979-1981	P-S
Lounge	33000-33024	(70)	25	1980-1981	P-S
Coach	34000-34101	75	91	1979-1980	P-S
Snack-coach	35000-35010	62	11	1979	P-S
Diner	38000-38038	(72)	39	1979-1981	P-S
Horizon Fleet					
Coach	54000-54071	78 or 82	72	1989	Bom
Handicap coach	54500-54551	72	14	1989	Bom
Dinette-coach	53000-53009	19 and (32)	8	1990	Bom
Dinette-handicap	53500-53504	1 and (48)	10	1990	Bom
Viewliner					
Sleeper	2300-2301	34	2	1987-1988	Budd-AMTK
Diner	8400	(48)	1	1988	Budd-AMTK
Cab-control cars					
Coach	809-828, 9630-9654	74	30	1967	Budd
Conference-club	9800	18 and 20	1	1967	Budd
Capitoliner					
Coach	800-889	56 or 76	26	1967	Budd
Turboliner					
Coach	80-97, 170-190	76, 72	18, 21	1973-1976	ANF, Rohr
Snack-coach	81-96, 171-189	52	13	1973-1976	ANF, Rohr
Miscellaneous					
Material handling	1400-1559	N/A	145	1986-1988	Thrall
Bilevel auto-carrier	9000-9040	N/A	40	1956	CC&F
Trilevel auto-carrier	9100-9120	N/A	21	1976	SLC

GENERAL NOTES

—Roster is for active equipment regularly used on scheduled passenger trains; it does not include special equipment such as office cars, technical training cars and work-train rolling stock, nor does it include equipment in extended storage awaiting disposal.

—Numbers in parenthesis indicate "non-revenue" (lounge and dining seats, etc.) capacities.

—The Amfleet I cars are in the process of being renumbered from the 20000 series to 40000 series; cars in the latter numbering have received train lines for push-pull operation.

Information for this roster courtesy of Amtrak and Elbert Simon

CODES: ACF = American Car & Foundry; AMTK = Amtrak; ANF = ANF-Frangeco; Bom = Bombardier Corporation; Budd = Budd Company; CC&F = Canadian Car & Foundry; NYC = New York Central; NEC = Northeast Corridor; P-S = Pullman-Standard; Rohr = Rohr Corporation; SLC = St. Louis Car Company; Thrall = Thrall Car Company

7/Amtrak Superstars

THE LONG-DISTANCE RUNNERS OF 1991

Say "passenger train" to the average middle-age American and they probably would be able to cite at least one or two famous celebrities, like *Super Chief* or *20th Century Limited*. Never mind that the greater part of the rail-traveling population in pre-Amtrak years were more likely to be found on a Long Island commuter train or a blue-collar intercity train like Pennsylvania No. 70, the Chicago-Cincinnati day run—it was the long-haul, grandly named conveyances that left their indelible mark on the traveling public

To think we almost lost the long-hauls (to say little of all other passenger trains)! Transportation soothsayers of the 1950's and 1960's predicted—with good reason—that U.S. intercity passenger trains would vanish by 1970. But Amtrak defied the prediction, and now more than 20 years later, the carrier fields a respectable fleet of named long-haul passenger trains—and, in terms of ridership and popularity, all are doing quite well, thank you.

Although far outnumbered by medium-haul namers and corridor trains, Amtrak's long-hauls are superstars which carry on the romance of North American rail travel. Ask your average American today about Amtrak and chances are that they'll know what Amtrak is—and if they're able to be even more specific, don't be surprised if they pull a name out of the hat, like *California Zephyr* or *Empire Builder*.

In the next 42 pages, we celebrate the survival of the long-haul name train in America. Some are continuations of traditional runs inherited by Amtrak in 1971; others are new creations, while some are even reincarnations. Regardless, they each have their own personality, and yet all carry on the spirit of the passenger train in America.

Representing the contemporary long-distance Amtrak train is No. 6, the eastbound *California Zephyr*, billowing out of a summer sunset in Western Nevada in 1984. The *CZ* has come to symbolize the hopes and dreams of those who embrace rail travel. Here is a train that died in March 1970 following a lingering illness diagnosed as hopeless: A way of travel designated as financially disastrous and outmoded. Americans, then, it was thought, no longer wanted—much less needed—the passenger train. Then, thirteen years later, the "impossible" happened: The *California Zephyr* was reincarnated. Though the image of a 1991 *CZ* is considerably different than that of the 1949 version, the spirit and romance have lured travelers back to the rails, and today it carries more passengers than its original ancestor. The popularity of all of Amtrak's long-distance runs proves that Americans still enjoy the lure of rail travel.—***Roger Puta, collection of Mel Finzer***

Nos. 1 & 2 *Sunset Limited*

New Orleans-Houston-San Antonio-Phoenix-Los Angeles

A pre-Amtrak *Sunset* prepares to depart Los Angeles Union Passenger Terminal in July 1969. Amtrak's *Sunset Limited* draws upon the ancestory of Southern Pacific's New Orleans-L.A. transcon of the same name, one of the oldest name trains still operating in North America.—*Mike Schafer; lighting by Jim Boyd*

Amtrak trains 1 and 2 continue a tradition established by the Southern Pacific Railroad in 1894 when the *Sunset Limited* was inaugurated between Los Angeles and New Orleans as the flagship train of the road's "Sunset Route."

The train was re-equipped with lightweight, streamlined equipment from the Budd Company in 1950 (interestingly, many of these same cars remained in service on single-level Amtrak trains into the 1990's). By the late 1960's—and despite the train's transcon status and its "Special Sunset Service Charge"—dining and lounge service was replaced with an "automatic buffet" car in which vending machines—not train personnel—dispensed food and beverages; sleeping-car service was also eliminated. Timekeeping went out with the amenities.

The *Sunset* of 1970 had come to symbolize the passenger train in peril; the train gained so much media attention that by 1971 the Interstate Commerce Commission ordered that dining, lounge and sleeping-car service be reinstituted to maintain certain minimal standards for interstate rail travel. In a sense then, the *Sunset* of early 1971 was a demonstration of what lay on the Amtrak horizon.

Today's *Sunset Limited* is a Superliner giant whose popularity is hampered only by its tri-weekly schedule—a problem that will probably be solved when ample new equipment becomes available later in the 1990's. And whereas most long-distance Amtrak trains have undergone route alterations through the years, while parent railroads have vanished through merger or abandonment, the *Sunset* is one of the few Amtrak trains that still plies virtually all of its original historical route, and still on the tracks of its original railroad.

Amtrak's *Sunset Limited* had the distinction of being the last Western long-haul to utilize steam-heated equipment; new bilevels came on line on the Sunset Route in 1981. Now, not only does this Sunbelt Superliner sport a full complement of diner, Sightseer Lounge, coaches and sleepers—including a through Chicago-L.A. sleeper delivered to and from the *Texas Eagle* at San Antonio—but it also features movies, games and hospitality hours. Food cars with vending machines? Unthinkable!

FACING PAGE, TOP: Number 2 snakes through southeastern Arizona near Pantano Wash in June 1988 as an SP freight heads west.—*Greg Brown*. ABOVE: In a namesake scene from 1978, the *Sunset* heads for the sunset near Cochise, Ariz.—*Mike Blaszak* LEFT: Triple ex-Union Pacific E-units head up No. 2 at El Paso in 1973; ex-Santa Fe Hi-Level equipment was the norm for the *Sunset* at that time.—*Mike Schafer* ABOVE: Signboard at Sanderson, Texas, in summer 1977 was a survivor of an earlier era.—*Brad Joseph*

TOP: **The mesa near North Guam, N.M., forms a background of pink for a silvery No. 4 cruising the desert on Dec. 27, 1986.**—*Joe McMillan* **RIGHT:** **The westbound *Southwest Chief* speeds over the Kankakee River near Lorenzo, Ill., on a fine spring day in 1987.**—*Mike Schafer*

Nos. 3 & 4

Chief

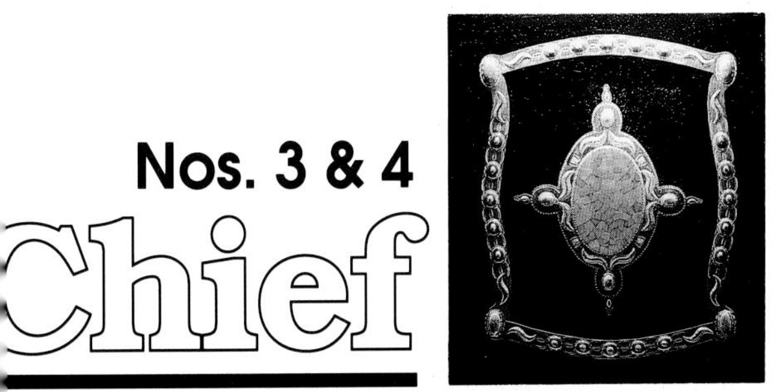

Today's *Chief* draws upon the heritage of Santa Fe's *Super Chief* and *El Capitan*; Turquoise Room emblem is from Pleasure Dome lounge-Turquoise Room dining room cars built in 1950 by Pullman-Standard for the 1951 rendition of the *Super Chief*.—*Jim Heuer*

Chicago-Kansas City-Albuquerque-Los Angeles

Quick now, what was the most-famous, luxurious American passenger train of all time? Half of you probably said New York Central's *20th Century Limited*; the other half probably said Santa Fe's *Super Chief*. Which is correct? It's an argument that undoubtedly will never be settled.

But to be sure, few trains could ever compare to Santa Fe's world-class, first-class, all-private-room *Super Chief* on the Chicago-Los Angeles route—not even today's *Southwest Chief*, which carries on the tradition of the legendary *Super Chief* principally through scheduling and routing. The *Super Chief* was introduced in 1936 as a diesel-powered heavyweight train and in 1938 became a lightweight streamliner. The *El Capitan* was born as a streamliner in 1938.

Amtrak assumed operation of the *Super Chief* and *El Capitan* from Santa Fe on May 1, 1971, maintaining the former's all-sleeper status (albeit usually combined with the all-coach *El Capitan*) and such exotic amenities as the Pleasure Dome with Turquoise Room private dining area and AT&SF's Champagne Dinner.

The *El Capitan* name was dropped in spring 1973 at which time the *Super Chief* officially became a coach-and-sleeper train. Sensing a trampling of long-established reputations, Santa Fe nixed Amtrak's use of the *Super Chief* moniker, and effective May 19, 1974, Nos. 3 and 4 were renamed *Southwest Limited*. The arrival of Superliner equipment ended the long-traditional mix of ex-Santa Fe Hi-Level cars and single-level cars, a trademark that harkened back to the days when Santa Fe ran the *Super* and *El Cap* combined.

The discontinuance of the Chicago-Kansas City-Houston *Lone Star* on Oct. 1, 1979, brought about the only major reroute on Amtrak's Chicago-Kansas City-Los Angeles run: On that date, the *Southwest Limited* was

TOP: One of the *Southwest Chief's* Indian guides, Teri Fraizer, takes a break from her description of tribal lands in No. 4's lounge to display some of her artistic handiwork.—*Bob Johnston* **ABOVE:** Crowds await boarding of No. 3 at Joliet, Ill., in 1987.—*Mike Schafer* **LEFT:** Except for the "yellow bonnet" F-unit buried in the motive-power consist, Amtrak No. 3 in December 1972 at Bannock, Calif., still resembles a pre-Amtrak operation (the yellow bonnet scheme was a brief product of the 1970's).—*Joe McMillan*

rerouted from the main line route through Ottawa Junction to the Topeka branch to maintain service to that city. Santa Fe is still the host railroad to Nos. 3 and 4 and its route is still the fastest between the nation's second- (L.A.) and third-largest (Chicago) cities. In fact, thanks to Automatic Train Stop signaling, 90 mph speed limits are still in force on certain segments of the *Chief's* trip, whereas 79 mph remains the top speed for most all other Amtrak Western long-hauls.

With Superliners came improved service on Nos. 3 and 4, with the thankfully brief exception of experimental no-frills food service early in the 1980's on all Western trains courtesy of government mandate. In October 1984, Santa Fe compromised on the name controversy, allowing Amtrak to again use the "Chief" (but apparently not "Super") trademark. More improvements followed: Expanding on a concept that had proved popular on the *Cardinal*, Amtrak introduced on-board live historical commentary provided by Indian guides native to the territory traversed by the *Southwest Chief* in Arizona and New Mexico.

This, in addition to the Superliner Enhancement Program (movies, happy hour, etc.) applied to all Western long-hauls, has made the *Southwest Chief* a classic of the Amtrak era. The sterling service of the *Super Chief* of yore may be past history, but the schedule is nearly the same and the Southwest scenery just as enchanting as ever. And, during the service stop at the Albuquerque (N.M.) Amtrak station, you can still purchase crafts from Indian traders from nearby pueblos, just as you could in the pre-Amtrak days of travel along the Santa Fe Trail.

FACING PAGE, TOP: The west-bound *Chief* wheels majestically through the rugged contours near Wooten, Colo., that make up Raton Pass.—*Steve Patterson* **FACING PAGE, LOWER: The former-Santa Fe Hi-Level lounge serving on No. 4 on July 27, 1990, at Lamy, N.M., is right at home on Santa Fe rails. The ex-AT&SF Hi-Level lounges tended to gravitate to assignments on Nos. 3 and 4 as well as the *Texas Eagle*.**—*Bob Johnston* **LEFT: The red noses of SDP40F's were a hallmark of Amtrak's formative years. On Dec. 9, 1974, SDP 524 and mates leading No. 4 meet No. 3 at Glorieta Pass, N.M., while the photographer enjoys the fresh mountain air from the Dutch door.**—*Joe McMillan*

When the original *California Zephyr* made its last Chicago-Oakland trips March 20-22, 1970—21 years to the day of its inaugural trips—America lost its "most talked-about train," a statement proclaimed by *CZ* operators Burlington, Rio Grande and Western Pacific.

The National Railroad Passenger Corporation had plans to in part revive the *California Zephyr* when Amtrak operations began on May 1, 1971; the main difference would have been the train's routing west of Salt Lake City: SP's spectacular Donner Pass line would carry the train through the Sierra Range rather than via WP's equally scenic (but less populated) route through the famed Feather River Canyon.

But Rio Grande surprised Amtrak at the Eleventh Hour by reneging on its plans to become an Amtrak member railroad. A tri-weekly *California Zephyr* did begin operation on May 1, combined with the daily *Denver Zephyr* between Chicago and Denver (except during peak travel days), but west of Denver found it on Union Pacific's Overland Route to Ogden even though the (rare) first Amtrak public timetable map shows the *CZ* as traveling through—not around—the Rockies. As a non-Amtrak-member railroad, Rio Grande was obliged to maintain Denver-Salt Lake/Ogden service with its little *Rio Grande Zephyr* domeliner, a train that had been implemented upon the *CZ*'s 1970 discontinuance as part of an ad hoc BN-

ZEPHYR

Chicago-Omaha-Denver-Salt Lake City-Oakland/San Francisco

When you take the best of two pre-Amtrak rivals, the *City of San Francisco* (LEFT) and the *California Zephyr* (FAR LEFT), you get one of the most-talked about trains in America today.—*Two photos, Mike Schafer* **ABOVE: That train is Amtrak's *California Zephyr*, wrapping around the Colorado River at Dell siding on the Rio Grande near Burns, Colo., on July 3, 1991.**—*Mel Patrick*

ABOVE: Of course, not all of a *California Zephyr's* journey is through mountain territory. In fact, more than half of the route is over desert or prairies, though mostly at night. After spending most of a day rolling through Iowa and Illinois, No. 6 accelerates away from its suburban Chicago stop at Naperville, Ill., on a December afternoon in 1983. Next stop, and end of the line—Union Station.—*Mike Schafer*

BELOW: Eastbound No. 6 glides through Reno, Nev., on an October evening in 1982 following an inspiring journey on Southern Pacific's line over Donner Pass. The original *CZ* of 1949-1970 operated between Salt Lake City and Oakland on the fabled Western Pacific Railroad, approaching the Bay Area through Northern California's magnificent Feather River Canyon. When Amtrak began, SP's Donner Pass route was selected over WP for the Chicago-San Francisco service, mainly because SP would be an Amtrak member road (WP was not eligible to join Amtrak, having given up the *CZ*—its last passenger train—in March 1970), but also because on-line Reno provided—and still does provide—a considerably greater traffic base.—*Mike Schafer*

D&RGW "California Service" coordinated with SP through a cross-platform transfer at Odgen with the Milwaukee Road-Union Pacific-SP *City of San Francisco.*

With the issuance of the July 12, 1971, Amtrak timetable, the *CZ* name was dropped, presumably forever, leaving trains 101 and 102 nameless until Nov. 14, 1971, when they were christened with a more-appropriate name from the past: *City of San Francisco.* On June 11, 1972, that name was traded in for *San Francisco Zephyr.*

The *SFZ* went daily on June 10, 1973; although Amtrak intended to revert the *SFZ* to tri-weekly service after the 1973 summer travel season, the train remained daily due to its popularity. Daily operation throughout the central Midwest-West Coast corridor made the *Denver Zephyr* name redundant, and it was quietly dropped on Oct. 28, 1973.

On June 7, 1977, the *SFZ* gained a new connecting train, the Salt Lake-Seattle *Pioneer*, at Ogden; similarly, Oct. 28, 1979, ushered in the startup of a Salt Lake-Los Angeles connection, the *Desert Wind.* By the end of 1980, Superliner equipment had been introduced on the *SFZ*, and as Superliner cars became available to equip the *Desert Wind* and *Pioneer* as well, they were extended to Chicago and combined with the *SFZ* east of Salt Lake City/Ogden.

The big news, however, came with the announcement early in 1983 that Rio Grande would finally "join" Amtrak, and the *SFZ* (and *Desert Wind* and *Pioneer*) permanently rerouted over D&RGW. In accordance with this change, scheduled to take place on April 24, 1983, Nos. 5 and 6 were rechristened *California Zephyr.* Major flood damage on the Rio Grande main line at Thistle, Utah, delayed the reroute until July 16. Festivities at Denver that day included the breaking of a bottle of champagne over No. 5's locomotive pilot by Mrs. James Bauman, a former Zephyrette who as Beaulah Ecklund had worked aboard the original *CZ* in the 1960's. Carrying her original announcement book, Mrs. Bauman provided p.a. commentary on route highlights as Amtrak 5 headed west on its new routing.

On Oct. 30, 1983, the *CZ* returned to yet another portion of its original route with a permanent reroute off the SP be-

CALIFORNIA ZEPHYR

tween Ogden and Alazon, Nev., and onto Union Pacific's former-WP main line between Salt Lake and Alazon. Now, Amtrak's *CZ* traverses some 2,000 miles of its original 2,525-mile route.

The formula that made the original *California Zephyr* so popular still works today: A transcontinental train scheduled to traverse the most-scenic portions of its route in daylight. Indeed, in some ways Amtrak's *CZ* is more popular than the original—more passengers ride the *California Zephyr* today than ever before. Watching Amtrak's *CZ* sprint the prairies west of Chicago, tackle the Front Range of the Colorado Rockies and slip into the night of a Nevada desert is testimony that—at least in the world of U.S. passenger trains—reincarnation is very real and that with Amtrak just about anything might be possible.

TOP LEFT: Many veteran train-riders mourn the loss of the classic Vista-Dome car on scenic-laden trains like the *CZ*, but the Superliner Sightseer Lounge, with its floor-to-ceiling windows, provides its own unique perspective for watching the passing geography. Passengers aboard westbound No. 5 in February 1987 enjoy a snow squall while climbing up Big Ten loops outside of Denver.—*Mike Schafer* **ABOVE LEFT: Lynn Joseph checks with the conductor of the *San Francisco Zephyr* at Chicago Union Station in 1983 for car assignments while her husband dutifully records the ritual, which will signal the start their honeymoon rail trip to California.**—*Brad Joseph* **ABOVE: A Southern Pacific SD45-2 provides an extra boost to the F40's handling 14-car *SFZ* over Donner Pass near Alta, Calif., in 1983.**—*Roger Puta, collection of Mel Finzer*

Nos. 7 & 8

Empire Builder

Chicago-Milwaukee-Minneapolis/St. Paul-Spokane-Seattle/Portland

ABOVE: The heritage of Amtrak's *Empire Builder* harkens to the *Builder* of GN, CB&Q and SP&S fame, with a touch of Milwaukee Road's *Hiawatha*'s. The "Big Sky Blue" version of the *EB* is shown at Rochelle, Ill., early in 1970.—*Mike Schafer*

Isn't it nice to know that, as of its 20th anniversary, Amtrak continues some traditions that are much older? Case in point: the *Empire Builder*, one of small cadre of long-distance Amtrak trains that represent continuous operation (versus reincarnation) of a particular train since its inauguration. (Others: *Broadway Limited*, *Silver Star* and *Silver Meteor*, *Sunset Limited*.)

Armed with a grandiose name (long-ago Great Northern President James J. Hill was known as the "Empire Builder") and a route through some of the finest geography in the Pacific Northwest, the *Empire Builder* since 1929 has captured the imagination of travelers—armchair or otherwise—long fascinated with places like Glacier National Park and the Cascade Range.

The majesty of Glacier Park has long been an attraction for travelers destined to the Pacific Northwest or to the park itself. The eastbound *Builder* on Aug. 8, 1980, revels in the breathtaking openess of Montana at Bison, some five miles west of Glacier Park station.—*Larry Zuetschel*

ABOVE: "Home" for the *Empire Builder* in Seattle is—as it has been for decades—King Street Station, formerly a joint facility of Great Northern and Northern Pacific (Burlington Northern after the GN-NP-CB&Q-SP&S merger of 1970). Westbound No. 7 poses under old and new elements of Seattle's impressive skyline on Nov. 22, 1989.—*Michael Shermetta* **TOP RIGHT: Highlight of the *Builder's* approach to or exit from Seattle is its promenade along Puget Sound for some 25 miles. Under the clearing skies of a February afternoon in 1988, patrons aboard No. 8, having left the bustle of the Pacific Northwest's largest city only a few minutes earlier, were afforded this peaceful view of the Sound.—***Mike Schafer*

When Amtrak began in 1971, Milwaukee Road was chosen over BN as the route between Chicago and the Twin Cities because of higher population and projected strong ridership. Thus, in the heritage of Amtrak's current version of the *Builder* hides another famous name from the past: the *Hiawatha*. Since 1934, *Hiawathas* have been speeding travelers between Chicago, Milwaukee and La Crosse, Wis., and the Twin Cities. Today's *Builder* holds that custom on the former-CMStP&P main—now owned by Soo Line—mimicking the schedules of the old *Afternoon Hiawatha* (westbound) and *Morning Hiawatha* (eastbound).

The *Empire Builder* route saw another reroute as of Amtrak's startup: a transfer from the former-GN main line between Spokane, Wash., and Seattle to that of the former Northern Pacific. Although also the result of population considerations and projected ridership, this route is no longer used and the main leg of the *Builder* has returned to BN's old Great Northern main between Spokane and Seattle.

From the very start, the *Builder* was a strong performer, not only by serving popular tourist destinations—Glacier Park and Seattle—but also providing a necessary transportation alternative to remote areas of North Dakota and Montana. By the time Amtrak reached its first anniversary, the *Builder* had been joined by a companion service, the *North Coast Hiawatha*, which during certain periods was combined with the *Builder* for portions of the run.

Funding considerations and equipment shortages resulted in the *Builder* being cut back to four times a week on Sept. 8, 1977 (whereupon it alternated with the *North Coast Hiawatha's* tri-weekly schedule), and then to thrice weekly upon the *Hiawatha's* discontinuance on Oct. 1, 1979. Thereafter, daily service was provided during peak travel periods until April 1982 when procurement of a mail contract permitted year-round daily operation.

The return to daily operation was not the only good news in terms of expansion of *Empire Builder* services. On Oct. 26, 1981, a Portland section had been established, splitting from the main-stem train at Spokane, Wash., and operating to Portland via a combination of BN's former Spokane, Portland & Seattle and NP main lines. This arrangement was in fact a revival of a pre-Amtrak operation, as the original *Empire Builder* had through cars to Portland. When the Portland leg debuted, the Seattle section shifted back to the original GN *Builder* route west of Spokane, via Wenatchee, for the first time in nearly a decade.

The *Empire Builder* has the distinction of being the first long-distance Amtrak train to go Superliner, which it did on Oct. 28, 1979. But regardless of equipment—be it the heavyweight *Builder* of the 1930's, the colorful orange-and-green domeliner of the 1950's or today's sparkling two-story version—the *Empire Builder* continues to delight passengers fascinated with the lore of the Northwest.

ABOVE: Dawn light baths the eastbound *Empire Builder* about to slip out of Great Northern Station in Minneapolis in September 1974. From here, No. 8 will skim the west bank of the Mississippi (at right in photo) for 140 miles to La Crescent, Minn., before crossing the river into La Crosse, Wis., to head through America's Dairyland.—*George A. Forero Jr.* **BELOW: Under the ghostly pinnacle of Mount Hood, No., 28, the eastbound Portland section—known as the "baby *Builder*" to local fans—scurries along the Columbia River near Avery, Wash., on the afternoon of May 11, 1985, en route to a rendezvous with No. 8 at Spokane.**—*T. O. Repp*

Coast Starlight

Nos. 11 & 14

Seattle-Portland-Oakland/San Francisco-Los Angeles

There almost wasn't a *Coast Starlight*. The original Amtrak route structure revealed on Nov. 30, 1970, did not include a Seattle-Oakland-Los Angeles run. Fortunately, in January 1971, Seattle-San Diego was added to the basic route system. It's all hard to believe when you consider that the contemporary *Coast Starlight* usually holds title to being Amtrak's most-popular long-distance train in terms of passengers carried.

No surprises here. The *Starlight* links the most-populous areas of California with the most populated region of the Pacific Northwest—and it does so on a super-scenic route made famous by two notable Southern Pacific trains: The *Coast Daylight* between San Francisco/Oakland and L.A., and the overnight *Cascade* between Oakland and Portland. Amtrak combined these two pre-Amtrak services with a new L.A.-San Diego *San Diegan* schedule and an existing Seattle-Portland run to form a new but unnamed long-distance triweekly Seattle-San Diego service, trains 11 and 12, supplemented by Oakland-L.A. trains

The *Coast Starlight*'s ancestory spotlights two trains in particular, both Southern Pacific: the Oakland-Portland *Cascade* (ABOVE RIGHT, shown just south of Portland in July 1969) and the San Francisco-Los Angeles *Coast Daylight* (BELOW RIGHT, shown westbound at Paso Robles, Calif., in July 1969.) The overall schedules of today's *Starlight* closely follow that of the old *Daylight* and *Cascade*.—*Both photos, Mike Schafer*

LEFT: A rare clear day in Oregon's Cascade Range bathes the northbound *Coast Starlight* with daylight on Sept. 3, 1989. Number 11 is at milepost 549 near Tunnel 11 on Southern Pacific's Shasta Route.—*Scott E. Odell* **ABOVE: Illustrating the contrast in scenery along the Los Angeles-Seattle run, the *Starlight* weaves through the arid confines of Santa Susanna Pass north of Los Angeles—and a long way south of the pine-forested mountainsides of Oregon—on Oct. 26, 1984.**—*Alan Tillotson*

98 and 99 (the old numbers of the famous *Coast Daylight* of SP days), which operated between those points on days that 11 and 12 didn't.

Numbers 11 and 12 were christened *Coast Starlight* on Nov. 14, 1971, with Nos. 98-99 renumbered 12 and 13 (as were the *Starlights* below Oakland because of the change in SP timetable direction at this point) and given the sacred SP *Coast Daylight* name. In addition, service was made daily south from Oakland all the way to San Diego. By the summer of 1972, through service to San Diego had ended; on June 10, 1973, the *Starlight/Daylight* became daily all the way from Seattle to L.A., and on May 9, 1974, the *Coast Daylight* name vanished from the timetable. Superliner equipment arrived during the winter of 1980-1981; by Feb. 1, 1981, the *Starlight* had officially become a member of the Superliner brigade.

On April 25, 1982, the *Starlight* underwent its only major reroute to date: a shift from the traditional route via Woodland, Calif., to that

More than a half century of railroading is represented in this 1983 scene at San Jose as the northbound *Starlight* with modern Superliner cars passes a Southern Pacific commute equipped with 1920's-era heavyweight "Harriman" suburban coaches. In a couple more years, the San Francisco-San Jose "CalTrain" commutes would likewise be converted to stainless-steel bilevels. The *Starlight* shares trackage with CalTrain runs for only about three miles, between Santa Clara and San Jose, so the passing of the two trains near SP's San Jose locomotive facility was a luck of the draw scene for the alert photographer.—*Ken Rattenne*

Coast Starlight

ABOVE: The volcanic profile of Mount Shasta crowns the F40's leading a tardy northbound *Starlight* through Macdoel, Calif., on a fine March morning in 1991. The *Starlight*'s path belts the famous mountain, but the train's passage in both directions is usually in the darkened hours.—*Greg Brown* BELOW: Amtrak serves America from sea to shining sea, and perhaps nowhere is this more poignant than on the *Starlight* route north of Los Angeles to San Luis Obispo, where the Coast Route turns inland to head up to the Bay Area. On a late summer day in 1981, No. 14 slices hazy air along the remote beaches south of San Luis Obispo.—*Roger Puta, Mel Finzer collection*

through Sacramento. In doing so, Amtrak added the California state capital to the *Starlight*'s route—not to mention a considerably greater market base.

Today, as Nos. 11 and 14, the *Starlight* remains one of Amtrak's all-time success stories in the long-distance train league. In 1990, more than 500,000 people rode the *Starlight*, whose 1,389-mile trail over Oregon's Cascade Range, through California's Central Valley and along the Pacific Ocean's misty shoreline connects widely varied Western scenery.

ABOVE: Superliner equipment was but a few weeks away for the *Coast Starlight* when this scene of southbound train 11 was recorded in October 1980 at Steilacoom, Wash. From Seattle south to Olympia, Wash., Burlington Northern's main line to Portland hugs Puget Sound. Note the dome cars, which had become a fixture on Nos. 11 and 12 by the late 1970's once SP had been convinced they would clear tunnels.—*Tom Carver* **LEFT: During Amtrak's infancy, former-Seaboard Coast Line observation-lounge cars were regulars on the *Starlight/Daylight*, as demonstrated by this scene of No. 13 at San Luis Obispo in May 1972. Ahead: a trip up Cuesta Grade over the Santa Lucia Range.**—
Mike Schafer

Nos. 19 & 20
Nos. 519 & 520

Crescent and Gulf Breeze

ABOVE LEFT: Amtrak's *Crescent* is a direct descendant of Southern's Washington-New Orleans flagship of the late 1960's and the 1970's, the *Southern Crescent.* It is shown at Birmingham, Ala., in 1978.—*Tom Nemeth* **LEFT:** The *Gulf Breeze* has some roots in the old joint PRR-SR-A&WP-WRofA-L&N *Crescent Limited,* pictured in the twilight of its life at Newnan, Ga., in August 1968.—*Mike Schafer*

Scenic water landmark of Norfolk Southern's Washington-New Orleans main line is the crossing of Lake Pontchartrain outside of New Orleans. Two F40's and eight Heritage and Amfleet cars comprising the northbound *Crescent* on a warm-looking morning in January 1986 approach the north end of the seven-mile trestle over the lake.—*David Hurt*

Amtrak's *Crescent* stands alone in Amtrak history as being the only long-distance train whose operation was acquired, more or less intact, from another carrier well after May 1, 1971. Among the railroads that opted not to join Amtrak on that date was Southern Railway. As a holdout, SR was obliged by law to continue its passenger fleet, the star of which was the *Southern Crescent*.

Unlike many passenger trains at that time, the *Southern Crescent* was a fairly recent phenomenon. It was the result of a 1969 part-and-parcel combining of two New York/Washington-New Orleans services: the *Southerner*, which operated on an all-SR route south of Washington, D.C. via Birmingham, Ala., and Meridian, Miss., and the *Crescent Limited*, a joint operation between SR, Atlanta & West Point, Western Railway of Alabama and Louisville & Nashville by way of Montgomery and Mobile, Ala.

Southern's post-May 1, 1971, operation of the *Southern Crescent* was noted by high service standards, attractive amenities and a spirit of cooperation: For example, SR and Amtrak featured through sleeping-car operation between New York and Los Angeles through New Orleans. Eventually economics dictated a change for SR, which, after watching NRPC grow up for nearly a decade, was confident Amtrak was now able to continue a fine tradition in the New York-New Orleans market. On Feb. 1, 1979, the *Southern Crescent*—minus the "Southern" in its name—became an all-Amtrak operation.

Although some unique SR-inspired traits slipped away such as the Atlanta-New Orleans dome car, the sleeper-lounge with shower-equipped master bedroom, and homemade biscuits in the diner, the new *Crescent* was not without improvements. Daily service west of Atlanta became a reality from Day One, and the introduction of all-electric Heritage Fleet equipment brought new levels of reliability and comfort. But one of the biggest improvements came on Oct. 27, 1989, when the *Southern Crescent* gained a Mobile section, thus restoring service to Montgomery, the Alabama state capital, which had lost its last passenger train ten years earlier upon the discontinuance of the Chicago-Miami/St. Petersburg *Floridian*. The new leg, which splits at Birmingham and travels over CSX to Montgomery and Mobile, is state-sponsored and enjoys its own name—*Gulf Breeze*.

Once again, as with certain other Amtrak runs, the *Crescent/Gulf Breeze* operations has certain unmistakable parallels to pre-Amtrak operations—in this case to SR's old New York-New Orleans *Southerner* via Meridian, and to the joint SR-A&WP-WRofA-L&N *Crescent Limited* via Montgomery. Now, as for a time in the 1960's, the two services run combined with each other for portions of their runs.

TOP: 'Twas the night before Christmas 1990, and No. 19/519 is awaiting highball from Charlotte, N.C. Who will reach New Orleans and Mobile first, the *Crescent* and *Gulf Breeze*, or Santa?—
Michael Shermetta **ABOVE: The *Gulf Breeze* restored rail passenger service to Montgomery, the Alabama state capital. Unable to utilize the classic old Union Station (left in background), the *Breeze* calls at a nearby converted grain elevator.—***Mel Fiveash* **LEFT: Number 19 booms past Southern freight 115 "in the hole" at Boligee, Ala., in April 1980.—***David Hurt*

TEXAS

ABOVE: Dead on time, the northbound *Texas Eagle* races auto traffic on old Route U.S. 66 and Interstate 55 through Lawndale in central Illinois on a May morning in 1990. The *Eagle* will alight at Bloomington and Joliet before returning to its "nest" at Chicago Union Station.—*Mike Schafer* **RIGHT: The *Eagle*, just in from Chicago, stands vigil at San Antonio below the imposing Hemisphere tower. The date in Feb. 18, 1983, and shortly the *Sunset Limited* will roll into town and pick up the *Eagle*'s through cars to Los Angeles.**—*Bob Johnston*

EAGLE

Nos. 21/521 & 22/522

Chicago-St. Louis-Little Rock-Dallas-Fort Worth-Laredo/Houston

Of all of Amtrak's long-distance trains, its *Texas Eagle* has perhaps the most-complex history of evolution. Today's service widely resembles that of Missouri Pacific's *Texas Eagle* operations of the 1950's and 1960's, with a bit of Gulf, Mobile & Ohio's *Abraham Lincoln* and Southern Pacific's *Sunbeam* and *Hustler*. Today's *Texas Eagle* is another case of how Amtrak has reincarnated a good idea.

The idea? That the burgeoning Sunbelt is a popular destination for Northerners. In few places is commercial and residential growth as spectacular as in Texas.

The *Texas Eagle* as we know it today was not a part of the original Amtrak system. Its Amtrak roots are in a little experimental train known as the *Inter-American*, whose tri-weekly all-Texas route—Fort Worth-San Antonio-Laredo—was inaugurated on Jan. 28, 1973, running on Santa Fe rails between Fort Worth and Milano, and on MP Milano to Laredo. The roundabout route via Milano was shortcutted in October 1975 when the train began operation on Katy tracks between Temple and Taylor.

The train was extended to St. Louis over MoPac rails on March 13, 1974—returning rail passenger service to the state of Arkansas for the first time since Amtrak—then to Chicago on Oct. 31, 1976, by combining it with existing Chicago-St. Louis schedules (schedules on this segment today are quite close to that of the old pre-Amtrak *Abe Lincoln*) on Illinois Central Gulf's ex-GM&O main. When the Chicago-Kansas City-Fort Worth/Dallas-Houston *Lone Star* was discontinued in October 1979, the *Inter-American* gained a Temple-Houston section so as to preserve Chicago-Fort Worth-Houston through service.

The *Inter-American* underwent a major transformation on Oct. 25,1981 when service to Laredo and Houston ended, Superliner status became official, through Chicago-Los Angeles cars commenced and the train became known as the *Eagle*. Service south of St. Louis remained triweekly.

On Nov. 15, 1988, the proud old MoPac name *Texas Eagle* (MP itself having been merged into Union Pacific by that time) was bestowed to Nos. 21 and 22 concurrent with the inauguration of a Dallas-Houston section, Nos. 521 and 522, operating via Corsicana, Texas, over Southern Pacific, approximating the schedule of SP's long-departed *Sunbeam* (southbound) and *Hustler* (northbound) on that segment. Finally, on Jan. 20, 1990, all *Texas Eagle* services with the exception of the L.A. through cars went daily.

Missouri Pacific's *Texas Eagle* network was once an institution in the Midwest-Texas rail corridor. Sadly, by the time the Amtrak bill was signed into law in 1970, the *Texas Eagle* had dwindled to a diminutive, coach-only "sparrow" between St. Louis and Texarkana, Texas. Piece by piece, Amtrak reconstructed the *Texas Eagle* tradition into the impressive operation it is today, much like the mythical bird—the phoenix—that rose from the ashes of destruction.

Amtrak 21/22 owes its heritage to several trains, notably MP's *Texas Eagle* (TOP, shown at St. Louis Union Station in 1970), GM&O's *Abraham Lincoln* (ABOVE, also at St. Louis) and two SP Dallas-Houston runs.—*Jim Heuer (top) and Mike Schafer*

In pre-dawn light, the northbound *Inter-American* awaits the departure hour from Laredo in spring 1981. Amtrak's *Inter-American* played a crucial role in the development of today's *Texas Eagle* network. The *I-A* was one of NRPC's early experimental routes, beginning only as an intra-Texas train and ending up as a Chicago-Laredo/Houston streamliner. One of the goals of the service was to re-establish connections with National Railways of Mexico passenger trains via the Laredo gateway, as had been popular in pre-Amtrak years, but connectivity remained elusive and significant tourist traffic to and from Mexico City never developed. Consequently, the run to the border was cancelled in the fall of 1981.—*Mike Schafer*

Nos. 25 & 26
PIONEER

Chicago-Omaha-Denver-Cheyenne-Ogden-Boise-Portland-Seattle

TOP: Off to Chicago: The *Pioneer* tiptoes out of the Rose City—Portland, Ore.—in February 1988.—*Mike Schafer* **ABOVE: For some 150 miles east of Portland, the *Pioneer* flanks the banks of the Columbia River. Number 25 is at Cascade Locks, Ore., in February 1991.**—*Scott Odell*

Union Pacific's *City of Portland* highballs west from Pocatello, Idaho, in July 1969.—*Mike Schafer*

Here's a recipe for a satisfying feast of scenery: combine a generous heaping of UP's famed *City of Portland* of yore, a good-size helping of the original *California Zephyr*, a dash of UP's *Butte Special* and *City of St. Louis*, and whaddya get? Amtrak's *Pioneer*.

The *Pioneer* was one of several new additions to the Amtrak system that resulted from a now-moribund congressional mandate that Amtrak began at least one new experimental route per year. For 1977, Salt Lake City-Portland-Seattle—which in part followed the Oregon Trail (hence the *Pioneer* name)—was that route. Thus on June 7, 1977, passenger service returned to a line known for its beautiful passage through the Blue Mountains of Oregon and the shoreline cruise along the spectacular Columbia River Gorge.

What began as a modest all-coach-and-dinette Amfleet train that connected with the *San Francisco Zephyr* at Ogden by Amtrak's 10th anniversary had evolved into a Chicago-Salt Lake-Seattle transcon Superliner, albeit combined with the *SFZ/CZ* east of Ogden (later, Salt Lake). Like Amtrak 5 and 6, the *Pioneer* originally operated via UP's Overland Route between Denver and Ogden, but was rerouted over the Rio Grande in 1983. The popularity of the Rio Grande routing, however, taxed the combined *CZ/Pioneer/Desert Wind*, and on June 16, 1991, the *Pioneer* began operating separately west of Denver to Ogden via the Union Pacific, restoring service to Wyoming that had been lost in 1983. The original *City of Portland* operated on a direct line between Green River, Wyo., and Pocatello, Idaho; today's *Pioneer* operates between those two points by way of Ogden (hence the *City of St. Louis* and *Butte Special* heritage).

But route matters aside, Nos. 25 and 26 capture the spirit of the old American West, and are reminders of a time when pioneers advanced against unknown territories and untold elements along the Oregon Trail to the great Pacific Northwest.

Nos. 35 & 36

Chicago-Omaha-Denver-Salt Lake City-Las Vegas-Los Angeles

LEFT: UP's *City of Los Angeles*, the legacy of today's *Desert Wind*, stands at the UP depot in Salt Lake City in July 1969. FAR LEFT: The *Desert Wind* serves the heart of Las Vegas; this 1981 view of downtown is from the front entrance of the Amtrak station and Plaza Hotel.—*Both photos, Mike Schafer* **BELOW: L.A.-bound No. 35 sweeps through Cajon Pass west of Summit, Calif.,on Feb. 23, 1989.**—*Steve Patterson*

Desert Wind

Like the *Pioneer*, the *Desert Wind* began as a connection to and from the *San Francisco Zephyr*, at Ogden, providing an overnight Ogden/Salt Lake City-Las Vegas schedule not unlike Union Pacific's Domeliner *City of Los Angeles* in later years.

As a through Chicago-Los Angeles train—which the *Desert Wind* officially became in spring 1981—Nos. 35-36 filled a void left by the discontinuance of the celebrated Chicago-L.A. *City* train in May 1971. Popularity of this routing increased significantly with the 1983 permanent reroute through the Rockies on the Rio Grande—so much so that the *Wind*'s diner, which had been operating only between L.A. and Salt Lake City, began running all the way through to and from Denver during peak travel seasons, supplementing the *California's Zephyr*'s diner.

High point (pun intended) of the *Desert Wind*'s jaunt over the old Los Angeles & Salt Lake Railroad is its crossing of famous Cajon Pass north of San Bernardino, Calif. (which, on Santa Fe trackage rights, is also traversed by the *Southwest Chief*). This monumental assault on the San Bernardino Mountains is one of the most notable rail engineering feats in Western railroading—and one of the busiest rail arteries leading to the Los Angeles Basin.

You can bet that the *Wind* is popular for more reasons than great scenery. Numbers 35 and 36 also serve one of the most well-known entertainment meccas in North America—Las Vegas, Nev., a destination which help makes the *Desert Wind* a high roller in terms of popularity and ridership.

Nos. 29 & 30
Chicago-Cleveland-Pittsburgh-Washington

Capitol Limited

ABOVE: Baltimore & Ohio was an American institution (not only was B&O the first common-carrier railroad in America, but the first to offer passenger service to the public) and so was its famed Chicago-Washington *Capitol Limited,* shown at Cumberland, Md., in 1968. Right up to the end on April 30, 1971, the *Capitol Limited* experience meant fine food and quality service. Though thought to be gone forever, the *Capitol* came back ten years later—and so did the fine food and quality service that was part of its heritage, including china and glassware in the diner.—*Mike Schafer* RIGHT: Amtrak's eastbound *Capitol Limited* makes a grand exit from Chicago in September 1990 as a Burlington Northern commuter likewise leaves behind the confines of Chicago Union Station.—*Doug Koontz*

Of all U.S. passenger trains that survived to Amtrak, few managed to maintain a reputation that was as honorable as Baltimore & Ohio's *Capitol Limited*. For years the "*Cap*" was *the* choice of rail travelers between Chicago and Washington, D.C., so it was with much emotional fanfare that the *Capitol* played out its final days of before Amtrak startup on May 1, 1971.

Morning sun and No. 30 meet in the elderly and elegant downtown area of Cumberland, Md., in October 1989.—*Duncan Richards*

The route structure of baby Amtrak provided for through Chicago-Washington service, but by way of an all-Penn Central (ex Pennsylvania Railroad) route and only in the form of through cars split from the Chicago-New York *Broadway Limited* at Harrisburg, Pa. In October 1975, the train-splitting operation was moved east to Philadelphia's 30th Street Station, which made for an even more circuitous passage (487 miles versus 397 on the original Amtrak routing) between Pittsburgh and Washington. Though done in the name of cost-effectiveness and freight-traffic congestion on the ex-PRR "Port Road" direct line along the Susquehanna River between Harrisburg and Perryville, Md., a Philadelphia overture meant 10-plus-hour travel time between Washington and Pittsburgh—or about twice the driving time.

Then, on Oct. 1, 1981, it all became moot. Taking a lesson from the past, Amtrak unveiled its own version of the *Capitol Limited*: a through Chicago-Washington streamliner operating between Chicago and Pittsburgh over Conrail's ex-PRR main, and from Pittsburgh to Washington over old-home-road trackage, the B&O. Initially, the *Cap* was combined with the *Broadway* between Chicago and Pittsburgh—and for a time carried a through Chicago-Miami coach—but an unexpected growth in mail and passenger traffic led to the *Capitol* becoming an entirely separate train all the way through effective Oct. 26, 1986.

The *Capitol* was the recipient of one of Amtrak's more-radical route changes when on Nov. 11, 1990, Nos. 29 and 30 were rerouted between Chicago and Pittsburgh through Toledo and Cleveland on Conrail's ex-New York Central main (Chicago-Cleveland) and ex-PRR Cleveland-Alliance-Pittsburgh line. Now Toledo and Cleveland have a direct link to Pittsburgh, Washington and the Southeast, the latter through reinstated through-car service via the *Silver Star*.

Gone are the blue-and-gray diesels and passenger cars of B&O days, and you won't find Lobster Newburg— a B&O *Capitol Limited* tradition—on the menu, but a lot of the spirit of the *Cap* of yore is alive and well on today's 29 and 30. Dome cars came back, just as the B&O *Capitol* sported in the 1950's and 1960's, and friendly crews still point out the Chesapeake & Ohio Canal, Civil War landmarks and the outstanding geography that make the east end of the *Capitol*'s journey a delight. Indeed, service aboard the *Capitol Limited* has received such accolades in recent years that some have called it Amtrak's best long-distance train overall.

Crossing from Maryland into Harpers Ferry, W.Va., No. 29 throttles back to make its station stop at the west end of the bridge over the Potomac. Here, in 1859, was the stage for John Brown's Raid, one of the opening scenes in the Civil War. The *Capitol Limited* traverses one of the most-historical regions of Eastern U.S. But isn't it nice to know that the *Capitol Limited* itself *isn't* history anymore?—*David Harrison*

Nos. 40 & 41

Chicago-Pittsburgh-Philadelphia-New York

Shortly after Amtrak celebrated its 20th anniversary in May 1991, one of its premier trains celebrated its 89th birthday and entered its 90th year of service. Thus to the *Broadway Limited* goes the award of being the nation's oldest, continuously operated long-distance passenger train.

Since June 15, 1902, the *Broadway* (originally named *Pennsylvania Special* until 1912) has been speeding passengers between New York and Chicago—close to 65,000 times! With its name of dual meaning (originally, it was named for PRR's multi-track "Broad-Way" main line, but most contemporary passengers are content to associate it with the famous Manhattan street of the same name), the *Broadway Limited* is one of those extra-prominent names in passenger-train history,

Today's *Broadway Limited* is a direct descendant of Pennsylvania Railroad's most-famous flagship, shown arriving Chicago Union Station in the summer of 1966.—*Mike Schafer*

ABOVE: Evening is setting in as the westbound *Broadway Limited* of Aug. 8, 1990, bridges one of the many tributaries to the Susquehanna River (background) near Duncannon, Pa. The *Broadway*'s former-Pennsy path is in a sense its own (with apologies to the late, great New York Central) "Water Level Route," following the Susquehanna and Juniata rivers west of Harrisburg to Altoona, Pa., to avoid excessively long and steep mountain grades.—*Don Jilson* RIGHT: Precisely on time following its all-night trek from Chicago on its new CSX route, No. 40 marches out of downtown Pittsburgh on the Conrail main to Harrisburg on June 19, 1991.—*Mike Schafer*

ABOVE: Clad in the "cigar band" scheme of the late 1970's, Amtrak E8 453 and three mates piloting the eastbound *Broadway* get fueled and watered at Crestline, Ohio, in the wee hours of a summer day in 1977. **LEFT:** Number 40, dropping downgrade from Cresson to Altoona, Pa., cants through Horseshoe Curve in June 1986. **BELOW:** Passengers aboard the eastbound *Broadway* in June 1987 enjoy comraderie —or solitude—in the lounge.—*Three photos, Mike Schafer* **FACING PAGE, RIGHT:** Filled with holiday travelers and bolstered with a healthy yield of head-end traffic, a twenty-car eastbound *Broadway Limited* sweeps through the rugged Pennsylvania countryside near Parkhill on the Fourth of July 1990 while a Conrail van train heads westward.—*Rich Ribarevski*

and its rise to prestige for preferred travel mode between the then-first and second-largest U.S. cities in the first half of the 20th Century was eclipsed only by its arch rival, New York Central's *20th Century Limited.*

The fierce competition between these two all-private-room trains ended abruptly with the *Century's* rather unceremonious termination in Dec. 3, 1967. The *Broadway* soldiered on, surviving not only the disastrous Penn Central merger (PRR + NYC) the following year, but also the wide swath of train-offs that marked the beginning of Amtrak. Instead, the *Broadway* on May 1, 1971, became Amtrak's chosen (and then only) new York-Chicago train—as well as its "new" Chicago-Washington train via through cars split from the train at Harrisburg. Almost immediately, Amtrak began infusing new blood into the *Broadway*: Twin-unit diners built for PRR's 1949 rendition of the Broadway (and other trains) were reinstated, Slumbercoach service was introduced and better cars (i.e., those from Western carriers such as UP) from Amtrak's "new" pool were rotated into *Broadway* consists.

On Amtrak's first birthday, May 1, 1972, the *Broadway* became the carrier's first refurbished train, wearing Amtrak's new red/white/blue/platinum mist (or stainless steel) exterior colors and "purple paisley" interior designs—ver-r-r-y Seventies. And, back again, was a regularly assigned sleeper-lounge observation car (ex-B&O), while a mid-train lounge sported VCRs showing contemporary-release movies. The *Broadway* had new lease on life.

And since then, life has been good for the *Broadway*, especially after PC successor Conrail rebuilt much of the *Broadway's* route between Chicago and Harrisburg, Pa. Rebuilt Heritage Fleet equipment was implemented in 1980, greatly increasing service reliability. The through cars to Washington eventually evolved into a whole new separate train (see *Capitol Limited* section), allowing the *Broadway* to grow on its own terms as a Chicago-New York run.

Until late in 1990, the *Broadway* also had the distinction of having continuously traversed—to within ten miles—its original 1902 route. Owing the Conrail's insistence on downgrading most of its old Pittsburgh, Fort Wayne & Chicago main line between those namesake points, Amtrak on Nov. 11, 1990, permanently rerouted the *Broadway* to CSX Transportation's ex-Baltimore & Ohio main line between Chicago and Pittsburgh. Though the change bypassed important stops like Fort Wayne, Ind., and Lima, Ohio, off the beaten path (the former still served by connecting bus), it added new population centers to the Amtrak map, notably Youngstown and Akron, Ohio.

But east of Pittsburgh, as it has for over 89 years, the *Broadway* still cruises over a serpentine steel spine along cool mountain streams, atop the crest of the Alleghenies around Horseshoe Curve, through well-to-do Main Line Philadelphia suburbs and into a middle-of-Manhattan terminal—a path fortified by a parent whose keystone symbol passed out of existence three years before Amtrak.

Lake Shore Limited

Nos. 48/448 & 49/449

Chicago-Toledo-Cleveland-Buffalo-Albany-New York/ Boston

There's a bit of NYC's *20th Century Limited* (above, at Chicago in 1966) and lots of its *New England States* in Amtrak's *Lake Shore Limited*.—*Mike Schafer*

Upon Amtrak's startup in 1971, the unthinkable happened: Through passenger service ended between New York and Chicago via Penn Central's former New York Central main line. Even in the 1960's, when passenger service was in precarious decline, the "Water Level Route" sported a wide array of through services between the two urban giants, highlighted by what may be arguably the most famous train in North American history: the *20th Century Limited.*

The *Century's* ignominious demise in December 1967 resulted in a nameless no-frills replacement train—in essence the remains of NYC's Chicago-Boston *New England States* with a New York section. Nonetheless, until Amtrak, there remained three Chicago-Buffalo-New York trains on the well-populated ex-

NYC route, so the absence of service west of Buffalo effective with Amtrak stunned rail advocates.

Fortunately, this major shortcoming (necessitated by woefully inadequate startup funding for Amtrak) was remedied when, only 10 days after Amtrak's birth, a through Chicago-Cleveland-Buffalo-New York train was established by some of the states it served (Illinois, Ohio and New York). As a 403(b) proposition, the *Lake Shore*—as it became known on Nov. 14, 1971—was doomed for lack of cooperation between the states and was discontinued on Jan. 6, 1972.

What the states could not accomplish on their own, Congress did in 1975 by mandating that Amtrak make Chicago-Cleveland-New York/Boston an experimental route. Amtrak built upon service patterns established by the erstwhile *New England States* and *20th Century Limited* and, borrowing a name used by New York Central predecessor railroads for a similar run dating from the turn of the century, on Oct. 31, 1975, unveiled the new *Lake Shore Limited.* And nobody has looked back since then.

No need to. The *Lake Shore Limited* has become one of Amtrak's strongest Eastern

FACING PAGE, TOP: Among the many bodies of water skirted by the *Lake Shore Limited*, perhaps none is so steeped in history and lore as the Hudson River. FL9 498 with train 48 heads south along the Hudson on April 26, 1990, for an appointment in Grand Central Terminal, some 50 miles downstream.—*Scott Hartley* **ABOVE: The eastbound *Lake Shore* wheels along the Mohawk River through Gulf Curve at Little Falls, N.Y., in June 1984.**—*John D. Bartley*

Lake Shore Limited

long-hauls, and today it would be unthinkable to not have Nos. 48/448-49/449 linking Chicago, New York and Boston with the likes of Syracuse, Rochester and Buffalo, N.Y., Cleveland and Toledo, Ohio, and Springfield, Mass. In addition, the extension of one Chicago-Detroit train to Toledo on Aug. 3, 1980, feeds Michigan traffic to and from the *Lake Shore Limited* at Toledo Union Terminal.

As with other Amtrak Eastern trains, the *Lake Shore* has be the beneficiary of both Conrail's major upgrade of main lines and of Amtrak's Beech Grove Shop Heritage Fleet rebuild program. Initial running time of the *Lake Shore Limited* between New York and Chicago in November 1975 was (eastbound) 23 hours; today that stands at about 19 hours— a testimony to the track and signaling improvements along the train's route, where east of Hoffman's, N.Y., and south to Poughkeepsie, N.Y., speeds of 100 mph are routine.

The *Lake Shore Limited* follows much of the same path it did when inaugurated in the mid-1970's, with three small but significant exceptions: (1) the return to the original main line between Albany and Hoffmans, N.Y., following the closing of an alternate route established by Penn Central before Amtrak; (2) the return to a reincarnated "Post Road Connection" between Albany/Rensselaer station and Post Road, N.Y., on Oct. 28, 1979, eliminating back-up moves and a circuitous routing via

Castleton Junction for the Boston section; and (3) the April 7, 1991, permanent reroute away from Grand Central Terminal in Manhattan to Penn Station via a revamped defunct former-NYC freight line south of Spuyten Duyvil, N.Y.

The Water Level Route slogan of NYC days is moribund, but not its meaning. The *Lake Shore Limited* does indeed skim many lake shores, most of all (Great) Lake Erie, as well as many historic waterways, notably the Mohawk River, Erie Canal and Hudson River in Upstate New York. The exception to the Water Level rule falls with the Boston section, trains 448 and 449, which must surmount the Berkshire Mountains in western Massachusetts on Conrail's former Boston & Albany main line.

If you squint a bit when you watch the glimmering stainless cars of the *Lake Shore*, you might see a bit of NYC's famed "Great Steel Fleet," which lives on in Amtrak's most-important Chicago-New York link. Might the *Lake Shore* become Amtrak's *21st Century Limited*?

FACING PAGE: The Boston section breezes through the Berkshires on a splendid fall day in October 1980.—*John D. Bartley* **ABOVE: Hold still! One of No. 48's cheerful car attendants does her best not to move while she and the *Lake Shore* pose at Toledo Union Station on New Year's Eve 1977.**—*Mike Schafer* **BELOW: Living up to its name, the westbound *Lake Shore Limited* heads in from across Sandusky Bay on Lake Erie in July 1984.**—*Bob Todten*

Nos. 50 & 51

Chicago-Indianapolis-Cincinnati-Washington-New York

TOP RIGHT: Thurmond, W. Va.—which has the CSX main line as its main street—is one of several remote towns served by the *Cardinal*, shown westbound on May 5, 1985.—*Terry Chicwak* **TOP LEFT: Departure board at Chicago.**—*Bob Johnston* **ABOVE AND RIGHT: C&O's *George Washington* (at Ashland, Ky., in 1969) and NYC's *James Whitcomb Riley* are ancestors.**—*Both, Mike Schafer*

Granted, Chicago to New York by way of Cincinnati, Huntington, W. Va., and Charlottesville, Va., is hardly in the realm of travel logic. but then the *Cardinal* is not your ordinary train. It has its own agenda, which is to serve out-of-the-way America—places bereft of mainstream air and bus service (and even interstates), and to provide riders a good time while doing so, with an ample helping of scenery.

Here is another Amtrak train with a convoluted history. The *Cardinal*'s heritage? Loosely defined, we can say it's a distant relative of New York Central's *James Whitcomb Riley* (Chicago-Cincinnati) and Chesapeake & Ohio's *George Washington* and *Sportsman* (Cincinnati-Washington/Newport News, Va., with the Newport News section separating from the main-stem train at Charlottesville). The *Riley* and the *George* were adopted by Amtrak on May 1, 1971, and by July 12 of that same year, the two services had been combined into one Chicago-Washington/Newport News streamliner which was known eastbound as the *George Washington* and westbound as the *James Whitcomb Riley*. Such a relationship had precedence, as NYC handled through cars from C&O trains at Cincinnati to Chicago into the 1960's.

From there, it should have been a success story, but that's not what happened. Track conditions in Indiana on the financially destitute Penn Central resulted in a myriad of "permanent" reroutes between Chicago and Cincinnati beginning in 1973, on alternate PC lines; on Aug. 1, 1974, the *James Whitcomb Riley* (the *George Washington* name having been dropped on May 19, 1974, in favor of a more-obscure personality—do *you* know who James Whitcomb Riley was?) settled into one of its longer permanent reroutes: Chicago-Cincinnati via Chicago & Western Indiana (Chicago-Hammond), Erie Lackawanna (Hammond-Griffith, Ind.) and Chesapeake & Ohio (Griffith-Cincinnati). On March 25, 1975,

the *Riley* was joined by a new service, the Chicago-Norfolk *Mountaineer*, which ran combined with the *Riley* between Chicago and Catlettsburg, Ky. That amalgamation ended on May 1, 1977.

Even the extremities of the new Chicago-Cincinnati route eventually changed, first in 1976 when a new path between Chicago and La Crosse, Ind., via Wellsboro, Ind., was implemented over Conrail, Baltimore & Ohio and C&O; and then in 1980 when the train was shifted to a B&O route between Cottage Grove, Ind., and Cincinnati.

On Oct. 30. 1977, following an infusion of new Amfleet equipment and major schedule changes, the *James Whitcomb Riley* was renamed *Cardinal*—the state bird of all states served by the train west of Washington, D.C.. On April 26, 1981, the train was extended to New York. A round of budget cuts later that year mortally wounded some Amtrak services, the *Cardinal* among them. But on Jan. 8, 1982, the *Cardinal* became the latest Amtrak phoenix and was revived (albeit tri-weekly) by popular demand.

Although the medium-size cities served by Nos. 50 and 51 in Indiana along the C&O route had demonstrated good patronage, its importance as a freight route for CSX had diminished, and CSX wanted to downgrade it. Additionally, Amtrak strongly preferred a reroute back through Indianapolis. Thus with the annual spring timetable change of 1986, the *Cardinal* returned to the Hoosier capital using a combination of Conrail (ex-PRR, Chicago-Maynard, Ind.), CSX (former Monon, Maynard-Crawfordsville), Conrail again (ex-Peoria & Eastern, Crawfordsville-Indianapolis), and more CSX (ex-B&O, Indy-Cincy).

To ride the *Cardinal* today is to embark on a sort of steel hiking trail. The essence of the train is its leisurely sojourn through some of the most rugged topography in the East, with highlights like West Virginia's New River Gorge and the climb over Blue Ridge Summit in neighboring Virginia. Emphasizing these important aspects of 50 and 51's colorful route are National Park Service guides, which on selected days provide on-board commentary.

The *Cardinal* is an alternative lifestyle to the speedy Chicago-New York trips of the *Broadway Limited* and *Lake Shore Limited*. Yet, it remains a popular run, one that is certain to warrant a return to daily operation once additional new equipment comes on line as Amtrak's 25th birthday in 1996 approaches. A run that proves that the fastest is not necessarily the bestest.

ABOVE LEFT: **Number 50 in the charge of a single F40 bursts from Stretchers Neck Tunnel near Prince, W. Va., on June 10, 1984. The *Cardinal*'s route over CSX's former-C&O main line is a wonderful journey through spectacular river valleys and over winding mountain passes.**—*Joe McMillan* **ABOVE: After Amtrak shifted Nos. 50 and 51 to the C&O Railway of Indiana between Hammond, Ind., and Cincinnati in 1974, the *Cardinal* gained a very scenic entrance to the Queen City by way of C&ORofI's Cheviot Hill line into the Ohio River valley. Here, on Dec. 28, 1977, General Electric P30CH No. 723 struts across one of several Cheviot trestles with the Chicago-bound *Cardinal*. This route has since been abandoned and the trestles dismantled, and Nos. 50 and 51 now enter Cincinnati over CSX's former B&O line through Hamilton, Ohio.**—*R. D. Acton Jr.*

Auto Train

Nos. 52 & 53
Lorton-Sanford

TOP: The southbound *Auto Train* flies high above the James River, Richmond, Va., in 1988.—*Doug Koontz* **ABOVE: Autos travel with passengers in special carriers.**—*Alex Mayes* **BELOW: The original *Auto-Train* in 1978.**—*Mike Schafer*

Amtrak has to its credit numerous feats of reincarnation, returning to the rails a multitude of trains that had vanished in those gray countdown years to May 1, 1971. *Auto Train* is one of those stars, but with a different twist: The original *Auto-Train* was not the vehicle of a railroad, but of a corporation dedicated to moving passengers and their cars between the Northeast (and later Midwest) and Florida. And, its first run was on Dec. 6, 1970, just months before Amtrak started.

Although initially wildly successful as a bold, new approach to rail passenger service, *Auto-Train* as a company was plagued by undercapitalization, high overhead, equipment shortages and internal problems. Cost-saving measures even included combining the Midwest *Auto-Train* with Amtrak's Chicago-Miami/St. Pete *Floridian* between Louisville, Ky., and Sanford, Fla. But, on April 30, 1981, *Auto-Train* made its final run, and the day after, the corporation filed for bankruptcy.

Noting that the original *Auto-Train* did not fail for lack of passengers, Amtrak felt the concept was still valid and began acquiring the old *Auto-Train* terminal facilities at Lorton Va., and Sanford as well as a number *Auto-Train* cars. On Oct. 30, 1983, a star was born, as Amtrak's *Auto Train* set sail from Lorton and Sanford for overnight journeys along the Richmond, Fredericksburg & Potomac Railroad and CSX's former-Atlantic Coast Line main.

Initially a triweekly operation, *Auto Train* in its first year carried more than 55,000 passengers; daily service came in 1984, and by the 1990's the mega-liner—with as many as 40 cars per run—was carrying well over 200,000 passengers a year. If the success continues, new routes may be in the offing.

Auto Train utilizes a combination of Heritage Fleet equipment (including several former-Great Northern, Milwaukee Road and Burlington full-length domes) and newer Amfleet II rolling stock. The train is targeted to eventually receive Superliners.

There's a little bit of "if you can't lick 'em, join 'em" in the *Auto Train* story. In the U.S., the automobile is the greatest competitor of the passenger train, but the auto-on-train concept is a supreme example of turning a liability into an asset.

MONTREALER

Nos. 60 & 61

Washington-New York-Montreal

ABOVE: Formalities are exchanged as Amtrak trainmen (left in photo) hand the northbound *Montrealer* over to their Canadian National counterparts at St. Albans, Vt. The Canadian crews will forward the train to Montreal.—*Scott Hartley*

The *Montrealer* is a study of contrasts. You step aboard No. 60 at Washington Union Station at the end of a day as thousands of people whose livelihoods are intertwined with the nerve center of the U.S. head for home in the suburbs or in cities up-line on the Northeast Corridor. Moments following departure, No. 60 is whirling along an electrified artery of transportation at 100 mph while you vie for space with business people in the popular Le Pub car. Later that night, as you tuck yourself in bed, turn off the lights and open the shade, all of wild, glimmering New York City lies biting at your feet as the *Montrealer* climbs away from Manhattan over Hell Gate Bridge.

When you wake up the next morning, the mood had done an about-face: The *Montrealer* is now sashaying along cool, leafy ponds surrounded by verdant mountain scenery. Here and there, you glimpse scenes of sparkling rivers spanned by wooden covered bridges—views that the night previous only seemed possible in drugstore promotional calendars. You are in (sigh) Vermont.

And then things change again as—*arrette!*—No. 60 comes to a halt, having delivered you to another world-class city. . . in another country. Pull out the bilingual dictionary; you are in French-speaking Quebec at the train's namesake metropolis, Montreal.

When the Pennsylvania, New Haven, Boston & Maine and Central Vermont railroads ended *Montrealer* service in 1966, few people dreamed it would ever return. But on Sept. 29, 1972, the *Montrealer* (southbound for a while it was called the *Washingtonian*) did just that, and amidst much fanfare. It was a clear signal that Amtrak could sometimes return what we thought we had lost forever during the dog days of the American passenger train. There were even some new twists, such as a seasonal through Montreal-Miami sleeper and a special lounge car, Le Pub, which with its live entertainment became the train's hallmark.

The *Montrealer*'s reign of popularity as an international link (and as a great way to get to Vermont ski slopes) was interrupted when deteriorating track conditions on the B&M between Springfield, Mass., and White River Junction, Vt., forced the train's suspension in April 1986. Following a heated battle between Guilford Transportation (operator of the B&M since 1981) and Amtrak and CV, service resumed on July 18, 1989, on a revised routing via New London, Conn.

As with the 1972 reincarnation, the 1989 *Montrealer* resumption brought about much celebration and media attention. Riders returned and Nos. 60 and 61 once again became a way of life in New England. Viva le *Montrealais*!

TOP: The southbound *Montrealer* pauses for passengers beside the main office building and former depot of the Central Vermont at St. Albans. At one time, a cavernous, ornate trainshed covered the tracks at this location; today, passengers utilize a smaller station building to the rear.—*C. W. Newton* **ABOVE: Covered bridges are synonymous with New England, and several dot the landscape along the route of the *Montrealer* as this view at Northfield, Vt., in early summer 1979 attests.** —*Mike Schafer*

City of New Orleans AND RIVER CITIES

Nos. 58/358 & 59/359

New Orleans
Memphis
Chicago
St. Louis
Kansas City

It would be natural to assume that Amtrak's *City of New Orleans* is a direct descendant of Illinois Central's *City*, but IC's *Panama Limited* is actually a closer relative. And the *River Cities* heritage? West of St. Louis, it's MP's *Missouri River Eagle*.—*Both photos, Mike Schafer*

Few trains conjure textured images of American railroading as much as that made famous by Arlo Guthrie in his 1972 hit "City of New Orleans. " The song's original version by the late songwriter Steve Goodman was released only a few months following the spectacular June 10, 1971, wreck of the *City* in downstate Illinois.

The song details, fairly accurately, a trip on what had been Illinois Central's pre-Amtrak *City*, whose high-speed (100 mph in some places) flight took it from Chicago to New Orleans in the space of a day. Its verses spoke of a rural America traversed by near-empty passenger trains of the 1960's, of "graveyards full of old black men" and of "changing cars in Memphis, Tennessee." Put on your Walkman as you ride today's *City of New Orleans*, and listen to the song. Some of it still applies (rural America), some of it doesn't (the *City* is a popular run that's not often empty).

Amtrak's first version of the *City of New Orleans* was almost exactly like that of predecessor operator Illinois Central; i.e., an all-day run from Chicago to the Gulf. Unable to maintain the demanding schedule of a day trip due to deteriorating IC track conditions, Amtrak on Nov. 14, 1971, switched to an overnight Chicago-New Orleans timing to which it ap-

ABOVE LEFT: The *City of New Orleans* meets the City of Chicago on a chilly February day in 1990. Number 58 is dropping down from the St. Charles Air Line and in a few minutes will position itself to back into Chicago Union Station.—*Mike Abalos*
ABOVE: The *River Cities* stands at Centralia, Ill., in 1984 while waiting for the *City of New Orleans* to arrive from Chicago. Is this Amtrak's most-diminutive long-distance train?—*Mike Schafer*

plied another well-known IC name, *Panama Limited*. IC's *Panama* was best-known as one of the last great all-sleeper trains in the U.S.

Perhaps Amtrak felt that the public had long ago lost any association with the *Panama Limited* name, which was derived from the opening of the Panama Canal early in the century. Certainly, the public related more to the *City of New Orleans* name (thanks again to Arlo and Steve), so on Feb. 1, 1981, the *Panama* was so rechristened.

The *City's* alter ego, the *River Cities*, came along some three years later, on April 29, 1984. To capitalize on the Louisiana Purchase Exposition that year, Amtrak inaugurated through Kansas City-New Orleans service in the form of a sleeper and dome coach piggybacked on existing schedules: on the *St. Louis/Kansas City Mules* along Union Pacific's ex-Missouri Pacific main line between Kansas City and St. Louis, and on the *City of New Orleans* via the Illinois Central between Centralia, Ill., and New Orleans. Between St. Louis and Centralia (later, Carbondale, Ill.), the *River Cities* is its own entity, returning rail passenger service along the Southern Railway (and a portion of Alton & Southern) between those two points for the first time in more than 30 years.

Vestiges of the original Illinois Central *City of New Orleans* remain on Amtrak's version in this scene of the southbound *City* descending into Kentucky from the Ohio River bridge in October 1971. Amtrak's "Rainbow Era" is in full swing as cars from Union Pacific, Louisville & Nashville and other carriers infiltrate the ranks of color-matched streamliners.—*Phil Gosney*

And what of the name *River Cities*? From Kansas City to New Orleans, Nos. 358 and 359 more or less parallel two great waterways, calling at communities that owe their lives to the Missouri and Mississippi rivers—places like Jefferson City (Mo.), St. Louis, Memphis and, of course, New Orleans.

The *City of New Orleans* is a living legend, working with the new-kid-on-the-block *River Cities* to form lifelines between America's heartland and one of America's most-legendary cities.

SILVER STAR and

Nos. 81-91 & 82-92

New York-Washington-Richmond-Raleigh-Jacksonville-Tampa/Miami

RIGHT: Bathed in morning sun, the northbound *Silver Star* glides into Hamlet, N.C., in November 1988.— *Michael Shermetta* **BELOW: Evening has set in at Lakeland, Fla., as No. 82, the Tampa section of the *Star,* arrows into the former-ACL depot in May 1987.—***Joseph L. Oates* **BOTTOM: Ruby-nosed SDP40F's make for a regal pose of the *Star* at Broad Street Station in Richmond, Va., in 1975, not long before Amtrak moved out of the venerable facility.—** *Mike Schafer*

Amtrak's "Silver Service" picks up where a conscientious carrier had to leave off. Seaboard Coast Line Railroad, the result of the 1967 merging of Seaboard Air Line and Atlantic Coast Line, was hailed as one of few shining stars of pre-Amtrak passenger carriers. And no wonder. Pre-merger ACL and SAL themselves were silver linings in the dark cloud of rail passenger service of the late 1960's.

Strictly speaking, the *Silver Star* and *Silver Meteor* were SAL trains, but today's versions adopt operations fielded by ACL as well. for example, Amtrak's *Meteor* now follows a route that is largely former ACL (Richmond -Charleston-Jacksonville), so there is a little bit of ACL/SCL's *Champion* echoed in today's *Meteor* format.

Seaboard Air Line introduced the *Silver Meteor* on Feb. 2, 1939, and the *Silver Star* in December 1947. Both trains operated between New York and Florida where they were split into Miami and St. Petersburg sections—which is how both trains operate today. They were enormously popular in the 1940's, 1950's and even the 1960's, and have always been strong operations for Amtrak.

At the time of Amtrak startup, SCL had been operating the *Silver Meteor* as strictly a New York-Miami train, the St. Pete section having been dropped in 1968. SCL's *Silver Star* followed the same route as the *Meteor*—on the former SAL via Raleigh, N.C., and Columbia, S.C.—but split at Jacksonville into two trains, with the St. Pete leg operating on the former-ACL main via Orlando. Amtrak for a time continued this format for both *Silver* trains, which through the first decade of Amtrak had various now-defunct companion Florida liners, including the *Champion*, *Florida Special*, *Miamian*, *Carolina Special* and *Vacationer*.

On Dec. 17, 1971, the *Meteor* was rerouted to the faster, double-track ACL route through the Carolinas where it has remained since. From June 11, 1972, to Dec. 14, 1972, the *Meteor* gained a St. Pete section when the New York-St. Pete *Champion* did not operate; interestingly, from Sept 10 through Dec. 14, 1972, the *Meteor* split into Miami

SILVER METEOR

Nos. 87-97 & 88-98

New York-Washington-Richmond-Charleston-Jacksonville-Tampa/Miami

and St. Pete sections at Savannah, Ga., with the Miami section bypassing Jacksonville on SCL's Baldwin cutoff. When the *Champion* returned on Dec. 15, 1972, the *Meteor* continued to bypass Jacksonville through April 27, 1973.

Throughout the 1970's, operations on the New York-Florida route were a complex array of seasonal and experimental services, some of which were combined with the *Meteor* during certain periods, and in some cases certain segments of the *Silver Star* were combined with the Chicago-Florida train. Budget cuts during the 1970's affected some Florida operations, but the Oct. 1. 1979, cuts mandated by the President Carter administration left New York-Miami/St. Pete service in the charge of two trains: the *Silver Star*, operating via Raleigh, and *Silver Meteor*, via Charleston.

Trackage rationalization by SCL successor CSX Transportation forced Amtrak to permanently detour the *Silver Star* between Petersburg, Va., and Raleigh via the old ACL route to Selma and the Southern into Raleigh effective Oct. 26, 1986. A smaller CSX route rationalization in Florida in 1988 put the Miami sections of both the *Meteor* and the *Star* onto a new route between Coleman and Lakeland, Fla., on June 12 of that year.

Amtrak's Northeast-Florida service is hardly a Mickey Mouse operation, although the carrier probably owes a lot to the slapstick rodent (with Walt Disney World as the Number One Florida tourist destination). Thanks to Mickey, warm Florida climates and seasonal winter homes away from homes, the Silver twins each continue to rack up celestial ridership counts in the long-distance market despite their nearly duplicative routes and the supplementation of *Auto Train* and the New York-Jacksonville *Palmetto*. Only the Seattle-L.A. *Coast Starlight* and the combined Chicago-West Coast service via Denver tend to carry more passengers on a yearly basis. On Amtrak, all that glitters isn't gold, but silver.

ABOVE LEFT: Husky E60 No. 600 is just into Newark Penn Station with the northbound *Silver Meteor*, about 45 minutes tardy and running at near capacity on May 16, 1991. TOP RIGHT: Today's "Silver Service" trains reflect the high regard travelers had for Seaboard Air Line and Atlantic Coast Line (later, Seaboard Coast Line) operations in the pre-Amtrak era. SAL's *Silver Meteor*, with its trademark observation-lounge that lasted well into Amtrak, has just arrived Miami in August 1965.—*Both photos, Mike Schafer* **ABOVE: The *Meteor* as it appeared during much of the 1970's. Number 97, the train's Miami section, is passing Lake Jackson near Sebring, Fla., on April 30, 1980. Rebuilt HEP (head-end power) consists and F40 locomotives are but months away.**—*Bob Schmidt*

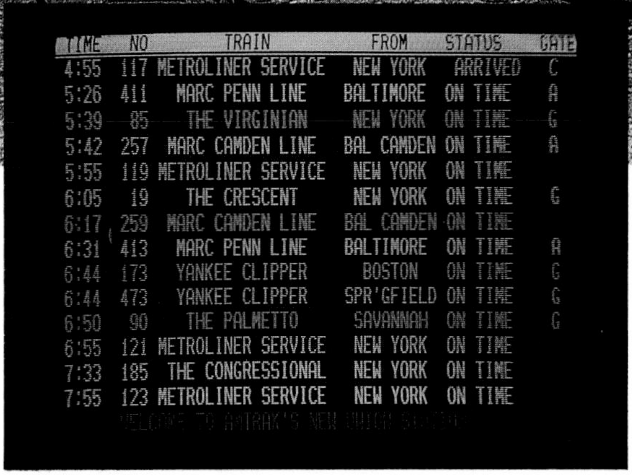

TIME	NO	TRAIN	FROM	STATUS	GATE
4:55	117	METROLINER SERVICE	NEW YORK	ARRIVED	C
5:26	411	MARC PENN LINE	BALTIMORE	ON TIME	A
5:39	85	THE VIRGINIAN	NEW YORK	ON TIME	G
5:42	257	MARC CAMDEN LINE	BAL CAMDEN	ON TIME	A
5:55	119	METROLINER SERVICE	NEW YORK	ON TIME	
6:05	19	THE CRESCENT	NEW YORK	ON TIME	G
6:17	259	MARC CAMDEN LINE	BAL CAMDEN	ON TIME	
6:31	413	MARC PENN LINE	BALTIMORE	ON TIME	A
6:44	173	YANKEE CLIPPER	BOSTON	ON TIME	G
6:44	473	YANKEE CLIPPER	SPR'GFIELD	ON TIME	G
6:50	90	THE PALMETTO	SAVANNAH	ON TIME	G
6:55	121	METROLINER SERVICE	NEW YORK	ON TIME	
7:33	185	THE CONGRESSIONAL	NEW YORK	ON TIME	
7:55	123	METROLINER SERVICE	NEW YORK	ON TIME	

ABOVE: Although hardly reflective of the diversity of Amtrak's Northeast Corridor, this 1989 panorama at Philadelphia on the New York-Washington line does epitomize the essence of American high-speed rail: a gutsy AEM7 electric leading a tube of stainless steel set against a dynamic, skyscraping skyline.—*Steve Barry* **LEFT: Video screens at Washington Union Station do show some of the route's variety, from long-distance Amtrak trains to MARC suburban runs to the famous *Metroliners*.** —*Mike Schafer*

8/Cruisin' Amtrak Boulevard

NRPC'S SHOWCASE: THE NORTHEAST CORRIDOR

BY BOB JOHNSTON

Though Penn Central's bankruptcy inflicted excruciating pain into daily Amtrak operations in the form of deferred equipment and track maintenance in the early 1970's, it also precipitated the National Railroad Passenger Corporation's first opportunity to own a piece of track from the ground up.

With a government-sponsored takeover of the moribund carrier looming, Amtrak President Paul Reistrup and his board of directors helped convince Congress that relieving newly created Conrail of its high-density passenger lines from Washington to Boston, Harrisburg to Philadelphia, and New Haven to Springfield made more sense than allowing the emerging company to retain ownership and operating responsibility but continue to receive payments from another government-subsidized entity. After all, the inability of passenger revenue to cover costs had helped sink the merged remnants of Pennsylvania, New York Central and New York, New Haven & Hartford in the first place.

So it was on April 1, 1976, that Amtrak became the landlord and Conrail the tenant over 363 of the 456 miles between Washington and Boston, with Conrail

(Metro-North Commuter Railroad after 1983, through ownership by New York's Metropolitan Transit Authority and Connecticut DOT) operating the segment west of New Haven to New Rochelle, N.Y. and Boston's MBTA owning but letting Amtrak operate the 38 miles from South Station to the Rhode Island state line.

Conveying the Northeast Corridor to Amtrak signaled another chapter of a story that originated with the laying of track prior to the Civil War along much of the route, tunneling under Baltimore in 1873, opening the Hudson and East River tunnels and New York's Pennsylvania Station in 1910 and completing the electrification from Washington to New Haven in 1935 (and to Harrisburg in 1938). With the Pennsylvania Railroad's venerable GG1 electric locomotives piloting both lightweight *Congressional* equipment as well as heavier strings of P70 coaches and Pullman-laden through trains south of New York, and Patrick McGinnis' New Haven vermilion and stainless-steel "American Flyer" cars pulled by FL9 diesel-electric/electrics and double-ended EP5 electric motors to the north, service patterns remained virtually unchanged from the early 1950's until Amtrak's inception in 1971.

But a parallel development in the 1960's would change the face of the Corridor forever and ultimately set the stage for Amtrak's creation and future persona for decades to come. After billions of dollars spent to build the nation's extensive Interstate Highway System had failed to make a dent in the Northeast's mounting road and air congestion, Rhode Island Senator Claiborne Pell prevailed upon his colleagues in Congress to pass the High Speed Ground Transportation Act in 1965, authorizing $90 million to fund a two-year demonstration project calling for new

The image most folks might have of the Northeast Corridor might be endorsed by the scene on the facing page, but the NEC has in fact its serene aspects, especially east of New Haven, Conn., where the former NYNH&H Shore Line hugs the Atlantic Ocean most of the way to Providence, R.I. A sunken trawler (lobster boat) at Wequetequok Cove near Stonington, Conn., adds to New England's postcard charm as Amtrak's westbound (appropriately) *Mayflower* skims toward New London in April 1990.—*Tom Carver*

The two principal offshoots of the Northeast Corridor are the ex-PRR "Main Line" (as it is formally known by even non-railroad-oriented locals) between Philadelphia and Harrisburg, Pa., and the former-New Haven Railroad Connecticut Valley branch from New Haven, Conn., to Springfield, Mass. TOP: Demoted from New York-Washington duties, a former Metroliner set flies past a SEPTA Budd Rail Diesel Car at Parkesburg, Pa., in 1984.—*Steve Barry* **ABOVE: The Springfield section of train 470, the *Yankee Clipper*, slips away from the Connecticut capital on May 3, 1990. Hartford Union Station was rehabilitated in the 1980's.**—*David Patch*

equipment and New York-Washington track upgrading. It was the country's first public investment in high-speed rail transportation.

Hatched from this seed money (of which only $2 million was ever spent) were four self-propelled, tubular cars with fluted stainless-steel sides. These prototypes were tested at speeds as high as 160 mph along a specially prepared stretch of the Corridor's grade-crossing-free tangent track in New Jersey, laying the groundwork for production models to follow. Entering revenue service on Jan. 16, 1969, at a modest 110-mph top speed, the initial 50-car Metroliner fleet built by Budd, General Electric and Westinghouse, cost Penn Central $57 million (including the railroad's share of track improvements) but cut New York-Washington running times to under three hours.

With conventional trains of the era limited to 90 mph producing a 3:50 New York-Washington running time at best, the all-reserved *Metroliners* represented the first concerted effort to compete directly with the Eastern Airlines shuttle for endpoint business and produced a marked improvement for travelers between the Corridor's intermediate points. As the self-propelled equipment arrived (eventually totaling 61 cars) and more 4- and 6-car round-trips were added, ridership rose from 605,000 in 1969 to 1.6 million in 1971.

Signifying the importance of this service to Amtrak's viability (and visibility), NRPC President Roger Lewis personally greeted the 3 millionth *Metroliner* passenger on July 29, 1971, at a Washington Union Station ceremony in which "roses for ladies and carnations for men were pinned on by three pretty Metromisses from Penn Central," according to one of Amtrak's earliest press releases.

By the Nov. 14, 1971, timetable change, Amtrak had upped the *Metroliner* ante to 20 daily trains including one round-trip to New Haven, carding three one-stop Washington-New York expresses making only either Capital Beltway or the newly constructed Woodbridge (N.J.) Metropark stop adjacent to the Garden State Parkway. Also by this time, with all Boston and Springfield trains having shifted from Grand Central Terminal to Penn Station on May 1, the beginnings of "memory" schedules further facilitated coordination of Corridor services. It was thus now possible to leave on the 1 p.m. *Metroliner* out of D.C., hit Gotham at 4 and be in Beantown by 8 p.m., thanks to a connection with the 4:15 p.m. *Turbo Yankee Clipper*, United Aircraft's bubble-topped "jet-powered" speedstar that lopped 45 minutes from New York-Boston running times.

The arrival of Amfleet equipment from the Budd Company in 1975-77, initially contemplated as a replacement for elderly conventional Corridor equipment, allowed for the revamping of 34 of the original self-propelled cars to begin in 1978. At that time, the term "*Metroliner Service*" was introduced to differentiate the schedules and reserved-seat status of the operation from the equipment used to protect it.

The search for something to pull the new cars resulted in 1976-77 comparative high-speed tests, when both French and Swedish locomotives sped down the Corridor. Dubbed the "Swedish Meatball," the ASEA Rc4a got the nod because its low weight-to-high-horsepower ratio made locomotive-hauled high-speed Amfleet trains a viable alternative to the original self-propelled cars, which had been experiencing overheating problems. As modified to include head-end electric power and the capability of switching from 25 hertz to 60 hertz (east of Harold Tower on the Hell Gate Bridge Route) 11,000-volt alternating current, the ASEA-licensed, GM Electro-Motive Division-built AEM7 consumed 20 percent less energy than the elderly GG1 it was destined to replace and 10 percent less than the GE E60 motors originally designed for freight or passenger use.

Though the first refurbished set of self-propelled cars began operating in 1979, the AEM7 made its initial revenue trip hauling *Metroliner Service* train 108, the 10 a.m. Washington departure, on May 9, 1980. By October 1981, AEM7/Amfleet *Metroliner Service* trainsets had effectively banished all of the original Metroliner cars to Philadelphia-Harrisburg service.

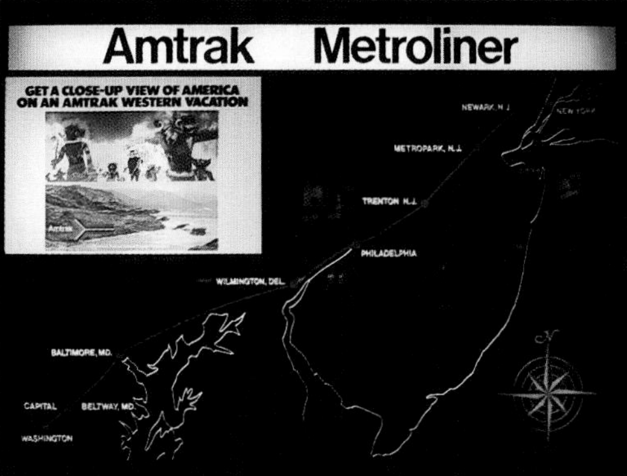

LEFT: Introduced in the late 1960's, *Metroliners* ushered in a new era of high-speed travel in the U.S. The highly touted multiple-unit cars served Amtrak well throughout the 1970's; this sign set off a special waiting area in Washington for *Metroliner* passengers in 1975.—*Mike Schafer* **ABOVE: Late-afternoon winter sun blushes the face of a Washington-bound *Metroliner* in 1980. Metroliner equipment went through heavy shopping in the late 1970's for general refurbishment and for refinements designed to alleviate cooling problems. The m.u.'s emerged with a eye-stopping car-end paint scheme that left little doubt to passengers witnessing an arrival as to who the carrier was.**—*Roger Puta, collection of Mel Finzer*

But perhaps the most important component of the 120 mph equation was the $2.5 billion authorized by Congress in 1976 for the Federal Railroad Administration's Northeast Corridor Improvement Project (NECIP). The stated goal of the initial Railroad Revitalization and Regulatory Reform Act was to achieve 2:40 New York-Washington and 3:40 New York-Boston running

ABOVE: AEM7 939 is framed by the latticework of Pelham (N.Y.) drawbridge in 1983.—*Bill Chaplik* FACING PAGE: Moments out of Manhattan, "Meatball" 944 and its Washington-bound corridor consist chase the setting sun on an afternoon in 1987. The units are also known as "toasters" because of their likeness to that appliance.—*Mike Del Vecchio*

times by 1981. Track had deteriorated to such an extent under cash-starved Penn Central that Amtrak attacked slow orders on the New Haven-Boston segment during the first month of its ownership of the line, lengthening schedules to account for single-tracking around maintenance sites, setting a pattern for Corridor slowdowns throughout the next decade.

With major work beginning in 1977, NECIP infused the Corridor with welded rail, concrete ties, rail grinding, high-speed surfacing, ballast cleaning, roadbed undercutting and development of the Automatic Track Laying System to efficiently expedite the process. Twenty-two highway crossings would be closed (none remain south of New Haven) or improved, and bridges, signals and stations repaired. Amtrak's Board separately allocated almost $5 million of non-NECIP funds for Philadelphia-Harrisburg and New Haven-Springfield tie and rail replacement in 1978. The construction season started at 11 different locations from Boston to Washington on April 2, 1979, prompting the Public Affairs department to offer a "travel forecast" telephone number discussing the week's work locations and resulting delays. Patronage suffered in 1980 when *Metroliner* schedules had been lengthened to 3 hours and 45 minutes.

But by 1981 the worst was over. Oct. 25 of that year saw the reintroduction of limited-stop all AEM7-hauled *Express Metroliner Service* between Washington and New York in "2 hours and 59 Civilized Minutes." Through *Metroliner Service* to New Haven was now possible again due to the locomotives' dual a.c. cycle capability, and double-headed Meatballs regularly cranked up long strings of non-reserved, heavy peak-period conventional trains like the *Senator* and *Yankee Clipper*.

As track speed, schedule reliability and equipment availability improved, so did Amtrak's "service" experimentation. For example, two *New England Metroliner* round trips were introduced in 1982 on under-four-hour New York-Boston schedules only to be dropped several years later in favor of non-reserved "Shoreline Service" which made a few more stops but did not even carry a club car.

Originally nameless New Haven-Springfield connections handled by "next generation" diesel railcars, SPV2000s, became "Connecticut Valley Service" in the mid-1980's until the designation was dropped with the practice of running through Amfleet coaches from Washington for points on the Inland Route at the front of trains, splitting them during the switch from electric to diesel power at New Haven; meanwhile, the mechanically unreliable SPV's were sidelined. West of Philadelphia, "Silverliner Service" became "Keystone Service" when the ex-Metroliner cars bumped their older cousins.

Another crucial component of upgrading Corridor speed, capacity and safety has been the complete overhaul of the former Pennsylvania Railroad's automated block and electric power systems. Though the cab-signaled line had been FRA-authorized for 125 mph over much of its route, trains were still being verbally passed between signal towers and times entered on dispatchers' train sheets in the same way they had been in the 1930's and earlier. With movements intermixed between 30-mph Conrail drag freights; MARC, SEPTA, New Jersey Transit and MBTA start-and-stop commuter service (into Washington-Baltimore, Philadelphia, New York, and Boston, respectively); 90 mph through trains to Montreal, Chicago and the South; and *Metroliner* speedsters, all superimposed over a physical plant expanding and contracting from two to six tracks thanks to tunnel and bridge constrictions, in 1981 the company commissioned a division of Chrysler to custom design a computerized train-control system based on the Corridor's unique operating needs.

Needless to say, there was nothing on the shelf that would meet specifications dictated by this complex task. But air traffic-control advances coupled with emerging video screen and computer technology resulted, by 1986, in the first on-line testing of CETC, Centralized Electrification and Traffic Control. From a darkened, windowless room eight floors above Amtrak's bustling 30th Street Station in Philadelphia, it was now possible for dispatch-

High up in 30th Street Station, Philadelphia, is a video "game" the likes of which you won't find at your neighborhood Blockbuster outlet. Here, one of two assistant chief dispatchers views the section of railroad from Washington Union Station to Perryville, Md., defined by color bands whose hues change according to block occupancy.—*Both photos, Bob Johnston*

Ron Krause studies graphic images of the Northeast Corridor projected on eleven video screens hung in a continuous array on the darkened room's walls in front of him. Though he can look from left to right scanning colored pencils of light that represent trains moving on the 130-mile section of track under CETC control between Washington and Philadelphia, he pays particular attention to the section between Gunpow Interlocking in Maryland and Ragan, west (south) of Wilmington, the portion of railroad under his control known as CETC-3. Jeff Metcheletti and Jane Glassing, CETC-1 and 2 dispatchers, are at consoles to his left and CETC-4's Bruce Davidson, who handles the railroad from Ragan into Philadelphia, is on the right. At 5:26 p.m. on May 15, these four people are responsible for 18 trains.

A constant murmur of radio traffic fills the room. Most is indistinguishable, and when Jeff, Jane and Ron respond to a transmission, it is in hushed tones. It's a different story with Davidson right now because he's learned that a SEPTA train waiting to flip back to Philadelphia at Marcus Hook has a mechanical problem and won't be able to move for a while. He has to let a lot of people know quickly that there is a problem, while planning ahead so that other southbound trains, *Express Metroliner* No. 223, the *Wall Street* (No. 185) and the *Silver Meteor* (87) with its lumbering E60 and heavy consist, don't get "stabbed" by the commuter train. The bathroom break will have to wait.

To Krause's left, Glassing studies the progress of No. 524, the new MARC local to Perryville, Md. She punches a few keys, touches the video screen, and seconds later a home signal flashes from two red horizontal lights to two vertical green ones near Edgewood, while gray lines change to green on her console and the big wall diagram, along with a tiny arrow that points in the direction of the cleared route. In back of the green line is an advancing red one, with a yellow "524" accompanying it.

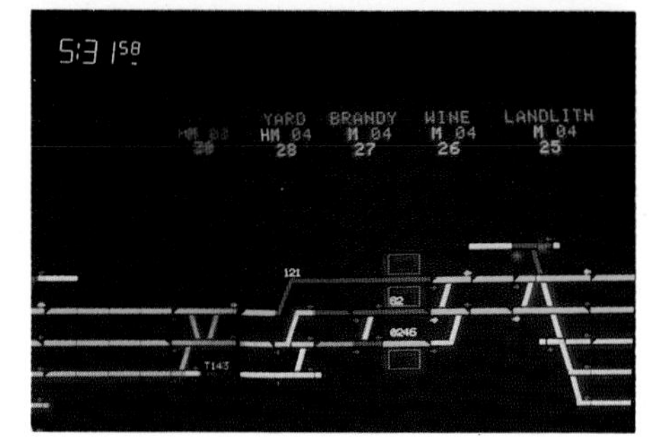

A freight track coming out of Conrail's Bayview Yard adjacent to the MARC local's path is shown in blue, the designation for a blocked route, because passengers must cross it when getting off the commuter train. Once the MARC train is past Gunpow, Glassing makes the blue line gray again, ready to accommodate a light (trainless) engine destined for Perryville when Chief Dispatcher Charlie Miller feels he can allow it into the mix.

After No. 524 arrives at Perryville and drops its passengers, CETC-3 dispatcher Krause touches the screen a few

ers to view displays of colored lines moving over the system and direct the trains they represented by entering computer commands to throw switches, clear signals and adjust power into a keyboard.

After a year of testing, the first segment was activated between New York Avenue (Washington) and Fulton (Baltimore) in May 1987, with control currently expanded up to Philadelphia. Meanwhile, a Boston CETC center became operational in 1989 covering the Boston-Cranston, R.I., segment. The $40 million initial investment for the new technology will be supplemented by $60 million more for extensions up to Morrisville (Trenton), N.J., and down to New Haven plus a New York facility handling New Rochelle (the Metro-North connection) to Morrisville.

If track and signal enhancements have vastly transformed the Northeast Corridor

times to quickly clear the commuter train into a siding. He's got two delayed E60-powered trains, the southbound *Crescent* (No. 19) and the northbound *Montrealer*, closing in on the crossover, but there should be plenty of time to avoid any yellow blocks. Once the local is in the clear, Krause punches some keys and No. 524 changes to 591, the southbound deadhead move, on the screens. The two heavy long-distance trains swirl past each other at Perryville, but the "dinky" isn't going anywhere because Krause notes southbound *Metroliner Service* 121 speedily changing green clear routes to red occupied ones, closing the gap on the much-slower No. 19. CETC-1 and 2 dispatchers Metcheletti and Glassing see this too on the big board, and it gives them a perspective on how to handle the two very different southbounds through the Baltimore tunnels and station.

Behind the four CETC dispatchers are their immediate supervisors, two assistant chief dispatchers, accompanied by clerks who handle data input as the trains' passage is automatically registered on printouts. In back of this tier of consoles are two power directors, responsible for 138,000-volt overhead transmission lines and the 12,000-volt catenary, and two "trouble desk" dispatchers who are in constant communication with maintenance people at trackside who deal with either electrical or operating irregularities. Key to the CETC system is a fault-tolerant computer where no single point of hardware failure can disable control.

But CETC is only part of the Philadelphia story eight floors above 30th Street Station's busy train concourse. The contrasts, transitional nature and uniqueness of the Northeast Corridor become more apparent with a look into the other offices.

Take the glass-windowed room off the dimly lit main CETC facility. It houses a standard Centralized Traffic Control board manned on this afternoon by Joe McArdle, who controls the Atlantic City line. He twists a few toggle switches to clear a route out of town for train 696, the 6:17 p.m. *Atlantic City Express* for Philadelphia.

Then, literally in a back room, Harrisburg line dispatcher Eric Schweitzer sits on a stool to view a large white train sheet. A loudspeaker crackles to life. The Bryn Mawr tower operator is describing a problem with the No. 9 switch on the center track at his location. A maintainer is on the scene, but the switch must be manually thrown, potentially forcing all Paoli and Harrisburg trains onto the local tracks. This could be a problem, because train 641, the New York-Harrisburg *Keystone State Express* may be delayed. While Schweitzer is mulling over this problem, though, Zoo comes on the line with a list of "OS" ("on sheet" or "on station") times he must enter on the sheet.

"Boop-beep-boop," goes the radio, and it's another tower checking in with times. Along the 104-mile Philadelphia-Harrisburg line, operators are "passing" trains along to the next tower the way they've been doing it for years. The same thing is happening eastward on the busiest piece of Corridor, Philly-New York, and beyond New Haven to where Boston CETC kicks in at Cranston.

How's 641 doing tonight, Tom?" Schweitzer asks a fellow sheet dispatcher in the other part of the room, responsible for bringing trains down from Trenton to Zoo and Philly.

"Eleven minutes late."

"Good, then we can bring along (SEPTA train) 573 on four," the Harrisburg line dispatcher tells the Bryn Mawr leverman.

Eric Schweitzer and Ron Krause are performing the same job on the Corridor. The two men are just doing it differently.—*Bob Johnston*

Eric Schweitzer dispatches Harrisburg line trains in the time-honored manner of monitoring train movement on paper through OS's supplied by lineside operators.—*Bob Johnston*

since the Amtrak takeover in 1976, so too have the destinations of the trains running over it. Conspicuous by their absence today are the large numbers of Conrail through freights, which have opted for ex-Reading and ex-Lehigh Valley trackage between New York and Harrisburg and on the former PRR Susquehanna River line down to Perryville rather than pay rent to Amtrak and be subjected to 30 mph speed restrictions or limited operating times and tracks. That trains of the Corridor's former owner are interloping intruders on the newly refurbished speedway was tragically drilled home on the chilly but sunny Sunday afternoon of Jan. 4, 1987, at Gunpow interlocking, Chase, Md., when an inattentive freight engine crew ran a red signal, then a switch, and got clobbered by the double-headed AEM7's of train 94, the the *Colonial*, racing north at

LEFT: Portal Interlocking is named for its location near the west end of the Hudson River tunnels. The swingbridge here carries the Northeast Corridor over the Hackensack River.—*Alan Tillotson* BELOW: Portal Tower on the evening of Sept. 29, 1988; Portal has since been closed and its functions moved to A Tower, Penn Station, Manhattan.—*Mike Del Vecchio*

Another day closes on the Corridor in 1983 as a cadre of E60's and a lone AEM7 stable up for the night at Race Street locomotive facility adjacent to Philadelphia's 30th Street Station. Some work-trains tie up here, as does the equipment of trains terminating at 30th Street or those changing from diesel to electric and vice versa, such as the ***Broadway Limited***.—*Steve Barry*

well over 100 mph. Sixteen people were killed and more than 175 injured in Amtrak's worst accident to date. The tragedy proved to be a catalyst for more restrictions on freight and additional safety appliances on passenger cars such as overhead baggage restraints.

The Corridor's passenger trains have expanded their horizons, too. Begun with a $200,000 feasibility study authorized by Congress in 1980, the $110 million upgrading of the New Jersey Department of Transportation-owned Atlantic City line, of which Amtrak contributed $30 million and has responsibility for maintenance and dispatching, opened in 1989 to host *Atlantic City Express*es which now go as far afield as Springfield, Mass, and Richmond, Va.

Today only 4 of 17 daily non-reserved conventional trains (in each direction) between New York and Washington both originate and terminate at those endpoints.

The Corridor envelope has been stretched to include eight trains each way running south of Washington, two Boston round-trips via Springfield, a morning *Metroliner* departure from Downingtown on the Harrisburg line to Washington, and even summer-only weekend service to Hyannis on Cape Cod. Commuter operations run under contract by Amtrak have also expanded to include Perryville (from Washington on MARC), Wilmington (SEPTA), Old Saybrook (Connecticut DOT), and Providence (MBTA).

With Amtrak becoming (by 1985) the largest single carrier in the combined air/rail market between New York and Washington, carrying more passengers than either the Trump or Pan Am air shuttle, capacity is strained to the utmost. A typical weekday after 5 p.m. at Philadelphia's newly remodeled 30th Street Station finds over 100 travelers crowding the track 2 platform ready to scramble aboard the 5:15 p.m. northbound train, the Washington-Boston/Springfield *Merchants Limited*, hoping to land a seat in the game of musical chairs that ensues when Philadelphia passengers get off. Others would be waiting, except that another 35 have paid at least 15 dollars more to get a "civilized" reserved seat on 5:18 p.m. *Express Metroliner* No. 218, which will beat the *Merchants* into New York. But wait. They're also lined up for the 5:22 *Pennsylvanian*, which will handle all local stops to the Big Apple, and still more passengers have reservations on *Metroliner* 120 departing at 5:33 p.m. Throw in a half-hour-late northbound *Silver Star*, and that makes five trains for New York within a half hour! At the end of the week, even lengthened consists and peak fare pricing can't prevent standees or sold out *Metroliners* on many trips when there are no more spare cars or locomotives to operate.

Effectively harnessing this kind of demand by splitting it into reserved and non-reserved departures and utilizing fare discount incentives for times when more equipment is available has led to an increase of over 300 million passenger miles on Northeast Corridor trains since 1977. At the same time, NEC trains' ticket revenue

TOP: In their hard-to-miss bright orange paint, Amtrak work equipment is a familiar sight on the Corridor, whether on assignment for a major rebuild project or for duties more routine. This Wire Extra at Trenton in 1980 features special platformed cars that provide easy access to the catenary.—*Bill Chaplik* **ABOVE: The Corridor is in essence a river of humanity, carrying nearly half of Amtrak's customers. During holiday periods, the flood of extra travelers requires borrowed equipment. What appears to be simply a (Boston) MBTA commuter train here is in reality an additional section of Amtrak's *Minute Man*, rifling through Branford, Conn., on the Sunday following Thanksgiving 1990. Amtrak leases equipment from MBTA, SEPTA and MARC for Thanksgiving, Christmas and New Year's holiday peak travel periods.**—*David Patch* **LEFT: Even during "off" periods of travel, corridor loads remain impressive. Witness this ample-size eastbound *Colonial* at Bridgeport in March 1986.**—*Scott Hartley*

has risen from $94.1 million in 1977 to $351 4 million in FY 1990.

Today, Northeast Corridor trains (excluding long-haul services that use the Corridor) account for 24.2 percent of the system's passenger miles (down from 26.7 percent in 1977) but deliver 40.1 percent of the ticket revenue (up from 36.2 percent then). Though the analysis doesn't allocate costs, it is easy to see the kind of contributions this piece of railroad makes to Amtrak's big picture.

As IMPRESSIVE AS THESE statistics may seem, the biggest gains may be yet to come. Congress has appropriated an additional $125 million of NECIP funds for extending the Boston's CETC center's dispatching control down to New Haven and other improvements to eliminate as much slow running as possible on the twisting double-track main through Connecticut and Rhode Island. Included are ballast decking of bridges, construction of a flyover connection with Metro-North at New Rochelle, high-speed crossovers at Old Saybrook and Kingston, R.I., and an engineering study to set design-build specifications for electrification, which will itself require additional capital funding.

A strong case can be made for expendi-

ABOVE: A blanked keystone emblem on the shanty next to Elmora Tower in Elizabeth, N.J., is about the only clue to the heritage of this portion of the NEC as a westbound heads from New York to Washington. Where Pennsylvania Railroad's leviathan GG1's once strode by with the likes of the *Afternoon Congressional* and the *General*, energetic but compact AEM7's whirl trains along with names like *Big Apple*, *Metroliner* and *Independece*. Nonetheless, some PRR names survive, so in 1991 you can still see a *Clocker* (the time-honored name for New York-Philadelphia short-hauls), *Congressional* or *Broadway Limited*.—*Alan Tillotson* **BELOW: Other names reflect the Corridor's New Haven Railroad heritage: *Bay State, Merchants Limited, Mount Vernon, Patriot*. A NYNH&H landmark on Amtrak's route east from New York City is Hell Gate Bridge, although technically it was a property of the New York Connecting Railroad, jointly owned by New Haven and PRR. A Manhattan-bound Amtrak train behind an AEM7 slices the haze of a summer day in 1986 as it heads down the east approach to Hell Gate. The train's flying high right now, but in a few minutes it will actually be passing *under* this same river to enter the bowels of New York City.**—*Mike Del Vecchio*

tures to string a 60-cycle, 25,000-volt catenary over the 160 miles between Boston and New Haven because eliminating the New Haven engine change and other improvements will cut travel times dramatically, hopefully triggering ridership and revenue increases paralleling the gains in the market share made between Washington and New York when that portion of the Corridor was speeded up. Also under consideration is the testing of state-of-art trainsets from Europe such as the Swedish X2000, which could further reduce running time by taking curves along the ocean-hugging Connecticut coastline at higher speeds. With 40 percent of Boston Logan Airport's flights destined for the New York area, Amtrak officials see perhaps the company's biggest unfulfilled marketing opportunity yet.

Over the past twenty years (and before), the Northeast Corridor has been a textbook example of how capital spending in improved physical plant and equipment has resulted in ever-expanding revenue and ridership dividends. As the interlocking towers operate side by side with, then abdicate to CETC, and as the heavyweight "Clocker" coaches have given way to Amfleet, the carrier's goal of providing better service has been achieved.

The original self-propelled Metroliner cars are a case in point. That initial investment before Amtrak's birth is still being felt around the entire system every time a *San Diegan*, or an Atlantic City, Detroit or Milwaukee train's F40 locomotive pushes a consist led by one of these ex-Corridor cars, denuded of electric pantographs and traction motors. As of press time, eight are being converted at Amtrak's Wilmington Shops into non-cab coaches for State of Michigan-funded service; another will be a guinea pig for the car design staff in Philadelphia.

But perhaps most noteworthy of all is an old cab car which has made a triumphant return to premium *Metroliner* service as club/conference car 9800. Built to test the market for business meetings on the go, the gleaming white-faced, upscale marketing experiment embodies the transformed character of the Corridor, and even Amtrak, today. Like the Corporation, the 9800 represents an initial investment made years ago that, with further capital expenditures now, is on the way to reaching its greatest potential ever.

Amtrak engineer DeAnn Rathbun.—*Bob Johnston*

Cab ride on the corridor

"You got 110 over there, Don?"

"I got 111, 113, 112."

"It's a little hotter than mine."

"Yeah, this thing was maybe a mile off when you were going 120."

Engineer DeAnn Rathbun on the right side and Transportation Manager Don Herman on the left are discussing minor calibration differences between the two speedometers in the cab of AEM7 907. There had been a 30 mph speed restiction at Bacon, a now-closed tower between Baltimore and Wilmington where maintenance-of-way crews pause long enough to let *Metroliner* 116, the 2 p.m. Washington departure of May 15, 1991, tiptoe through the crossovers back onto its heavy welded-rail-and-concrete-tie speedway.

"You get on the wooden ties, there's a definite difference," Rathbun explains, only momentarily glancing away from the onrushing track ahead. "Concrete, it's much firmer."

Now De Ann has again reached track speed, the AEM7 having responded effortlessly to her clicking throttle urgings, with only a revving whining sound increasing in pitch and volume, hinting at the massive transformation of electric power into physical energy that is taking place. On the straightaway a light appears, and 20 seconds later, whoosh! southbound *Metroliner* 115 rushes by, the combined speed of the two trains over 200 mph. But there's not the trademark "thump" of bowing windows *Metroliner* passengers experience when two of the speedsters pass.

Gliding over the heavily ballasted roadbed south of Newark, Del., there's practically none of the vibration and sway associated with even a 60 mph F40 cab ride on some of the lines over which Amtrak operates. Viewing the track ahead is more like the race car video game "Pole Position," where a weaving road ahead rushes on while the would-be driver remains perfectly static.

The 907 hurtles across the two-track Susquehanna River bridge at Havre de Grace, and the engineer marks the time in her notebook.

Back up to 125. More bugs splatter the windshield. The whine of the locomotive gets higher, punctuated by an intermittent scream of the alerter siren, silenced when the engineer touches a control on the desk. Now she moves the throttle back on the left and brake handle on the right with a soft clanking sound, and a few seconds later a yellow "110" sign hung in the catenary flashes overhead.

"Well, did you see our sly fox on the way up?" asks Rathbun.

"Mr. Palumbo is out there somewhere with his radar gun," explains Don Herman of another transportation manager based in Baltimore. "He's probably around here doing speed or signal tests."

Twenty minutes later, the Wilmington station slips into view. The AEM7's friskiness has been tamed by some more skillful lever movements and the train of five Amfleet Metroliner coaches glides along the platform with the well-dressed clientel waiting to board showing appropriate respect by standing well behind the yellow line. It's been a trip of contrasts: waiting for a shifter to move cars from the track ahead at Washington, creeping through Baltimore's ancient tunnels, skipping across the interlocking at Gunpow, 125, 110, 90, 110 and 125 mph running as well as 30 and 65 mph slow orders. And now these people are waiting to board at Wilmington as if nothing unusual has happened.

It hasn't. Just another day on the Corridor.—*Bob Johnston*

9/Rank-and-file Amtrak

A TRIBUTE TO THE COMMON-FOLK CORRIDORS AND MEDIUM-HAUL TRAINS

Some accounts of rail travel might have you believing that just about everyone during the first half of the 20th century swept about the country aboard the likes of the *Super Chief, 20th Century Limited* or *City of San Francisco*. In reality, in the "good 'ole days," those trains could only be afforded by America's elite. In fact, Pullman travel in general was extraordinarily expensive, proportionately more so than sleeping-car service is now, taking into account inflation and such.

No, back then and even well into the second half of the century, most rail travelers rode secondary trains like Santa Fe's economy-minded *Grand Canyon*, PRR's *Pennsylvania Limited* and Illinois Central's *Hawkeye*. Too, the greater number of passengers were riding medium-haul and corridor trains. For every passenger that booked passage aboard the *Olympian Hiawatha* for a trip across the country in 1950, probably 75 boarded a North Shore *Electroliner* seven times a day for an 85-mile Chicago-Milwaukee trip.

The demographics have changed since those days, since even Amtrak's most-"prestigious" long-distance trains are all-class conveyances where supersaver All-Aboard Fare coach passengers comingle with those splurging on their own deluxe bedroom. Yet, a great number of Amtrak passengers travel not on the *Empire Builder, Silver Meteor* or *Southwest Chief*, but on more workaday runs like the *Palmetto, State House* or *San Joaquin*. Case in point: During March 1991, 478,947 passen-

Two widely divergent forms of transport are in evidence at Del Mar, Calif., on a September afternoon in 1990 as a southbound *San Diegan* skims the coast of the Pacific Ocean toward its namesake city.— *Dan Munson*

ABOVE: For nearly 140 miles Amtrak's Empire Corridor hugs the east shore of the storied Hudson River. It's land of contrasts, from the home of George Washington Irving ("The Legend of Sleepy Hollow"), which predates the railroad, to sleek Turboliners such as the *Hudson Highlander* whining through Ardsley-on-Hudson in the autumn of 1985.—*Mike Schafer* RIGHT: FL9 485 shoots through Breakneck Tunnels with the northbound *Electric City Express* in April 1989.—*Tom Carver* BELOW: The scenery doesn't run out west of Albany, where Empire Corridor trains streak through elderly Upstate cities and along other waterways. Amtrak train 280, the *Mohawk*, cruises along its namesake river at Amsterdam, N.Y., on a July morning in 1990. Glimpses of the fabled Erie Canal are also part of the fun of riding the Empire Corridor.—*Jim Conroy*

gers rode the long-distance trains highlighted in chapter 7 ("Amtrak Superstars"), yet a whopping 1,482,944 Amtrak passengers rode something other than a long-distance train. Even if you subtract the number of Northeast Corridor passengers that month (973,614), that still leaves 509,330 people who rode other corridors and short- and medium-haul runs. That's what this chapter is all about.

New York-Albany/Rensselaer-Buffalo-Niagara Falls: The spine of giant New York Central's passenger network was this route, which in the Amtrak era is known as the Empire Corridor. The route interconnects several important medium-size Upstate cities with the U.S.'s largest metropolis, which is why outside the Northeast Corridor the Empire Corridor is

The westbound *Maple Leaf* is at St. Catherines, Ont., in May 1989, crossing another transportation "corridor"—the Welland Canal. This 20-mile north-south waterway takes Great Lakes vessels from Lake Ontario to Lake Erie, bypassing Niagara Falls. At this point, Amtrak is using Canadian National trackage, also traversed by VIA's Toronto-Niagara Falls (Ont.) trains. The current version of the New York-Toronto *Maple Leaf* replaces what had been a transfer arrangement at Buffalo between Amtrak and a Toronto, Hamilton & Buffalo-Canadian Pacific (later, VIA) Budd car.—*Mike Schafer*

Amtrak's busiest with nearly a dozen trains in each direction south of the state capital of Albany (the station for which is actually across the Hudson River in Rensselaer); some corridor trains extend beyond Albany to Schenectady, Syracuse and Niagara Falls. (As a side note, from March 1, 1972, to April 29, 1979, Amtrak trains used a bypass route around Schenectady.)

When Amtrak assumed the route's passenger operations from Penn Central on May 1, 1971, Buffalo was the end of the line. Niagara Falls (N.Y.) became the new western endpoint for the corridor on Oct. 29, 1978. Conrail now owns most of the route's trackage, but Amtrak owns 7.8 miles of the direct line through Schenectady. April 1991 was an important turning point for the Empire Corridor as the southern terminus was shifted from famous Grand Central Terminal to Pennsylvania Station, concentrating all Amtrak Manhattan station operations in one location.

The State of New York has been heavily involved in the development of the corridor, and track-improvement projects have netted some 110 mph trackage. Almost all of the major cities on the Empire Corridor feature new depots: Albany/Rensselaer, Schenectady, Syracuse, Rochester and Buffalo (Depew). Utica's station is a handsomely restored Italian Renaissance structure which also serves various bus lines, while the Niagara Falls facility is a cleverly converted freight depot.

Not until April 10, 1974, did Empire Corridor trains receive individual names, monikers which reflect the territory's history (the *Washington Irving*, *Hendrick Hudson*) and geography (the *Bear Mountain*, *Palisades* and *Water Level Express*).

Turboliners are king of the road on the Empire Corridor, but Amfleet still reigns on some trains like the *Maple Leaf* (see next entry) while Heritage Fleet holds down the *Lake Shore Limited*, the only long-distance train on the route.

New York-Toronto: In pre-Amtrak days, this international route was a joint effort between New York Central (New York-Buffalo-Welland, Ont.), Toronto, Hamilton & Buffalo (Welland-Hamilton, Ont.) and Canadian Pacific (Hamilton-Toronto). Trains connected at Buffalo, and until 1970 there was through sleeper service.

Today's service is an extension of what in earlier Amtrak days had been a New York-Buffalo corridor train. After Amtrak started, TH&B-CP continued to operate a Budd RDC between Toronto and Buffalo, where connection was made to Amtrak's *Empire State Express* (later renamed *Niagara Rainbow*). On April 26, 1981, this arrangement was supplanted by a new through New York-Toronto train, the *Maple Leaf*, jointly operated by Amtrak and VIA Rail Canada. The TH&B train was dropped and the new train began operating through Niagara Falls and on VIA's Canadian National route to Hamilton

New York-Albany-Montreal: On Aug. 6, 1974, Amtrak and the State of New York launched a day train between Manhattan and Montreal, the *Adirondack*. The pre-

Amtrak precedence was a joint New York Central (Penn Central after Feb. 1, 1968)-Delaware & Hudson day run known as the *Laurentian* (there was also an overnight train, the *Montreal Limited*). South of Albany in both eras, the trains at times have run combined with Empire Corridor trips.

Passengers on the route are treated to two major waterside vistas: the Hudson River between New York and Rensselaer, and Lake Champlain between Whitehall and Rouses Point, N.Y., and the *Adirondack* can also be used as a step-off point for nearby Adirondack Mountain resorts.

When it first started, the *Adirondack* operated north of Albany/Rensselaer on D&H trackage through Mechanicville, N.Y., and on D&H subsidiary Napierville Junction Railway between Rouses Point and the outskirts of Montreal. On Oct. 29, 1976, the *Adirondack* began serving Schenectady proper by traveling west from Rensselaer on Conrail to Schenectady before entering the D&H. On Jan. 12, 1986, a new route into Montreal from Rouses Point went into effect, via Canadian National.

During the *Adirondack*'s first few years, it achieved celebrity status among passenger-train aficionados because it featured mostly D&H locomotives (Alco PA's) and cars, at the behest of Delaware & Hudson whose equipment for the run had been rehabilitated with help from the State of New York. But since the latter half of the 1970's, the *Adirondack* has operated with Turboliners or Amfleet.

Boston/New York-Richmond-Newport News: Rail passenger service to the Tidewater area (Norfolk/Virginia Beach/Hamp-

BELOW: The *Adirondack* shares the morning sun with a commuter train in Canadian Pacific's Windsor Station, Montreal, on New Year's Day 1986. In less than two weeks, the *Adirondack* will be shifted to CN's Central Station.—*Don Jilson* BOTTOM: The southbound *Adirondack* sweeps along Lake Champlain near Port Henry, N.Y., on a frigid day in February 1991.—*Gary Knapp*

ABOVE: Following two relatively unsuccessful attempts at serving Virginia's Tidewater area, Amtrak finally came up with a winner with its Boston-Washington *Colonial* and northbound Newport News-New York City *Tidewater.* The latter train is shown at the former-Chesapeake & Ohio station at Lee Hall, Va.—the step-off point for the U.S. Army's Fort Eustis—on the Fourth of July afternoon of 1984. The *Tidewater*'s late-Sunday-afternoon departure in place of the *Colonial*'s daily-except-Sunday morning northbound schedule affords tourists a longer weekend stay in northeast Virginia.—*Frank S. Novak*

ton Roads/Newport News/Portsmouth) in pre-Amtrak days included Norfolk & Western with its Norfolk-Cincinnati runs, and Chesapeake & Ohio with Newport News-Cincinnati-Chicago services. Seaboard Air Line snuck in from the south with a train from Jacksonville. Surprisingly, direct Northeast-Tidewater service then was nil.

When Amtrak started, the Tidewater area was served, as before, by a connection off a Midwest-East train, the *George Washington/James Whitcomb Riley*. Service to Tidewater doubled on March 25, 1975, with the inaugural of the Chicago-Norfolk *Mountaineer*. The Newport News section never did very well and was dropped effective June 15, 1976, and the *Mountaineer* succumbed on May 31, 1977. However, Tidewater still had a train, for concurrent with the discontinuance of the *Riley*'s Newport News section, Amtrak extended its westbound Boston-Washington *Colonial* and eastbound Washington-Boston *Betsy Ross* to Newport News (this was later joined by a Sunday companion train called the *Tidewater*).

Since then, the tide has turned on rail ridership into the populous north Virginia coast, a region rich in history (the *Colonial* and *Tidewater* serve Williamsburg, Va., only a few miles from Jamestown, the first non-native settlement in America) and a focal point of U.S. Navy operations.

A relatively new train that shares a portion of the *Colonial/Tidwater* route is the Richmond-New York *Virginian*. Its introduction on Oct. 28, 1984, gave Virginia's largest city an early morning schedule to Washington and New York, with an evening return—a timing popular with business people. The *Virginian* perhaps addresses the inevitable: that the Richmond-Fredericksburg-Alexandria-Washington route will someday be an integral part of the Northeast Corridor.

New York-Jacksonville: With the popularity of its New York-Miami/St. Petersburg long-hauls, Amtrak learned early on that a supplemental local service was necessary to serve Virginia and the Carolinas. Its first experiment in this realm was the overnight New York-Savannah (Ga.) *Carolina Coast*,

The northbound *Carolinian* is less than an hour into its all-day trek to New York City as it sprints across the lazy Yadkin River near Spencer (Salisbury), N.C., in June 1985. Like its sister train, the *Palmetto*, the *Carolinian* penetrates a populous area of the Southeast sunbelt. Charlotte, N.C., a city which has become a major industrial and business force in the Southeast, is home to the *Carolinian*, which links Charlotte and Raleigh (the state capital) by way of the tobacco belt. The *Crescent* also serves Charlotte, but only during the day's small hours.—*Doug Koontz*

which ran during the summer of 1972 on Seaboard Coast Line's old Atlantic Coast Line route between Petersburg, Va., and Savannah, Ga. It reappeared the following summer as the *Carolina Special*, but operating all the way to Jacksonville over the old Seaboard Air Line between Petersburg and Savannah via Raleigh, N.C.

Amtrak really scored with the introduction of the New York-Savannah *Palmetto* (borrowing an old ACL name) on June 15, 1976—made possible with the then-recent delivery of Amfleet cars. Intended as another summer-only venture, the day run was a hit with local travelers and has remained in service since. On Nov. 15, 1988, the *Palmetto* was extended to Jacksonville.

New York-Charlotte: There is no precedence in recent pre-Amtrak history of New York-Charlotte service by way of Richmond and Raleigh, which is what makes this North Carolina 403(b) operation so interesting. The *Carolinian* had its first incarnation on Oct. 28, 1984, as a Charlotte section to the *Palmetto*, splitting from that train at

As a day run serving Virginia, the Carolinas and Georgia—four states burgeoning with retirees and businesses fleeing from colder climes—the *Palmetto* is an important supplement to the *Silver Meteor* and *Silver Star*. ABOVE: Southbound 82 is at Selma, N.C., located on CSX's ex-ACL main line. This is the point at which the New York-Charlotte *Carolinian* and the New York-Florida *Silver Star* turn west to Raleigh, N.C., on the Southern.—*Doug Koontz* **BELOW: On a sterling October afternoon in 1986, the southbound *Palmetto* cruises down the well-manicured double-track artery of the Richmond, Fredericksburg & Potomac Railroad at Potomac Creek, Va. The RF&P hosts some 14 Amtrak trains a day.**—*Mike Schafer*

TOP: It's 3:48 p.m. on July 18, 1989, as an average-size *Pennsylvanian* cuts its way through Johnstown, Pa. When autumn colors permeate the region, passengers will flood the train, swelling its consist to eight or more cars.—*David Baer* ABOVE: Hot—er, cold—on the heels of autumn comes the winter, strongly in evidence in this frosty scene of the westbound *Pennsylvanian* poppin' out of one of Allegheny Tunnel's two bores at Gallitzin, Pa., on Dec. 8, 1981. This mountaintop burgh marks the crest of the Alleghenies on Conrail's Philadelphia-Pittsburgh main line. Westbound trains generally use Allegheny Tunnel, while eastbounds descend through single-bore Portage Tunnel a short distance to the south. The *Pennsylvanian*'s overall schedule is not unlike that of Pennsylvania Railroad's *Duquesne*.—*Alex Mayes*

Richmond, Va., and running on the old SAL route through Henderson, N.C., to Raleigh. There, the train turned west onto the Southern for a trip through Durham and Burlington to Greensboro, N.C., where it entered SR's Washington-New Orleans main line (the *Crescent*'s route) to reach Charlotte. Due to funding problems, the train was dropped effective Sept. 2, 1985.

The *Carolinian* revival on May 12, 1990, brought a new *modus operandi*: The train was, again, combined with the *Palmetto* out of New York, but the split took place at Rocky Mount, N.C., on CSX's old ACL main line, since most of the former-SAL main between Petersburg and Raleigh had been abandoned. From Rocky Mount, the *Carolinian* proceeds south to Selma, N.C., on CSX, then west on SR to Raleigh where it picks up the former-*Carolinian* route. The success of this second incarnation has led to the train operating separately all to the way to and from New York, and an additional 403(b) Charlotte-Raleigh operation is in the works as this book goes to press.

New York-Pittsburgh: It began as a little two-car Amfleet train and today it's three or more times that size. The *Pennsylvanian* also has the distinction of being perhaps the only state-supported train that is covering its fully allocated costs.

In pre-Amtrak times, the New York-Philadelphia-Pittsburgh route was a busy avenue for Pennsylvania Railroad's fleet of Blue Ribbon trains like the *General, Broadway* and *Spirit of St. Louis.* But PRR was also aware of the need for solid workhorse day trains to cater to short-haul travelers, and that's the kind of yeoman duty its *Juniata* and *Duquesne* performed.

The *Duquesne* (Doo-KANE) survived into Amtrak and was renamed *Keystone* on Nov. 14, 1971. Unfortunately, it did not do well and was discontinued on April 30, 1972. The *National Limited* picked up some of the slack by making some of the *Keystone*'s station stops. But then, in 1979, the *National,* too, became history.

PennDOT was an early champion of the 403(b) provision in the Amtrak law, having funded Harrisburg-Philadelphia service, and now it wanted a cross-state train to fill the *National*'s void. (The *Broadway*, which shares the route with the *Pennsylvanian*, is or has been largely a night run in at least one direction.) Since its first run on April 27, 1980, the *Pennsylvanian* has led the good life, with increasing patronage and an excellent financial status. In less than a decade, ridership doubled, from 83,109 passengers in 1980-81 to 167,904 in 1988-89.

For a short time, the *Pennsylvanian* had another 403(b) sibling, the *Fort Pitt.* Serving the Pittsburgh-Altoona market, this run lasted from April 26, 1981, to Jan. 30, 1983.

The scenic attributes of Conrail's steel boulevard through the Allegheny Mountains prompted PennDOT to have National Park Service rangers ride the train on selected days to provide historical and geographical commentary to passengers. This has proved so popular that individuals and groups sometimes ride the *Pennsylvanian* just for the entertainment value!

Chicago-Grand Rapids: In pre-Amtrak days, Chesapeake & Ohio operated this 184-mile route, which also had a Holland-Muskegon, Mich., connection. As an Amtrak-Michigan DOT endeavor, the *Pere Marquette* (the name previously used by C&O for Chicago-Grand Rapids and Grand Rapids-Detroit services) remains a modest but popular operation. Michigan has long been involved in 403(b) experiments, and this one started on Aug. 4, 1984. East of Pine Junction, Ind., it follows the same route used by pre-Amtrak *Pere Marquettes*: Conrail (ex-NYC) to Porter, Ind., then CSX's ex-C&O line to Michigan's second-largest city.

ABOVE: It's summer in the city—Chicago, that is, and 95 degrees to be exact—as the Toronto-bound *International* negotiates South Branch lift bridge and 21st Street junction in August 1988 as a virtually on-time *Cardinal* saunters in from the East Coast. Two sets of equipment are necessary to protect *International* schedules, one provided by VIA and one by Amtrak. The VIA set usually consists of an F40 and an LRC trainset (the one that Amtrak borrowed for a few years in the 1980's, now rebuilt and decommissioned of its tilt-body mechanisms), and that's what's on No. 364 today, but with an Amtrak F40 assisting. As a day operation between Chicago and Toronto, the *International* continues a popular pre-Amtrak GTW tradition, the *Maple Leaf.*—*Mark Jones*

RIGHT: Amfleet and Heritage Fleet rolling stock make up this day's westbound *Lake Cities* out of Toledo and Detroit on Sept. 30, 1984. Look for the clue that reveals the heritage of Amtrak's Detroit corridor in this scene near Augusta, Mich. You have eagle eyes if you spotted the "M.C.R.R. 1923" that appears in relief on the concrete shed at the base of the abandoned coaling tower, which we can presume was constructed in that year. This was once a speedway for the Michigan Central Railroad, which became a subsidiary of New York Central in 1930. When riding Amtrak from Detroit to Chicago, you follow the old MC as far west as Porter, Ind., where Detroit-line trains now enter Conrail's former-NYC main line. In earlier days, Detroit-Chicago passenger trains stayed on the MC all the way to the Illinois Central main line at Kensington (115th Street) on the south side of Chicago.—*J. P. Baukus Jr.*

ABOVE LEFT: Depots on the Chicago-Detroit corridor run the gamut of elderly classics to ultra modern, the latter being an apt description for the new Battle Creek station, built as part of a line-relocation project. The westbound *Wolverine* is at the home of Kellog's Corn Flakes in summer of 1983.—*Mike Schafer* ABOVE RIGHT: Eastern terminus of the Michigan corridor is at the huge old MC depot/office building near downtown Detroit. Amtrak is using a temporary facility nearby until plans for a new station are finalized. The *Twilight Limited* is shown in 1981.—*J. P. Baukus Jr.*

Chicago-Port Huron-Toronto: An early Michigan 403(b) train was the *Blue Water*, commencing service between Chicago and Port Huron, Mich., on Sept. 15, 1974. In a break from pre-Amtrak service between those two points, the *Blue Water* operated via Penn Central's old NYC route between Chicago and Battle Creek, Mich., where it used a new connection to swing onto the Grand Trunk Western for the remainder of the run to the Canadian border. In pre-Amtrak days, it was an all-GTW route.

Although the *Blue Water* terminated just across the St. Clair River from Sarnia, Ont., the western terminus of a Canadian National (later, VIA) corridor out of Toronto, there were no direct connections without an overnight stay. The push for a through train between Chicago and Toronto—a void left by the coming of Amtrak on May 1, 1971—gained momentum and became reality on Oct. 31, 1982. The *International* supplanted the *Blue Water* and a VIA Sarnia-Toronto round trip.

Chicago-Detroit-Toledo: In New York Central years, Chicago-Detroit was a bustling corridor, in part because the route serves several medium-size cities (Kalamazoo, Battle Creek, Jackson and Ann Arbor) and also because this was NYC's alternate main line between Chicago and Buffalo. So, aside from corridor-type runs like the

Michigan and *Motor City Special*, there were through trains from Manhattan, such as the *New York Special* and *Wolverine*. What Amtrak acquired from NYC-successor Penn Central on the 284-mile Chicago-Detroit section were two of the three sad, nameless remnants of this fleet—running on a considerably deteriorated line. There was nowhere to go but up.

And that's the direction Amtrak went. Better equipment was assigned and food service added, along with names (*Wolverine* and *St. Clair*) in November 1971. A Detroit-Jackson state-sponsored quasi-commuter run, the *Michigan Executive*, was added in January 1975, and later the same year an additional Chicago-Detroit round trip was instituted as was Turboliner service. The addition of Chicago-Port Huron service in 1974 meant eight trains a day on the Chicago-Battle Creek segment. The Michigan Corridor had come back to life.

Michigan DOT became increasingly involved in operations and, together with Amtrak and Conrail—the former having purchased the Porter-Kalamazoo segment on April 1, 1976, and the latter having superceded PC on the same day—track and station improvements brought the corridor to new high standards. Later in 1976, Amfleet equipment began protecting some schedules. By late 1978, Chicago-Detroit running time had been reduced from over 6 hours to under 5½. On Aug. 3, 1980, the *St. Clair* was extended beyond Detroit to Toledo via Conrail to connect with the *Lake Shore Limited*, thus providing Michiganders with travel options to the East Coast; in the process, the train gained a new name (borrowed from the defunct Erie Railroad), *Lake Cities*.

With splendidly renovated depots at Kalamazoo, Niles, and Jackson, new facilities at Battle Creek, Ann Arbor and Dearborn (an important new suburban Detroit stop in 1977), the Michigan corridor has become a showcase hampered only by lack of a permanent facility at Detroit; Amtrak was forced to evacuate the former-Michigan Central depot in the late 1980's, and as of press time the carrier and Michgian DOT continue to ponder solutions.

Chicago-Indianapolis: In the first years of Amtrak, this city pair was connected by two long-distance trains, the *South Wind* (later, *Floridian*) and the *George Washington/James Whitcomb Riley*, operating via Illinois Central from Chicago to Kankakee, Ill., then over Penn Central's ex-NYC line to Indianapolis. Deteriorating track conditions on that PC line put them on another PC line in 1972—the former-Pennsylvania route between Chicago and Indy through Logansport and either (at the host railroad's discretion) Lebanon or Anderson, Ind. When *those* lines were closed on Aug. 1, 1974, account of track conditions, the two trains fled to completely different routes that did not include Indianapolis.

PRR and NYC both had direct Chicago-Indianapolis service in pre-Amtrak days, with NYC's *James Whitcomb Riley, Indianapolis Special* and *Sycamore*, and PRR's *South Wind* and *Kentuckian*. Until 1959, Monon Railroad was also an entry in the Chicago-Indianapolis corridor with its *Hoosier* and *Tippecanoe*. As of Aug. 1, 1974, though, Indianapolis and Chicago were no longer directly linked by passenger trains. The situation was aggravated by the 1979 discontinuance of the *National Limited*, which took Indianapolis completely off the Amtrak map. Amtrak no longer had a convenient means of ferrying equipment to and from Beech Grove Shops.

This all prompted Amtrak to add a new short-haul train to its Chicago hub on Oct. 1, 1980: The *Hoosier State* returned direct service between Chicago and Indy. The routing was an altogether new combination: Conrail's former-PRR route out of Chicago to Maynard, Ind., Louisville & Nashville (now CSX) to Crawfordsville—the old Monon main line—and Conrail's ex-Peoria & Eastern main from Crawfordsville to the outskirts of Indy.

Now here's something motorists probably won't challenge as they cruise the streets of Lafayette, Ind.—Amtrak's *Hoosier State*. For nearly 150 years, trains have wandered down 5th Street in Lafayette, Ind., home of Purdue University. Middle-of-the-road operation, in fact, was a way of life for the Monon Railroad, formerly the Chicago, Indianapolis & Louisville, which passed down—not across—the streets of a number of Indiana cities. Amtrak's *Hoosier State* and *Cardinal* maintain that archaic (but fascinating) tradition in Lafayette as they traverse CSX's former-Monon route between Maynard and Crawfordsville, Ind. But hurry if you want to observe this practice; Amtrak is scheduled to move to a new joint CSX-Norfolk Southern private right-of-way along the Wabash River through downtown Lafayette by the mid-1990's. (Trivia: Where else does Amtrak take to the streets? Oakland and Fresno, Calif., Ashland, Va., and Springfield, Ill., to name four examples.)—*Mike Schafer*

LEFT: Slam, slam! One can almost hear the northbound *Illini*'s F40 batter the crossings of CSX (ex-Baltimore & Ohio) and Union Pacific (ex-Missouri Pacific and Chicago & Eastern Illinois) at Tuscola, Ill., during the summer of 1988.—*Eric Coleman* BELOW: In more-urban surroundings, the southbound *Illini* overtakes an Illinois Central Gulf/Metra suburban train at the 55th-56th Street stop in May 1986.—*George A. Forero Jr.*

Chicago-Carbondale: In the years leading to Amtrak, Illinois Central dubbed this 307-mile (309 for Amtrak) route the "Mini-Corridor." Once the domain of brown-and-orange Illinois Central streamliners and coachliners, the largely rural route lacks the two characteristics common to most corridor operations—i.e., well-populated stops and a large anchor city at both ends. Yet it has always been a well-traveled artery. Why? Because of on-line colleges.

First and foremost is the University of Illinois, at Champaign/Urbana; another popular college, Southern Illinois University, provides the "anchor" for the south end of the corridor. And in between is Eastern Illinois University at Charleston, just east of the on-line stop of Mattoon. Most students at these three state colleges hail from Chicago and, along with Chanute Air

Force Base at Rantoul, thus provide an ongoing supply of passengers .

During IC's Mini-Corridor era, when radio spots touting the service were common on Chicago's famous AM station WLS (during an era when passenger-train advertising was almost nil), most trains operated on memory schedules—for example, Chicago departures were at 8 a.m., 8:40 a.m., and 3, 5, 7 and 9 p.m. Trains like the *Shawnee, Illini* and *Mid-American* sped over a double-track line at speeds of up to 100 mph, making the trip to Carbondale in little over five hours for an average speed of about a mile a minute, stops included.

Although the route has since fallen from such esteem, what with the single-tracking of the IC, the lowering of speed limits, the state's cutback of 403(b) monies and the completion of parallel Interstate 57, Amtrak still dispatches two trains (*City of New Orleans* and *Illini*) in each direction over the entire route. On weekends while college is in session, standing-room-only crowds still pack multi-car *Illinis* as students head back to Chicago for a fix of civilization—or to other campuses for a weekend of revelry.

Because of UofI's proximity to Chicago (129 miles), Amtrak and Illinois DOT for several years fielded a third train, the *Illini* (at that time, the Chicago-Carbondale train was known as the *Shawnee*), between Chicago and "Cham-Bana." This train was extended to Decatur, Ill., via Tolono and the Norfolk & Western on July 2, 1981, but was retrenched on July 10, 1983. Budgetary cutbacks which took effect on Jan. 12, 1986, forced the discontinuance of the Chicago-Champaign train altogether; the *Illini* (ee-LIE-ny) name was transferred to a restructured Chicago-Carbondale run. Periodically, talk surfaces of extending the *Illini* to Memphis, to serve as a day partner to the overnight *City of New Orleans*.

Chicago-St. Louis-Kansas City: Chicago-St. Louis was once one of the most hotly contested rail corridors in the nation. At one time, no less than four railroads—Alton (Gulf, Mobile & Ohio after 1947), Wabash, Illinois Central and Chicago & Eastern Illinois—competed for traffic between the two major cities. Chicago-Kansas City was also a major-league route, with Santa Fe and Burlington vyeing for the bulk of the traffic.

As the only carrier to still have Chicago-St. Louis runs as of May 1, 1971, GM&O was clearly the winner in the competition. GM&O's two day trains, the *Limited* and *Abraham Lincoln*, were retained by Amtrak, which since then—and with the aid of Illinois DOT—has applied modest efforts to bolster the corridor's standing.

Early developments included extension of the *Limited* (renamed *Prairie State*) and *Abe* beyond Chicago to Milwaukee on Nov. 14, 1971, together with an infusion of high-quality equipment—Vista-Domes, diners and parlor-observation cars. The through service officially ended with the introduction of unnamed Turboliner service in October 1973, at which time another round trip, with conventional equipment, was added to the fleet, the Illinois-financed *State House*. This three-each-way frequency on the Chicago-St. Louis route has remained much the same since, although schedules have varied considerably over the years.

The Turbos were removed in February 1976 as some then-new Amfleet equipment went into use; at this time the *Abraham Lincoln* name was resurrected—as was another old Alton name, *Ann Rutledge*. A major change came later that year when, on Oct. 31, the St. Louis-Laredo *Inter-American* was extended to Chicago, supplanting the *Ann Rutledge*. Although GM&O had ferried through cars to and from other railroads at St. Louis, this was the first time in recent history that the route had hosted a long-distance train. This evolved into a full-blown Superliner operation now known as the *Texas Eagle*.

The next major change came in October 1979 when the *Ann Rutledge* (the obscure name had been revived once more, this time inexplicably to replace the well-recognized *Abe Lincoln* name in October 1977) was extended west of St. Louis to Kansas City to fill the void left by the discontinuance of the New York/Washington-K.C. *National Limited*. The St. Louis-K.C. portion of

Train 22, the ***Eagle***, begins its 282-mile flight from St. Louis to Chicago by tunneling under a portion of the Gateway Arch park that fronts the Mississippi River at St. Louis. It's June 1984 and this is a "short" day for the ***Eagle***, which, south of St. Louis then operated through to and from Texas on a triweekly basis. On non-through days, the ***Eagle*** was simply an Amfleet Chicago-St. Louis corridor train. Since the mid-1960's when it was completed, the arch has been a symbol of the city's role as a gateway between East and West. (St. Louis lies smack in the midrift of the Midwest, over 600 miles from the East, which ostensibly begins at Pittsburgh, and some 700 miles from the West, which perhaps begins at the Colorado-Kansas border. But in earlier days, St. Louis generally was as far west as Eastern roads got, and vice versa.)—*Bob Schmidt*

<u>LEFT</u>: While the Gateway Arch is a symbol for St. Louis, the Illinois state capitol building at Springfield has some symbolism for this scene of the morning northbound St. Louis-Chicago Turboliner in the summer of 1975. The State of Illinois has been instrumental in developing service along the corridor, providing funds for 403(b) trains and station and track rehabilitation. In the late 1980's, the State helped avert a crisis by loaning money to the route's then-financially frail owner Chicago, Missouri & Western for major trackwork and repairs. Had this not been done, Amtrak would have moved to an alternate route, which would have been a blow to on-line communities like Bloomington and Springfield.—*Mike Schafer* <u>BELOW</u>: The combined *Kansas City Mule-River Cities* negotiates the High Line at State Line Junction west of Kansas City Union Station in March 1990. Just in from New Orleans and St. Louis, the train has disembarked its passengers and is being turned for its late afternoon eastbound departure as the *St. Louis Mule-River Cities*. The *Mules* are Missouri 403(b) operations.—*Keith Wilhite*

the new-version "Annie" remains a Missouri 403(b) operation. The re-emergence of St. Louis-Kansas City as a corridor—once the flight pattern of the *Missouri River Eagle, Colorado Eagle* and other Missouri Pacific varnish—was further strengthened with another 403(b) debut on Oct. 26, 1980, the *Kansas City Mule* and *St. Louis Mule*. Beginning on April 19, 1984, the *Mules* were combined with a new K.C.-New Orleans train, the *River Cities*.

Backing up to Aug. 10, 1980, we find the start of a short-lived branch off the Chicago-St. Louis route at Chenoa, Ill. The *Prairie Marksman*, another Illinois 403(b) run, split from the Chicago-St. Louis line at Chenoa onto the Toledo, Peoria & Western to reach metro Peoria, the state's third-largest city. Budgetary constraints ended this potential operation on Oct. 4, 1981. The most-recent major service change on the Chicago-St. Louis route was the April 27, 1986, inauguration of another state-sponsored run, the *Loop*, between Chicago and Springfield, the Illinois state capital.

The busy Chicago-St. Louis-Kansas City corridor has weathered a multitude of ownership changes during Amtrak's first 20 years. Although ownership of the St. Louis-K.C. segment has changed but once—from MP to Union Pacific in the mid-1980's—the Chicago-St. Louis end has changed three times, from GM&O to Illinois Central Gulf in 1972, to Chicago, Missouri & Western in 1987 and then to Southern Pacific in 1989. It appears this most-recent change will be the most-beneficial to a corridor with vast potential (like Chicago-Carbondale, it has several on-line colleges), as SP continued major line-upgrading through state assistance.

Chicago-(West) Quincy: Quincy, Ill., with a modest population of 42,000, seems an unlikely terminus for a passenger train. But, as with the state's Chicago-Carbondale line, it's the on-line colleges that play a crucial role here. Knox College at Galesburg, Western Illinois University at Macomb and Quincy College all provide a good traffic base for the *Illinois Zephyr*.

LEFT: Until Amfleet equipment became available, the *Illinois Zephyr* was a repository for all sorts of exotic rolling stock. Waving at trackside spectators, revelers on the eastbound *IZ* leaving Mendota, Ill., in 1974 are standing in coach-lounge-dome-observation car *Linoma*, built by Budd in 1948 for C&O's planned *Chessie* streamliner between Cincinnati and Washington/Newport News. Ahead of that car is one of Burlington's two "pattern" dome cars homebuilt in the company's Aurora (Ill.) shops. A straight coach separates the pattern dome from a UP diner, which was being used on this day, not as a food-service car, but a "study hall" car for students on the move.—*Mike Schafer*
ABOVE: A more-routine *Illinois Zephyr* of the 1990's roars down Burlington Northern's triple-track main line through Hollywood, Ill., home of world-famous Brookfield Zoo in suburban Chicago.—*Doug Koontz*

The *IZ* was one of the earliest new Amtrak trains, and Illinois' first 403(b) operation. This descendant of Chicago, Burlington & Quincy's Chicago-Kansas City domeliner *Kansas City Zephyr*, which had been cut back to a Chicago-West Quincy (Mo.) local by the time Amtrak started, began service on Nov. 14, 1971.

The *IZ* shares the BN main line with the *California Zephyr/Pioneer/Desert Wind* as far as Galesburg, hence its nickname, "Baby Zephyr." Beyond Galesburg—the Midwest hub of BN—the IZ heads for the remote southwestern part of the Prairie State, terminating not in Quincy, Ill., but across the Mississippi River in West Quincy, Mo., where BN has servicing facilities.

In the early 1970's, the IZ was a catch-all for all sorts of equipment, from dome-observation cars to the ex-C&NW bilevels to French Turboliners. It was long an Amfleet train—and during holiday periods when schools let out, a *long* Amfleet train at that—and today operates with Horizon Fleet coaches and an Amcafe, with Superliners occasionally helping shoulder heavy loads during peak travel periods.

Los Angeles-San Diego: Outside of the Northeast Corridor, this 129-mile route is one of the all-time biggest success stories for Amtrak. . . and the State of California, which has also been instrumental in the route's development. The Surf Line, as it is sometimes known, was a bustling operation for pre-Amtrak Santa Fe, which introduced streamlined equipment to the route in 1938. World War II accelerated growth along the corridor, thanks largely to the Navy's strong presence in San Diego. Service peaked with seven round trips, but one by one beginning in 1957, schedule frequencies were reduced. After 1965, there were but three L.A.-San Diego round trips, which is what Amtrak inherited.

Amtrak's Seattle-San Diego train, which debuted with the carrier on May 1, 1971, was the route's first long-distance train in recent history. This tri-weekly train supplanted one of the regular daily L.A.-San Diego round trips, so in essence there was a reduction in service frequency—from 21 trains weekly in each direction to 17. This was the (fortunately short-lived) low point in the corridor's life. On Nov. 14, 1971, the Oakland-San Diego end of the through train, now named the *Coast Starlight/Daylight* (*Coast Starlight* north of Oakland, *Coast Daylight* south), went daily.

Effective June 11, 1972, the through operation retrenched to L.A., and everything south of there simply again became *San Diegans*, with schedules catering mostly to long-distance-train connections at L.A. Ridership stabilized to just under 400,000 passengers per year. Then, the State stepped in, largely through the efforts of Senator James Mills, and things haven't been the same since—in a good way, of course. On Sept. 1, 1976, California's first 403(b) operation was born in the form of a fourth L.A.-San Diego round trip. On April 24, 1977, a fifth round trip began, followed by a sixth train on Feb. 15, 1978. By the end of 1979, 1.2 million passengers were riding the corridor in the space of a year. It was an important lesson: Schedule frequency had doubled, but ridership had tripled, the axiom being that convenience expands exponentially to schedule increases.

Growth continued in the 1980's with a seventh round trip added on Oct. 26, 1980, and an eighth in the spring of 1988—the highest frequency count ever in the corridor. Five of the eight round trips are 403(b) runs. Although schedules have remained constant since then, the long-talked about extension of San Diego service through L.A. to Santa Barbara finally occurred on June 26, 1988. Caltrans (California Department of Transportation) officials were stunned at the number of passengers who took to the new format, which permitted quick passage through auto-choked Los Angeles, and a second train was extended to Santa Barbara in 1990.

During the first half of the 1970's, the L.A.-San Diego corridor was one of the last holdouts for Santa Fe's aged fleet of F-units, which Amtrak had been leasing pending the arrival of its own locomotives. When photographed in spring 1973, the warbonnetted locomotives were still a familiar face at the San Diego depot, although the rolling stock was decidedly "foreign." On the *San Diegan* at left, for example, the-ex Wabash *Blue Bird* coffee-shop combine provides the food service, while the rest of the train is comprised of coaches from one-time rival Southern Pacific. For Santa Fe, the Los Angeles-San Diego corridor was an important extension of its fleet of transcontinental trains, with many runs scheduled to connect with the likes of the *Super Chief* and *Grand Canyon*. From pale beginnings in 1971, Amtrak and California DOT (Caltrans) have built a prestigious corridor that defies the state's perceived auto prejudice.—*Mike Schafer*

Though mention of California brings visions of Malibu mansions on Pacific beaches, the San Joaquin valley reveals another, less-remarked side to the Golden State's amazing geographic variety. In this hot, sometimes barren and surprisingly flat 300-mile-or-so valley lies a crucial facet of California's position on the U.S. economy: agriculture. Too, the San Joaquin valley serves as a base for industry—a sort of industrial back yard hidden from the more-glamorous oceanfront vistas normally associated with Calfiornia. Nonetheless, the industry and agriculture have brought in the population necessary to sustain six daily *San Joaquin* trains, with the prospect of more on the horizon. *San Joaquin* No. 708 is at Middle River, Calif., in February 1985. For this area near Stockton, rivers and irrigation channels are a regular part of the scene.—*Joe McMillan*

The impressive growth was made possible by other enhancements. A bill in 1979 raised capital for improvements, including a number of station rehabilitations and the coordination of connecting transit services. Track improvements resulted in higher speeds and shortened running times, and with increased momentum on the part of state thanks to the passage of a pro-rail referendum in 1990, work continues into the new decade to further enhance operations on the coast-hugging route.

Oakland-Bakersfield: On March 6, 1974, the *San Joaquin* revived service in the Golden State's San Joaquin Valley, home to several medium-size cities important to the state's industry and agricultural base, including Stockton, Modesto (served through Riverbank) and Fresno.

The *San Joaquin* route follows Southern Pacific's Oakland-Sacramento main line as far as Martinez and then strikes out on SP's Mococo line to Port Chicago. There, 36 miles out of Oakland, a connection transfers the trains to the Santa Fe for the remaining 276 miles to Bakersfield. Except for the SP segment, Amtrak/Caltrans' *San Joaquin* service is not unlike that of Santa Fe's *Golden Gate*s of the pre-Amtrak years, although those Oakland-Bakersfield runs had vanished by the time Amtrak was born. As of April 30, 1971, there was but one train on the route, the Chicago-Richmond *San Francisco Chief*.

The first *San Joaquin* was one of Amtrak's early "experimental" routes, which it was required by law to establish. Not until 1977 did the state become involved in the train's operation after Amtrak threatened to discontinue it because of a budgetary flap. The 1979 cuts that affected many parts of the Amtrak system threatened the *San Joaquin*, as well, but this time California intervened in a big way, not only saving the run but appropriating additional funds for a second round trip, which went into operation on Feb. 3, 1980. Predictably, the doubling of service resulted in a ridership boom. A lack of equipment prevented expansion until new Horizon Fleet cars became available, after which the third *San Joaquin* was launched on Dec. 17, 1989. The Horizon Fleet cars bumped Superliners on the *San Joaquin*, which in turn had supplanted Amfleet.

Because of the slow, circuitous, congested rail route over the Tehachapi Mountains, buses have long been the transport

Under the looming watch of its namesake peak, the *Mount Rainier* hastens southward between Puyallup and Tacoma in June 1977. This is the evening Seattle-Portland train, which in pre-Amtrak days was Northern Pacific's contribution to the Pool Train service. In the latter half of Amtrak's first decade, locomotives and cars still sported the wide red-and-blue striping—*T. O. Repp*

mode for rail passengers traveling beyond Bakersfield to and from Los Angeles—in Santa Fe days as well as today. Although there has been talk of extending at least one of the *San Joaquins* through to L.A., the connecting buses provide speed and maximum flexibility because of the wide variety of destinations they offer. A single *San Joaquin* is sometimes met in Bakersfield by as many as a dozen buses.

The continued success of the San Joaquin Valley corridor is expected to result in yet more trains, with extensions to Sacramento, the state capital, as well to San Jose on the west end. Plans are also afoot that may shift the *San Joaquins* to an all- or mostly SP route between Stockton and Bakersfield so that Modesto can be served directly and to take trains off a segment of time-consuming street-running in Fresno. If these developments occur, what started as a shaky operation in 1974 will have developed into a premier corridor.

Seattle-Portland: The 186 scenic miles separating these two world-class cities in the Pacific Northwest are both a bane and a blessing to Amtrak. Alas, the rugged topography hinders a true high-speed corridor operation; but, the four-hour ride features a splendid helping of vistas, from volcanic mountain peaks to shimmering bays and waterways.

In the days before Amtrak, the route was a joint operation by Northern Pacific, Great Northern and Union Pacific. Rather than compete, the three carriers cooperated on scheduling and ticketing. For years this "Pool Service," as it was known, consisted of just three trains. These lasted until—and into—Amtrak, although one of the heretofore daily runs became a part of the new tri-weekly Seattle-San Diego train thus for a time actually reducing Seattle-Portland frequencies.

All three runs got names on Nov. 14, 1971; the through train became the *Coast Starlight*, of course, while the other two were christened *Puget Sound* and *Mount Rainier*. The corridor was in effect extended north to Vancouver, B.C., with the July 17, 1972, start of the *Pacific International*, a run which lasted nine years. The *Starlight* went daily in June 1973, increasing frequencies on the Seattle-Portland route.

Then on June 7, 1977, the *Pioneer* was inaugurated between Seattle and Salt Lake City, replacing one Seattle-Portland local round trip. From then on, two long-distance trains served as two of the route's three "corridor" round trips, with the *Mount Rainier* being the sole surviving direct descendant of a pre-Amtrak Pool Train.

For a time, the corridor was extended south to Eugene, Ore., as well, when that state introduced double-daily Portland-Eugene *Willamette Valley* service on Aug. 3, 1980. These schedules were co-ordinated with Portland-Seattle runs; in fact, the *Mount Rainier* name and schedule was in part incorporated into the Eugene extension. Following mixed reviews and performance, the two Oregon 403(b) round trips were cancelled effective April 25, 1982, leaving only the *Starlight* on that route.

Chicago-Milwaukee: In 1957, rail travelers had a choice of some 40 weekday trains *each way* between Chicago and Milwaukee on three different roads (Milwaukee Road, North Western and North Shore Line). By 1971, this had dwindled to about eight trains each way divided among C&NW and Milwaukee. Amtrak retained the latter's route and four round trips, one of which was the newly rerouted (off the Burlington) *Empire Builder*.

The climb back to respectability has been a slow one for this highly potential route, but it started relatively quickly, on Nov. 14, 1971, when Amtrak innovatively implemented Milwaukee-Chicago-St. Louis through service and made the new (in July 1971) Chicago-Seattle *North Coast Hiawatha* a separate train out of Chicago. The net of all this was an increase in Chicago-Milwaukee frequencies from four to seven each way—the best it's ever been in the Amtrak era, particularly considering most runs then had full dining and parlor service and dome cars.

In October 1972 the local runs became collectively known as *Hiawatha Service* trains. Through service to St. Louis ended in 1973 along with most of the amenities it had brought. Eventually this setback was tempered by the introduction of long-awaited Turboliner service on the route in the fall of 1975, an event which made front-page headlines in the Milwaukee *Sentinel*; one of the two Turboliner-equipped round trips was a short-lived Detroit-Chicago-Milwaukee run-through. The remainder of the *Hiawatha Service* fleet was "Turbo-ized" on June 15, 1976.

After that, the number of Chicago-Milwaukee options fluctuated either through periodic local travel restrictions on the *Empire Builder* or outright discontinuances and/or re-establishments of Chicago-Milwaukee local trains in response to budget crisis of the moment. In 1980, the local trains received their own names; Turboliners were removed from the route the following year and replaced with Amfleet and ex-C&NW bilevels.

Things took a major plummet with 1981 budget cuts that reduced frequencies to three each way and ended all food and beverage service on the local trains; it was the nadir of the corridor. But through the rest of the 1980's, service slowly improved, with the biggest gain occuring in October 1989 when Wisconsin and Illinois began jointly sponsoring two Chicago-Milwaukee runs, bringing the total back to 6-7 round trips (depending on the day of the week). As with other corridors, the increase in service ushered in impressive gains in ridership, and today the spartan corridor, despite the lack of innovation and capital improvements enjoyed by, say, the California corridors, survives reasonably well.

AMTRAK'S YEOMAN TRAINS, runs like the *San Diegans*, the *Carolinian* and the *Ann Rutledge*, represent a sometimes unremarked side of our national rail passenger system. Yet, these corridor and medium-distance runs yield about a quarter of Amtrak's ridership—more than even the high-profile long-distance trains that are frequently spotlighted in the travel media. That's something to remember next time we're tempted to say, "Oh, that's just another Amfleet train!"

Check out the roofline of this train! GP40TC 194 leads an Amcoach sandwiched by two about-to-be-retired ex-C&NW bilevels on the northbound *Radisson*, heading for Wisconsin's largest city, Milwaukee, in March 1989. For a time, GP40-TC's—former GO Transit units built in 1966—were common on the route, but F40's reign again. All local Chicago-Milwaukee trains operate in push-pull configuration (the rear bilevel is a cab-control coach), which in part allowed the states of Wisconsin and Illinois to increase service on the line in October 1989. Prior to push-pull, Amtrak either operated an F40 at each end of a consist, or turned locomotives at Milwaukee, an operation involving an hour-and-a-half round trip to a wye in North Milwaukee.—*Eric Coleman*

ABOVE: Arguably one of the finest rail passenger facilities in North America, Los Angeles Union Passenger Terminal in 1989 celebrated its 50th anniversary. The event followed renovation of the Spanish mission-style complex that was once home to the likes of Santa Fe's *Super Chief*, Union Pacific's *City of Los Angeles* and Southern Pacific's *Coast Daylight*. Today, LAUPT is home for Amtrak's *Coast Starlight, Sunset Limited, Southwest Chief, Desert Wind* and eight *San Diegans*.—*Steve Patterson* **RIGHT:** Amtrak has made a concerted effort to standardize on some of the signage for station grounds, although depot buildings themselves vary wildly. This attactively landscaped sign stands at the entrance ot the Kirkwood (Mo.) depot in suburban St. Louis.—*Paul Fries*

10/Amtrak, call home

THE STATIONS AND SHOPS OF NRPC

BY BOB JOHNSTON

"The *Inter-American* arrives and departs at Travis Street and the MP Railroad tracks." So explained the reference mark in Amtrak's 1973 timetables, a footnote that spoke volumes of one of the carrier's several predicaments upon its inception. Back then a street crossing next to an empty field—"the rabbit patch" as some wags dubbed it—was the best San Antonio stop available for the Fort Worth to Laredo tri-weekly train. The Missouri Pacific station had been demolished, and to utilize the massive, mission-style depot where the *Sunset Limited* stopped would have required another crew, longer running times and negotiations with the station owner Southern Pacific.

Today, a daily *Texas Eagle* comes down from Fort Worth along the same route the *Inter-American* took, but now terminates at the SP's facility. Though the rails into town now belong to Union Pacific and through cars of the Superliner-equipped train connect with the *Sunset*, what hasn't changed is that Southern Pacific still owns the station, an arrangement that has made sense in San Antonio for 20 years.

RIGHT: Amtrak inherited several "barns"—large derelict depots that, although once appropriate for passenger-train fleets of yore, were much more than necessary for the skeletal remains that operated after May 1, 1971. A classic example was Buffalo Union Terminal, once host to dozens of trains of New York Central, Pennsylvania and Toronto, Hamilton & Buffalo. Young Amtrak had barely the resources to maintain the huge weed-infested complex (shown in October 1977) and early in the 1980's moved to a new station at nearby Depew, N.Y.—*C. W. Newton* **BELOW RIGHT:** Amtrak's first new depot—that is, one built to its own specifications—was at Cincinnati. The little building opened on Oct. 29, 1972, was expanded a few years later when the *Shenandoah* was also using it, and closed when Amtrak returned to Cincinnati Union Terminal on July 29, 1991.—*Mike Schafer*

For Amtrak, the saga of stations and maintenance bases has been an ever-changing collage, with facilities in each city dictated by what the carrier inherited, whether the host railroad wishes to hold on to its property, if public or private ownership is a factor, how commuter rail impacts operations and if there is commercial development potential.

Where the trains stopped or were serviced was almost incidental in 1971; Amtrak had bigger fish to fry. But almost immediately, operating costs came under close scrutiny from a management that needed its scarce resources for new cars and locomotives. "Return on investment" financial theory identified some easy targets: large, antiquated, high-maintenance venues like Cincinnati Union Terminal, Great Northern Station in Minneapolis, Cleveland's Terminal Tower and stations in Richmond, Jacksonville and Miami, to name a few. First in Cincinnati, and eventually in the other cities, Amtrak found the best way to control costs was to build its own facility, more suited to the level of service being provided at the time. In smaller communities, too, Amtrak's initial inclination was to build a spartan shelter rather attempt to resuscitate and maintain a previously closed or dilapidated building for, frequently, one train per day. And if no station existed, utilizing a small bus-type shelter was, after all, better than boarding passengers from a "rabbit patch."

But other combinations of station ownership became viable as Amtrak's performance and perceived importance grew through the 1970's and into the 1980's. Facilities in Grand Rapids, Mich., Altoona, Pa., and Bridgeport, Conn., for example,

LEFT: Although Cincinnati was Amtrak's first station built to its specifications, all work was subcontracted. Eventually, NRPC established its own design and architectural arm. Here, an Amtrak architect in the railroad's original headquarters at L'Enfant Plaza (Washington, D.C.) assembles a scale model of a proposed new depot. As did most railroads earlier in the century, Amtrak has developed a series of standardized depot styles. Compare the photo at left, taken in April 1975, with those below of the St. Paul station to note how some of the component styles have been carried through on the real thing. **BELOW:** The new Twin Cities Midway Station under construction in 1977.—*Two photos, Mike Schafer* **BOTTOM:** The completed Midway Station in 1978.—*Steve Glischinski*

ABOVE: Interiors of most new Amtrak depots exhibit a family resemblance with such items as seating, signage and counter arrangement. This is the inside of the Hammond/Whiting (Ind.) depot, new in 1982. Most trains to Michigan points and the East Coast call at the southeast suburban Chicago stop, and for certain trains the station serves as a transfer point such that passengers off a Chicago-bound Michigan train can transfer to, say, the eastbound *Capitol Limited*, thus avoiding a trip all the way into Chicago Union Station.—*Mike Schafer*

were all rebuilt by the cities themselves, with some additional investment from the private sector. Over $400,000 of community money was spent (plus $90,000 from Amtrak) to help restore the ornate Spanish Mission Revival-style station in Orlando, Fla., with 1,200 volunteers from over 70 organizations performing work.

The stations utilized by Amtrak in Santa Barbara, Calif., and New London, Conn., on the other hand, are privately held. Commuter authorities own and maintain stations as widely disparate as Newark (New Jersey Transit) and Summit, Ill. (Chicago's Metra), while railroads themselves continue to own some properties, such as the new, BN-built, turn-of-the-century-style depot at Galesburg, Ill., and Union Terminals in Denver, Los Angeles and New Orleans.

Alas, sometimes there's no easy solution, such as Lafayette, Ind. There, Amtrak trains trundle through town down the ex-

Continued on page 164

TOP: Not all major terminals Amtrak inherited were candidates for abandonment. Several still served a large number of trains. King of them all is Penn Station, New York, where there are still literally hundreds of Amtrak, Long Island Rail Road and New Jersey Transit movements every 24 hours. E60 No. 605 heads up the Chicago-bound *Broadway Limited* at Penn Station on May 18, 1991; adjacent, the *Crescent* loads. The view is from the gantry of "A" Tower.—*Mike Schafer* **ABOVE: Inside "A" Tower is a combination of new technology and ancient but time-proven control apparatus dating from Penn Station's construction by the Pennsylvania Railroad in 1910.**—*Bob Johnston*

From the sublime to the ridiculous. . . Amtrak boarding points represent a full spectrum of marvels. **RIGHT:** In Lafayette, Ind., the Chicago-bound *Hoosier State* on June 21, 1991, cruises 5th Street, one of downtown's main drags, to a storefront gift shop that served as the city depot until it closed a few weeks later.—*Mike Schafer* **BOTTOM:** Unable to utilize the classic Montgomery (Ala.) Union Station nearby, Amtrak has patrons arriving at the state capital off the *Gulf Breeze* detrain at a concrete grain elevator-turned-depot.—*Larry Richards* **BELOW:** Meanwhile, the new first-class Metropolitan Lounge at Chicago Union Station represents a much more luxurious aspect of waiting for the train.—*Bob Johnston*

Convenience is the keyword for the Amtrak depot in Las Vegas, Nev. Not only is it located at the foot of the gambling capital's downtown section, but it doubles as the lobby of the Plaza Hotel. No airport limousines necessary here! And, while the *Desert Wind* pauses twice a day at the joint facility (built by Union Pacific, incidentally), passengers just passing through can still disembark to challenge the slot machines inside.—*Mike Schafer*

The 1980's thankfully ushered a trend that spread into the railroad industry: the extensive renovation of classic structures. Several stations Amtrak owns or uses have been rehabilitated, sometimes down to the most faithful detail. Here, on a December evening in 1985, Pennsylvania Station in Newark, N.J., looms in majestic renaissance. The former-PRR building, with its interesting curved trainshed, hosts dozens of Amtrak Northeast Corridor trains as well as those of the building's owner, New Jersey Transit. Though the Pennsylvania had been gone for nearly 18 years when this scene was made, Newark Penn Station's renovation maintained many PRR details, such as keystone logos on waiting-room benches and the road's Tuscan and gold colors on interior trim.—*Mike Del Vecchio*

Even in the 1990's, Amtrak stations are a panoply of fascinating polarities, from the ultra-modern (ABOVE, at Irvine, Calif.) to the traditional (LEFT, at Manassas, Va.). Contrasts like these only further enhance the intrigue of rail travel in the U.S.— *Above, Stanton Hunter; left, Ken Kraemer.*

Monon (now CSX) line smack in the middle of 5th Street. With the old Monon station at the edge of the business district sold to private interests long before Amtrak came into town, the *Cardinal* and the *Hoosier State* paused for years in front of the Lahr Hotel. Passengers utilized the lobby as a waiting room. Then the hotel closed, and trains began stopping at the Potpourri Gift Shop down the street. But now that establishment has gone out of business, and travelers must find another place to wait, at least until the city completes a massive railroad relocation project that will put Amtrak back into the former Big Four (New York Central) depot.

Contrast the Lafayette experience with what has been happening in some of Amtrak's key cities, where the prospect of

The former-Pennsylvania Railroad station at Harrisburg, Pa., where PRR GG1 electrics were once swapped for sturdy K-4 Pacific steam locomotives, was extensively rehabbed in the mid-1980's to its original splendor. The City of Harrisburg spearheaded the project, and funded most of it. The depot serves as an example of how Amtrak and Greyhound have turned rivalry into cooperation, benefitting travelers and carriers alike. Greyhound uses a portion of the depot, where a former PRR GG1 resides on display under the ornate trainshed.—*Don Jilson*

commercial development in a busy station has helped fund renovation of an older facility, making it a pleasant place to catch a train. Washington's grand old Union Station languished for years after an attempt to turn it into a National Visitors Center flopped. Then Amtrak invested $70 million for modernization and restoration of the building's architectural details, a private developer came forward with $50 million to tastefully convert large portions of the station into retail space, and the city chipped in $40 million for a parking garage. Opened in 1988 to rave reviews as a multi-purpose mecca of shops, movie theaters and restaurants served by both Amtrak and the subway system, Washington Union Station confirmed that there was life, indeed, for the massive structures built to serve the nation when railroads had a monopoly on intercity travel.

Now, in large measure because Amtrak has been doing a good job of wooing the previously lost business back, the big city station is making a comeback. Over $100 million has been spent at Philadelphia's 30th Street with the aid of tax-free industrial development bonds, an urban development action grant, and contributions from Amtrak and private investors for new passenger facilities, multi-level retail shops and over 250,000 square feet of office space. Boston's South Station, Los An-

ABOVE: The former-Rio Grande depot in Salt Lake City serves Amtrak and houses a restaurant and museum. Amtrak moved from the UP depot to the Rio Grande depot to alleviate switching problems.—*David C. Warner* **LEFT:** Dallas Union Station has been heavily re-habbed and incorporated into a whole new complex called (cleverly) ReUnion Center. Union Station can be seen at left, while the glass-faced Hyatt Hotel stands across the tracks; it is directly accessible to Union Station via an undertrack pedestrian walkway.—*Mike Schafer* **BELOW:** Vestiges of an earlier era—original neon—still guided passengers at King Street Station, Seattle, Wash., in 1977.—*Brad Joseph*

RIGHT: The eastbound *Colonial* pokes its nose out of the new depot in Providence, R.I., on a summer evening in 1988. Amtrak traded the former New Haven Railroad depot here for a new facility built and owned by the city. The new station constructed at the foot of the state capitol building (out of photo at right), required an extensive line relocation that allowed Amtrak to vacate and sell the valuable grounds of the old facility.—*Scott Hartley*

The spirit of the season is conveyed at the former Missouri Pacific stone depot at Kirkwood, Mo., as the westbound *Ann Rutledge* from Chicago and St. Louis takes on holiday travelers for Jefferson City, Sedalia, Independence and Kansas City on New Year's Day 1989.—*Bob Schmidt*

geles' Union Passenger Terminal, Pennsylvania Station in New York and Chicago Union Station have all gone through a transformation fueled by the prospect of retail rental revenues and large or increasing commuter traffic to provide a ready market for the shopkeepers and defray Amtrak's infrastructure renewal cost. Chicago has been a particularly ambitious project, since completely new traffic patterns, a mezzanine for commuters and a posh first-class lounge for sleeping-car passengers was created in the basement of a 1970 high rise, on the site of the old CUS concourse building, that was originally designed to handle only suburbanites on their way to and from work.

A tight economy and difficult financial markets have limited the scope of some of these station rehabilitations. The movement apparently came too late for Kansas City's grand old lady, where Amtrak sustained itself within a plastic bubble to keep the heat in and falling plaster out, until it could not wait any longer. Today the old station sits dark and forlorn, sans tracks, while the *Southwest Chief, Ann Rutledge, River Cities* and *Mule*s depart from the new facility next door.

But proof that "what goes around, comes around" is alive and well and living in Cincinnati, where Amtrak in the summer of 1991 closed the first station it built. The reason: After several stabs at redevelopment, private and public funds have reincarnated the Art Deco Cincinnati Union Station to house two museums, movie theaters, shops and, for a rental maintenance fee, the "new" Amtrak station. No longer will trains have to make a time-consuming, complicated back-up move down to River Road. Instead the *Cardinal* will glide to a halt next to the main line under what many thought was one of the country's last great monuments to passenger train travel. Now, thanks to Amtrak, it has company.

ALTHOUGH AMTRAK STOPS AT 568 stations, its most important "homes" may be the servicing facilities and shops where equipment is maintained and rebuilt. Every day, 58 to 69 passenger cars are out of service for scheduled maintenance. If a car's maintenance is more than seven days late, its tardiness hits the morning report that goes all the way to Mr. Claytor's office.

Though "running repairs" may be made as needed anywhere on the system, eleven preventive-maintenance locations are assigned specific cars for which they are responsible. It is up to the equipment sched-

RIGHT: Car 54 where are you? Terminal Supervisor Don Crimmin in the tower of Amtrak's 14th Street Coach Yard in Chicago enlists the aid of binoculars to monitor movements and car location on a January day in 1987. The sprawling complex represents one of Amtrak's largest rags-to-riches projects of its first decade as the former-Penn Central (ex-Pennsylvania) engine terminal and coach yards in Chicago were transformed from a downtrodden battlefield to a gleaming new servicing center. **LOWER RIGHT:** Focal point for the facility is the car shop and office building with its seven-story control tower.—*Two photos, Mike Schafer* **BELOW:** A northward view from the tower on an August evening in 1990. The Chicago River is at right; the Sears Tower, a block east of Union Station, dominates the skyline.—*Steve Rathke*

F40 294 rests between assignments at Burlington Northern's Interbay Yard engine terminal at Seattle in 1984. Amtrak contracts with host railroads to service equipment that is beyond the reach of its own maintenance locations.—*Dan Munson*

uler to get coaches, baggage and material-handling cars back to their home base every 180 days, and sleepers, lounges, diners, table cars and dorms to their assigned facility every 120 days. The inspection begins with a specific maintenance analysis program (MAP) developed for that type of equipment. Voltages are checked, brake tolerances examined and interiors fumigated, to name a few of the tasks.

Some of the key maintenance bases? Washington, D.C.'s Ivy City is responsible for 331 Amfleet I coaches, clubs and snack cars. Brighton Park in Chicago's Bridgeport neighborhood, which used to be the headquarters for the ANF-Frangeco Turboliner fleet, handles the chores on all 139 Superliner coach and coach-baggage cars and all 68 Superliner sleepers, along with 30 Amfleet I and 37 Amfleet II cars. All 25 Sightseer and Hi-Level lounges and 39 Superliner diners are assigned to the newly opened preventive-maintenance facility in Los Angeles between the 8th Street Coach Yard and the station. Other periodic repairs occur at Hialeah (Miami), Sanford and Tampa in Florida; Boston's Southhampton Street; Rensselaer (N.Y.); Sunnyside (New York City, assigned every material handling car); Oakland; and the Penn Coach Yard in Philadelphia (which is, temporarily at least, "home" to the still-under-test Viewliners so they can be observed closely by Amtrak's mechanical department, headquartered in Philly).

On the locomotive side, most F40s call the 16th Street Engine Terminal in Chicago "home," regardless of their regular assignment. Getting far-flung *San Diegan* service units back to Chicago is a challenge for Philadelphia-based power desk personnel, but most locations are only one trip away from the Windy City. All of the remaining General Electric P30 fleet is maintained at New Orleans, adjacent to the locomotives' typical *Sunset Limited* duty; the remainder had been serviced at Sanford, Fla., as a part of the *Auto Train* pool.

Major rebuilding, wreck repair and complete interior overhauls for Heritage, Horizon, Amfleet and Superliner cars and diesel locomotives take place at Beech Grove, in Indianapolis. It was originally a New York Central shop conveyed to Amtrak in 1974, and represents one of the company's first and most persistent efforts to get a handle on quality control. All of the crucial head-end power conversions were performed

The acquisition of Beech Grove Shops from Penn Central in 1974 was a strategic move on Amtrak's part. It provides the carrier with its own major repair center as well as a revenue-generating contract shop. RIGHT: Although Beech Grove tends to be synonymous with passenger rolling stock, shop forces can handle major locomotive repairs and rebuilds as well.—*Mike Schafer* **BELOW:** The Beech Grove city limit sign reveals the importance of Amtrak's presence in the community.—*David C. Warner*

here, and a standard was established for the entire system. Other projects have included assembly of the two Viewliner sleepers and one diner as well as cars for Washington's Metro rapid-transit system on a contract basis.

In 1976, the Wilmington Shops were acquired from Penn Central as part of the Northeast Corridor. Reprising its historical role as the Pennsylvania Railroad's electric motive-power headquarters with complete AEM7 and E60 responsibility, Wilmington has also handled ex-Metroliner cab-car repair, conversion and retrofitting (most recently making straight coaches out of them for use in Michigan and building the Metroliner Conference Car).

In 1984 the Bear, Del., facility was purchased originally to host the Northeast Corridor's orange fleet of track-maintenance cars and locomotives. Located 4.8 miles from the junction with the main line at Newark, Del., on Conrail's Delmarva Secondary, the installation has grown in stature to become one of Amtrak's most multi-functional homes. The 213,000-square-foot shop added switch-frog rebuilding in 1986, a complete Amfleet I refurbishing production line a year later, then a concrete ballast deck-bridge conversion operation and a paint shop for all work done in Wilmington. It will also be home to the new Roadrailer testing program over the next few years; the first of these special truck-on-rails vehicles, which Amtrak intends to use for mail service, were delivered in the summer of 1991.

Administratively, Bear is the control point for Amtrak's fleet of 1,244 highway vehicles and the expenses they incur, where managers keep an eye on all credit card purchases of gasoline and diesel fuel.

Finally, of course, there's corporate headquarters in Washington, D.C., and many other offices, from dining-car commissaries to the room at the Santa Fe station in La Junta, Colo., where *Southwest Chief* crews check in. Together with the shops and stations, all of these places are "home," to Amtrak's most important asset, people who are ultimately responsible for the product the carrier delivers every day.

Electrician Michael Sharpe wires air-conditioning starter panels for Michigan-funded ex-Metroliner cab-control coaches being rebuilt at Wilmington Shops on May 16, 1991.—*Bob Johnston*

ABOVE: Display trains such as this at Naperville, Ill., in 1985 have gone a long way in making Amtrak more public-aware.—*David H. Thompson* **LEFT**: New uniforms, 1972.—*Robert Malinoski*

11/Making the trains worth traveling again

A SAMPLER OF PROMOTIONS AND MARKETING

BY KEVIN McKINNEY

The years leading to the creation of Amtrak were almost totally devoid of railroad passenger advertising. Except for a few notable efforts, such as Santa Fe's ongoing television spots and newspaper ads, or Grand Trunk's radio campaign in the late 1960's, railroads only advertised for two reasons. One was the small, token ad, usually just placed prior to presenting a train-off case, that permitted the railroad to state to the Interstate Commerce Commission "Yes, we advertised the train but there was no increase in ridership." A one-column-inch Erie Lackawanna ad in a Chicago newspaper typified that category. The other occasion was the corporate image ad that said, "we really don't want to discontinue passenger service, but we have no choice." Memorable in that category was a full-page Illinois Central ad featuring a teary-eyed conductor mourning the potential loss of the *Panama Limited*.

It wasn't always that way, of course. Railroads once had won numerous awards for creative advertising on posters, billboards and in newspapers and magazines. By the mid-1950's however, optimism over the future of the passenger train had largely faded, and advertising budgets evaporated. So when it came to marketing and advertising, Amtrak had to start from

<u>RIGHT</u>: Amtrak wasted no time in letting the public know that it had accomplished a major breakthrough by accepting credit cards; this announcement appeared in newspapers and in the national timetable issued on Jan. 16, 1972. A Seaboard Coast Line E-unit with its nose herald blocked out had the honors of posing in this bit of memorable (at least for those old enough to remember Amtrak's early years) advertising.—*Courtesy Amtrak*
<u>BELOW RIGHT</u>: With the Rohr Turboliners came this classy color brochure that pushed the high-tech aspect train travel could have.—*Zephyr Graphics & Editorial: Andy McBride*

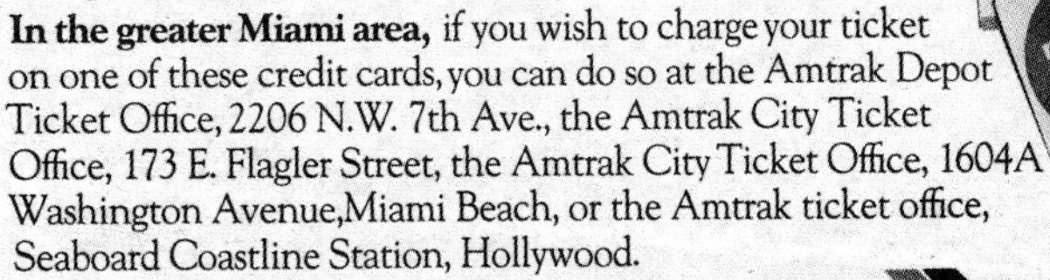

scratch, at the same time needing to overcome some very negative images.

The airlines, with their slick marketing and advertising, became the model for Amtrak to emulate. The customer-oriented airlines accepted every credit card then available while most railroads accepted none, except for the obscure Rail Travel Card. Airlines offered toll-free information and reservation numbers; railroads did not. Airline commercials were on TV and radio with catchy jingles. To make matters worse, in the public mind of 1971, railroads were thought of as a dying industry, with passenger trains rapidly fading toward oblivion, and Penn Central, the nation's largest railroad, bankrupt and falling apart. Even the creation of Amtrak, a positive event, was seen as a negative by many people, since May 1, 1971, meant the end of more than half of America's remaining passenger trains.

Initial Amtrak advertising was basic. Newspaper advertisements in cities that retained intercity rail passenger service merely said in bold headlines, "Now Amtrak trains speed you to . . . with intermediate stops." In time, more-elaborate ads were produced for the print media in an attempt to explain the positive things Amtrak was doing to reverse the decline of rail passenger service. Sometimes, the ad copy was downright apologetic: "How's the food these days? Right now, to be honest, we're only concerned that you get a real good meal every time you step into our dining cars. And that even a snack in an Amtrak coach is always fresh and tasty. But there's a gourmet streak deep inside us that's going to come out in the future and surprise you." The ad (see page 73) went on to tout the slashing of red tape in ticketing and reservations and the improvements in scheduling that were being implemented as the year 1971 progressed.

AMTRAK. WE'RE MAKING THE TRAINS WORTH TRAVELING AGAIN

(All we ask from you is a little patience)

Amtrak Passenger Representative with a model of a modern Amtrak passenger car now in service

What is Amtrak? We're America's first nationwide passenger rail system.

When President Nixon signed the Rail Passenger Service Act, it gave us the responsibility for managing the country's intercity rail network starting May 1, 1971.

That meant merging the services and solving the obstacles of what had been 22 different passenger railroads, each with its own built-in problems. While at the same time running 1300 trains a week over 20,000 miles of track to 340 cities in the U.S.A.

It may not be the country's biggest headache. But it's close. That's why when we took over we made only one simple promise. To make the trains worth traveling again. It's going to take time, and work. But we're going to do it. Just be patient, please.

You're going to ride the best 1200 cars in the country. You can't run a good railroad without good railroad cars. So our first order of business was to take stock of our rolling stock. We examined all 3000 passenger cars formerly in service. And we're keeping only the 1200 best, most of them stainless steel.

You talk—we listen. For the first time there are passenger representatives riding our trains just to get your ideas about rail service. You've already made it clear that you want your trains a lot cleaner than in the past. And they will be.

Eat a little better. Right now we're concerned with making sure that you get a real good dinner every time you enter our dining cars. And that even a snack in an Amtrak coach is always fresh and tasty.

We want to save you time, money and aggravation. Some of the most annoying problems of going by train take place before you even step aboard. And we know it. That's why we're putting such a high priority on faster and simpler reservation and ticketing procedures. We don't like red tape any better than you do.

People who care are caring about you. If you've been aboard an Amtrak train lately, perhaps you've noticed how attentive our personnel are. Nobody has a greater stake in the success of Amtrak than the people on our trains. After all, their future is riding on it.

All this, of course, is only a very small start on a very big job. But we are making progress—and we're proud of it. Come aboard an Amtrak train this fall and see for yourself.

We're making the trains worth traveling again.

Amtrak

LEFT: The ad that started it all. This 1971 advertisement which appeared in the famous Nov. 14, 1971, national timetable (Amtrak's first true in-house timetable) and in full-page newspaper space throughout the country featured a lead-in phrase that was destined to become legendary: "We're making the trains worth traveling again." An actual Amtrak Passenger Service Representative, R. Paul Carey, rather than a professional model, posed in an ad that has become an Amtrak classic.—*Collection of Mike Schafer* **BELOW LEFT**: Early newspaper ads issued right after Amtrak was born were fairly generic.—*Courtesy Amtrak*

It took some time to make the trains worth traveling again, but steady progress was made throughout the 1970's against a backdrop of budget battles that threatened the carrier's very exisitence. By the time the Superliners began to arrive at the end of the decade, Amtrak finally had something it could really advertise.

And advertise it did, with a new generation of sophisticated print and television ads. There was at last a good story to tell and Amtrak successfully revived the spirit of railroad advertising in the heyday of railroading. A headling stating, "Not everyone was meant to fly" captured the advantages of rail travel and ended with the comment, "So next time your'e planning to travel somewhere, think about taking the train. See how good it feels to fly without leaving the ground." Ads extolling the faster, more frequent *Metroliner* service in the Northeast Corridor promoted trains as the civilized way to travel. Later, well into the 1980's, television promos featured spectacular vistas as seen from the train along with views of Western Amtrak trains winding through scenery that far surpassed the "See the U.S.A. in your Chevrolet" spots of the 1950's and 1960's. Some of these won advertising awards.

In the realm of marketing, Amtrak first set out to copy the airlines. Indeed, it forced itself into the computerized systems used by the airlines and travel agents (at first opposed by the airline industry) in 1985, a move that has greatly increased Amtrak usage by the travel industry. Then it set out to differentiate the positive aspects of rail travel compared to competing modes. The result is an on-target approach to promoting rail, one that has only been hampered by the lack of a truly adequate budget over the years.

Nevertheless, when one considers the combined advertising budgets of the railroads in 1970 (a figure not available, but one not likely to have too many digits) and the user-friendly state of rail service at the time, the progress has been substantial.

NOT ALL OF AMTRAK'S PROMOTION has been through the TV, radio and periodical media. Readers who have visited railroadiana shows or "flea markets" know of the existence of a vast array of promotional paraphernelia distributed by the railroads during their golden years, with company logos, train names and such incorporated into the items. There are playing cards, baggage tags, pens and pencils, ash trays, cocktail glasses, blankets, swizzle sticks, travel bags and even specialty items, such as the lapel pin Illinois Central presented to *Panama Limited* customers who ordered the famous King's Dinner.

Railroads also used publishing to their advantage. Folders touting specific trains or new equipment were commonplace, and route brochures could still be found on Santa Fe trains right up until Amtrak.

The purpose of all these items is significant, yet subtle: They kept a railroad's name (or one of its trains) in front of the public eye—perhaps subliminally, but there nonetheless. This subtle form of train advertising was completely revived by Amtrak. Pens, balloons, buttons and the like remain great giveaway items, and Amtrak also offers a complete line of catalog merchandise, from jackets to HO scale train sets (Amtrak models, of course) to cocktail glasses and travel bags.

One of the most-requested items by passengers has been route brochures; these reappeared early in the Amtrak era and remain a regular item on selected long-distance trains. In fact, before Amtrak had its own promotional department in place, it simply contracted Santa Fe publish route brochures—which is why early Amtrak route guides have the nose of Santa Fe locomotives on them and look an awful lot like Santa Fe guides of the 1960's. Amtrak has also issued folders promoting new equipment: a sleek, slender and stylish folder accompanied the introduction of new Superliner cars in the late 1970's; a Viewliner folder, though much more austere, was issued when the three Viewliner prototypes went into revenue service in the 1980's.

With perhaps the exception of television, the parallels between Amtrak's current promotions and those of the 1940's and 1950's is startling, and it is as though we have entered another golden era of the passenger train—admittedly of a much smaller scope, of course. But there is one difference. Advertising and promotion apparently had limited affect on the downward tide of the passenger train in the post-World War II years; in the Amtrak era, ridership has mostly been on the rise. Whether it's because of playing cards decked with photos of Superliners, or a memorable visual message during a *Family Ties* commercial break, or a colorful brochure luring people out of their autos for a trip on the *Broadway Limited* or *Empire Builder*, or just the desire of a travel option brimming with mystique and adverture, the people are coming back to the passenger train.

TOP LEFT: Amtrak collectibles from the first decade include postcards with French Turboliners, E-units and people seated in a Southern Pacific diner, and travel folders, pens and the now-rare SDP40F locomotive soap bars. The playing cards are from the 1980's.—*Zephyr Graphics & Editorial: Andy McBride* **TOP RIGHT: Amtrak is wise to make an impression on schoolchildren—people who will someday grow up to decide on their own whether to drive, fly or take the train. This group of exuberant youngsters just off the *Lake Shore Limited* at Albany/Rensselaer is bedecked in Amtrak engineer hats handed out by train crews.**—*Mike Schafer* **ABOVE: A billboard along the freeway (and railway) into Atlantic City, N.J., in 1989.**—*Steve Barry*

1970

1/18: DOT announces plans for a quasi-public rail passenger network.
5/1: The "Railpax" bill is introduced.
5/6: Senate approves the bill, 78-3.
10/14: House presents its version of Railpax; Senate accepts.
10/30: President Nixon signs Railpax bill; National Railroad Passenger Corporation is born.
11/30: Preliminary system endpoint map unveiled.

1971

1/28: DOT unveils Final System map.
3/22: Specific routes connecting Final System endpoints are announced.
4/19: NRPC replaces "Railpax" working name with "Amtrak."
4/28: Roger Lewis named first president of NRPC.
4/30: Most U.S. passenger trains make or begin last runs.
5/1: Amtrak begins; first train is New York-Washington "Clocker" No. 235, departing New York Penn Station at 12:05 a.m. Overnight railroad-operated trains arrive at their terminals for the last time.
5/2: Railroad-operated transcons arrive their terminals for the last time.
5/10: Chicago-Cleveland-New York 403(b) train added.
5/17: Boston-Springfield-New Haven Bay State begins.
6/5: Chicago-Butte-Seattle run on.
6/10: *City of New Orleans* derails at 98 mph at Tonti, Ill., killing 13.
7/12: Amtrak issues its second timetable.
9/8: Washington-Parkersburg *West Virginian* added.
11/14: First true in-house timetable issued, with many revised schedules and operations, new train names and new runs—Chicago-West Quincy *Illinois Zephyr*, third *San Diegan.*
12/9: Amtrak introduces uniforms.

1972

1/5: Chicago-Cleveland-New York *Lake Shore* makes last trip.
1/10: Amtrak begins accepting national credit cards.
1/23: *Floridian* detoured off original Amtrak route through Indiana.
3/6: Amtrak trains using Central Station, Chicago, move to Union Station as the former closes.
4/30: New York-Pittsburgh *Keystone* discontinued.
5/1: Amtrak's first birthday, celebrated with refurbished *Broadway.*
7/17: Seattle-Vancouver (B.C.) *Pacific International* begins.
9/29: Washington-Montreal service via Vermont begins.
10/29: New station at Cincinnati opens, Amtrak's first.
11/2: SDP40F's ordered from EMD.
12/28: Acquisition of UA and French Turbos announced.

1973

1/28: Fort Worth-Laredo Inter-American begins.
3/26: 15 GE E60's ordered.
4/15: First central reservation office opens at Bensalem, Pa.
5/1: Second anniversary of Amtrak.
5/7: Washington-Parkersburg service truncated to Cumberland.
6/22: SDP40F's make first passenger run, on *Super Chief.*
10/1: Chicago-St. Louis *State House* added.
10/12: 57 Amfleet cars ordered from Budd; also 70 more SDP40's from EMD and 11 E60's from GE.
10/16: *James Whitcomb Riley/George Washington* detoured from its original Indiana route.
12/17: Chicago-Champaign/Urbana *Illini* debuts.

1974

2/14: Chicago-Rockford-Dubuque *Black Hawk* added.
3/6: Oakland-Bakersfield *San Joaquin* begins.
3/13: *Inter-American* extended beyond Fort Worth to St. Louis.
5/1: New Turbo maintenance facility opens at Brighton Park, Chicago; third anniversary of Amtrak.
5/19: Seattle-Spokane *Expo '74* inaugurated for World's Fair, Spokane.
6/5: 200 more Amfleet cars ordered.
6/21: Four more French Turbos ordered.
6/24: Amtrak orders 25 P30CH's from General Electric.
6/27: ARTS computer system become fully operational.
7/26: Seven Turboliners ordered from Rohr Corp.
8/1: *Floridian* shifted to L&N Chicago-Evansville-Nashville route; *James Whitcomb Riley* begins using C&O through Indiana.
8/6: New York-Albany-Montreal *Adirondack* begins.
9/15: Chicago-Port Huron *Blue Water* introduced.
10/25: More Amfleet ordered: 35 cars.
10/31: New York-Buffalo-Detroit *Empire State Express* begins.

1975

1/20: Detroit-Jackson *Michigan Executive* added.
3/1: Paul Reistrup becomes Amtrak's second president; *Bay State* discontinued.
3/25: Chicago-Norfolk *Mountaineer* starts operation.
4/1: Amtrak acquires Beech Grove Shops from Penn Central.
4/2: Superliners are ordered—235 cars—as well as 200 additional Amfleet cars.
4/15: Minneapolis-Superior *Arrowhead* inauguration special; revenue service begins on following day.
4/27: *Floridian* shifted to L&N's ex-Monon line through Indiana; third Chicago-Detroit train added.
5/1: Fourth anniversary of Amtrak.
5/8: Thirty F40PH's ordered from EMD.
5/15: Third Chicago-Detroit frequency begins.
7/1: Chicago-Houston *Lone Star* gains Fort Worth-Dallas leg.
8/7: Amfleet cars enter service in NEC.
10/25: Turbos bumped from St. Louis corridor; *Abe Lincoln* returns.
10/26: *Inter-American* rerouted onto Katy between Temple and Taylor, Texas.
10/31: Chicago-Cleveland-New York/ Boston *Lake Shore Limited* debuts.
11/24: First E60 electric accepted.
11/30: Washington section of *Broadway* rerouted between Harrisburg, Pa., and Perryville, Md., via Philadelphia.

1976

3/1: USARail pass born.
4/1: Amtrak acquired Northeast Corridor and Porter (Ind.)-Kalamazoo (Mich.) line from Penn Central.
4/4: F40PH's enter service.
5/1: Fifth anniversary of Amtrak.
5/21: Los Angeles-Las Vegas *Las Vegas Limited* begins service (Friday/Sundays only).
6/15: Newport News section of *Riley* makes last trip; Boston-Newport News *Colonial* begins; New York-Savannah *Palmetto* debuts.
7/29: Original Superliner order boosted from 235 cars to 249.
9/1: Fourth *San Diegan* begins.
10/29: *Adirondack* rerouted through Schenectady, N.Y.
10/31: Washington-Cincinnati *Shenandoah* begins; Washington-Cumberland *Blue Ridge* ends; joint *Auto-Train*/Amtrak (*Floridian*) service begins between Louisville and Sanford.
11/1: *Floridian* begins running combined with *Auto-Train* Louisville-Sanford; begins using A-T station at Louisville.
11/24: Superliner order boosted again, from 249 cars to 284.

1977

1/19: Severe winter weather conditions suspend service throughout much of Midwest.
3/2: Weather-related service suspensions fully lifted.
3/31: Northeast Corridor Improvement Program starts.
4/22: Ten more F40PH's ordered.
4/24: Fifth L.A.-San Diego round trip implemented.
5/1: Sixth anniversary of Amtrak.
5/15: GG1 4935 makes inaugural run in its PRR heritage scheme.
5/26: Heritage Fleet program officially starts with work on 25 sleepers.
6/1: Washington-Catlettsburg (Ky.) *Hilltopper* begins; replaces Chicago-Norfolk *Mountaineer.*
6/7: Salt Lake City-Seattle *Pioneer* starts.
6/9: Amfleet ordered completed.
6/12: *James Whitcomb Riley* rerouted between La Crosse, Ind., and Chicago via Wellsboro, Ind.
9/8: Joint Amtrak-Auto-Train service ends.
9/28: First batch (8 units) of AEM7 electrics ordered.

1978

2/15: Sixth *San Diegan* goes into service.
3/1: New Twin Cities station opens; all Amtrak trains put on new route through Minneapolis/St. Paul.
5/1: Washington-Philadelphia 403(b) *Chesapeake* begins; seventh anniversary of Amtrak.
6/1: Alan S. Boyd becomes Amtrak's third president.
7/17: *Cardinal* between Cincinnati and Cottage Grove, Ind., via Hamilton, Ohio.
8/13: *National Limited* goes HEP and Amfleet.
9/28: Second batch (15) of AEM7's ordered.
10/27: First Superliner is accepted by Amtrak.
10/28: Washington section of *National Limited* rerouted between Harrisburg, Pa., and Perryville, Md., via Philadelphia; Empire Corridor extended to Niagara Falls, N.Y.

1979

2/1: Operation of *Southern Crescent* conveyed by Southern to Amtrak.
2/26: Superliners enter service in Midwest on corridor trains.
4/29: Amtrak returns to direct route through Schenectady, serving new station at that city.
5/1: Eighth anniversary of Amtrak.
7/25: Third batch (15) of AEM7's ordered.
9/30: *Silver Meteor* rerouted between Jacksonville and Savannah via former-ACL main.
10/1: Trains failing route-criteria evaluation process are discontinued: *National Limited, Champion, Hilltopper, Floridian, North Coast Hiawatha, Lone Star.* "Stay of execution" trains begin Newton (Kan.)-Fort Worth and Chicago-Butte-Seattle.
10/2: *Southwest Limited* rerouted between Newton and Kansas City, Kan., via Topeka; *Empire Builder* rerouted between Twin Cities and Fargo, N.D., via Staples, Minn.
10/8: Temporary Newton-Fort Worth connection to *Southwest Limited* discontinued.
10/15: *Lake Shore Limited* becomes HEP Heritage train.
Oct. 27: *San Francisco Zephyr* begins bypassing Cheyenne, Wyo.
10/28: *Empire Builder* becomes first long-distance Superliner train; *Inter-American* gains Temple-Houston leg; *Desert Wind* begins between Ogden and Los Angeles; "Post Road" connection reopens, allowing *Lake Shore* Boston section direct routing east from Rensselaer.

1980

2/3: Second *San Joaquin* begins.
2/27: Amfleet II cars ordered.
2/28: Fourth batch (17) AEM7's ordered.
4/27: *Pennsylvanian* debuts between Philadelphia and Pittsburgh.
5/1: Ninth anniversary of Amtrak.
5/9: First AEM7 enters revenue service.
8/3: *St. Clair* extended beyond Detroit to Toledo as *Lake Cities*; *Willamette Valley* service begins Portland-Eugene, Ore.
8/9: Chicago-East Peoria *Prairie*

TIME LINE

Marksman begins.
10/1: *Hoosier State* revives Chicago-Indianapolis service.
10/26: Missouri/Amtrak *Mules* begin Kansas City-St. Louis runs; seventh *San Diegan* added.
11/30: Last steam-heated equipment operated out of Chicago.

1981

1/6: First Superliner lounge enters long-distance service, on *San Francisco Zephyr.*
1/29: *Coast Starlight* completely converted to Superliner.
4/26: New York-Toronto *Maple Leaf* and Pittsburgh-Altoona *Fort Pitt* begin.
5/1: Tenth anniversary of Amtrak.
7/2: Chicago-Champaign *Illini* extended to Decatur, Ill.
7/30: Last Superliner sleeper, *George M. Pullman*, enters service as builder Pullman-Standard exits passenger-car business.
9/8: French Turbos retired from Midwest service.
9/26: New Chicago 14th Street maintenance facility dedicated.
9/30: *Black Hawk, Cardinal, Shenandoah, Pacific International, Beacon Hill* and Houston section of the *Inter-American* make last runs.
10/1: *Capitol Limited* begins between Washington and Chicago; *Inter-American* renamed *Eagle* and through Chicago-L.A. sleeper added.
10/4: *Prairie Marksman* discontinued.
10/15: New Albany/Rensselaer station opens.
10/25: *Spirit of California* begins overnight L.A.-Sacramento service; *Express Metroliner* Service begins; *Keystone Service* name applied to Philadelphia-Harrisburg runs, now protected by demoted Metroliner cars.
10/26: Portland section of *Empire Builder* implemented; *Empire Builder* rerouted between Spokane and Seattle via Wenatchee.
11/1: ARROW reservation computer goes into service.
11/11: First Amfleet II cars unveiled by Budd at Red Lion (Pa.) plant.
12/31: *Willamette Valley* trains end.

1982

1/8: *Cardinal* returns to service.
3/10: Amtrak becomes "all electric" as *Silver Star*'s steam-heated equipment is replaced.
4/25: *Coast Starlight* rerouted through Sacramento.
5/1: Amtrak turns eleven.
7/2: W. Graham Claytor Jr. becomes fourth president of Amtrak.
9/11: New major south suburban Chicago station opens at Hammond/Whiting, Ind.
10/31: Chicago-Toronto *International* replaces *Blue Water Limited*; *New England Metroliners* begin limited-stop service between New York and Boston.
11/20: *Silver Palm* begins linking Miami and Tampa.
12/16: New Grand Forks, N.D., depot opens.

1983

1/1: First Amtrak train and engine crews to be directly employed by Amtrak, on Northeast Corridor.
1/29: New Ann Arbor (Mich.) depot opens.
1/30: *Fort Pitt* discontinued.
2/1: Nationwide Amtrak Express package service begins.
3/9: First Superliner scrapped, account fire damage.
3/15: First HEP dome car released from Beech Grove.
4/24: *California Zephyr* revived.
6/27: Train Manager/Train Chief program begins on long-distance trains.
7/10: *Illini* retrenched from Decatur, Ill.
7/16: *California Zephyr* rerouted over Rio Grande.
9/30: *Spirit of California* makes last trips.
10/30: *California Zephyr* rerouted between Salt Lake City and Alazon, Nev., via UP (ex-Western Pacific) main; switching of *CZ/Pioneer/Desert Wind* shifted from Ogden to Salt Lake City; Amtrak Auto Train commences; Annaheim, Calif., gets new depot.
11/12: *Eagle* derails in Texas, killing four.

1984

1/13: *Michigan Executive* makes final run.
1/31: *Silver Meteor* and *Silver Star* cut back from St. Petersburg to Tampa.
4/29: Kansas City-New Orleans *River Cities* begins; New Orleans-Mobile *Gulf Coast Limited* starts; *Metroliner Service* begins between L.A. and San Diego.
5/1: Amtrak becomes a "teenager."
6/9: Classic "railroad-style" depot replaces Burlington station at Galesburg, Ill.
6/15: New Tacoma (Wash.) depot dedicated.
7/7: *Montrealer* derails in Vermont, killing five.
8/4: *Pere Marquette* restores Chicago-Grand Rapids service; Chicago-Milwaukee *Badger* begins.
8/24: New Omaha station dedicated.
10/28: *Carolinian* starts between Charlotte and New York via Raleigh; *Bay State* restores Boston-New Haven service via Inland Route; *Virginian* begins Richmond-New York run; mail trains 12 (*Fast Mail*) and 13 (*Mail Express*) added on Northeast Corridor; Saturday-night-only *Encore* added Chicago-Milwaukee.

1985

1/6: *Gulf Coast Limited* discontinued.
4/27: L.A.-San Diego *Metroliner Service* ends.
5/1: Amtrak celebrates 14th birthday with upgraded *Southwest Chief.*
9/1: *Carolinian* makes last run.
9/7: New Santa Ana (Calif.) transportation center opens.
10/26: St. Paul-Duluth *North Star* makes last run.
12/2: New Kansas City station opens.
12/4: Last transcontinental sleeper (L.A.-New York) operates.
12/12: New Quincy, Ill., depot opens.

1986

1/1: *Blue Ridge* operation transferred to Maryland Rail Commuter.
1/12: *Adirondack* rerouted onto CN between Rouses Point, N.Y., and Montreal Central Station; new through-car service eliminates need to change trains at New Haven; Chicago-Champaign *Illini* discontinued and name applied to Chicago-Carbondale *Shawnee*; Chicago-Valparaiso (Ind.) *Indiana Connection* discontinued. Other budget-related cuts reduce frequencies on several routes.
4/27: *Cardinal* rerouted between Chicago and Cottage Grove, Ind., via La Fayette and Indianapolis; *Desert Wind* rerouted Los Angeles-San Bernardino via Fullerton; Chicago-Springfield (Ill.) *Loop* added.
5/1: Amtrak turns 15.
6/16: New Providence (R.I.) station opens.
7/3: *Cape Codder* brings trains back to Cape Cod, Mass.
7/11: New Altoona (Pa.) depot dedicated.
10/26: *Silver Star* rerouted Petersburg, Va.-Raleigh, N.C., via Selma, N.C.; *Broadway* and *Capitol* become separate trains between Chicago and Pittsburgh.

1987:

1/4: *Colonial* collides with Conrail locomotives at Chase, Md., killing 16.
4/6: *Montrealer* suspended.
5/1: Amtrak turns sweet 16.
8/24: Rebuilt French Turbos enter service on Empire Corridor.
10/5: Amtrak returns to rebuilt Southwest Corridor main out of Boston following eight-year detour on normally freight-only Dorchester branch.
10/7: First Viewliner enters test service.
10/25: Eighth *San Diegan* enters service; nonstop Washington-New York *Metroliner Service* established.

1988

5/1: Seventeen years old—Amtrak.
6/7: Purchase agreements announced for Horizon Fleet cars
6/11: *Silver Meteor* Miami section rerouted Coleman-Auburndale, Fla., via Lakeland.
6/26: One *San Diegan* extended north of L.A. to Santa Barbara.
9/9: Guilford Industries sells B&M line in Vermont and New Hampshire to Amtrak/Central Vermont, allowing restoration of *Montrealer* following year.
9/29: "New" Washington Union Station unveiled.
11/15: *Eagle* gains Dallas-Houston leg; *Palmetto* extended to Jacksonville.

1989

4/11: Horizon Fleet cars unveiled.
5/1: Amtrak turns 18.
5/23: Atlantic City revenue service begins.
7/18: *Montrealer* reinstated, but via New London, Conn.
10/21-22: Newly renovated Boston South Station dedicated.
10/27: *Gulf Breeze* inaugural between New York and Mobile (revenue service begins on 10/29); Amtrak moves into new Pittsburgh station.
10/29: Two Chicago-Milwaukee 403(b) round trips added.
12/17: Third *San Joaquin* goes into service.

1990

1/15: *International* rerouted London-Toronto via Stratford, Ont.
3/29: New York-Syracuse *Mohawk* begins service.
5/1: Amtrak turns 19.
5/12: *Carolinian* revived, but via Selma, N.C.
6/1: Atlantic City-Philadelphia *Atlantic City Express*es extended to Philadelphia Airport; new Irvine (Calif.) station opens.
6/10: New Bloomington/Normal (Ill.) station opens.
9/8: Experimental F69's enter revenue service.
10/29: *New England Express*es enter limited-stop service on New York-Boston line.
12/10: Amtrak and United Air Lines enter joint marketing agreement
11/11: *Broadway Limited* rerouted Chicago-Pittsburgh via CSX through Napanee, Ind., and Youngstown, Ohio; *Capitol Limited* rerouted between Chicago and Alliance, Ohio, via Cleveland.
12/26: Amtrak announces order for 52 new locomotives from GE.

1991

1/8: *Atlantic City Express*es retrenched from Philadelphia airport.
1/15: New Columbia (S.C.) station opens.
2/27: *Atlantic City Express* service extended to Harrisburg.
3/11: Amtrak releases report on feasibility of Jacksonville-New Orleans service.
4/1: Richmond-Atlantic City train added.
4/6: Last Amtrak trains depart from legendary Grand Central Terminal in Manhattan; all operations consolidated at Penn Station following day.
4/7: *Carolinian* and *Palmetto* begin running separately; through Chicago-Miami car begins service on *Capitol* and *Silver Star.*
4/ : 140 new Superliners ordered.
5/1: Amtrak celebrates its 20th anniversary.
5/3: Chicago-Valparaiso *Calumet* makes last run.
6/16: *Pioneer* rerouted through Wyoming.
6/14-16: Newly renovated 30th Street Station, Philadelphia, celebrated.
7/29: Amtrak returns to Cincinnati Union Terminal.

Space does not permit a fully comprehensive time line, but corrections and other additions from readers would be welcomed for possible future reprintings of this book.

ALL ABOARD AMTRAK

Bob Johnston photo

PUBLISHED BY
Railpace Company, Piscataway, N.J.

BOOK DESIGN, LAYOUT AND ART PRODUCTION
Mike Schafer/Zephyr Graphics & Editorial, Waukesha, Wis.

EDITORIAL ASSISTANCE
Bob Johnston, Mike McBride

PRODUCTION ASSISTANCE
Andy McBride, Tom Nemeth, Chris Kimler, Joy Buslaff

PROMOTION, MARKETING AND DISTRIBUTION
Denis Connell

COLOR SEPARATIONS
Litho-Tech, Inc., Franklin, N.J.

PRINTING
Kutztown Publishing Company, Kutztown, Pa.

DEDICATION

To my mom,
Doris Anna Madalyn Nelson,
who in 1953 had the
foresight to take my sister and me
on our first trip to Chicago by train,
to experience the ambiance and
excitement of rail travel

Bob Johnston photo

MIKE SCHAFER's affinity for railroading in general and passenger trains in particular goes back to his childhood in Rockford, Ill., where he was born in 1949. After growing up around the likes of Illinois Central's *Hawkeye* and *Land O' Corn*, Burlington *Zephyrs* and Milwaukee Road *City* Streamliners, he graduated with an art degree from Northern Illinois University, De Kalb, Ill., in 1971 and immediately entered the publishing field, with a focus on railroading. He spent eight years in the book and art departments of Kalmbach Publishing Co. before starting his own company, Zephyr Graphics & Editorial, in 1980. Through ZG&E, he took on the production and design of PTJ Publishing's growing book line and its *Prototype Modeler* and *Passenger Train Journal* magazines, the latter of which he became editor of in 1983. Although Mike states that editing *PTJ* was his favorite job ever, he returned to the world of self-employment in 1991, reviving Zephyr Graphics and forming an alliance with Andover Junction Publications of Andover, N.J., with a goal of "bringing higher standards of quality and design into railroad book and magazine publishing." Although ALL ABOARD AMTRAK is the first book he has authored, he has edited and/or designed a number of other railroad titles since 1971. Mike, who is also a big fan of roller coasters, Steak 'n' Shake restaurants, 1950's and 1960's music, Americana and the paranormal (ghosts and related phenomenon) resides in Waukesha, Wis., with his dog, Max.

ACKNOWLEDGMENTS

As with any endeavor of this nature, there are many individuals whom were instrumental in making it all possible. First of all, I would like to thank the Railpace fellows—Tom Nemeth, Denis Connell, Bill Chaplik and Jim Clarke—for approaching me first when the idea struck them to do an Amtrak anniversary book. No book on Amtrak is possible without the help of the people of that company, and in particular I would like to thank Amtrak's Cliff Black and Bruce Heard for their unending patience, support and comraderie; their knowledge of and devotion to the National Railroad Passenger Corporation give Amtrak a human side that other railroads can only dream of. In addition, Amtrak's Sue Martin and NRPC President W. Graham Claytor Jr. provided the extra measures necessary to make ALL ABOARD AMTRAK an accurate recount of the carrier's first 20 years.

Every book needs an editor, and though I am in part an editor by trade, one should not edit his or her own book. For this, I enlisted the able assistance of another passenger-train aficionado, Amtrak fan and very accomplished writer—Bob Johnston. Bob's long hours of proofreading at the Zephyr Graphics drawing board and his input at several idea-bashing lunch and dinner work sessions down the street at Waukesha's Depot Restaurant (and also aboard the *Capitol Limited* and *Broadway Limited*) were invaluable to the building of the book's personality and its readability.

There's more. Many thank-yous are in order for: Elbert Simon Jr., who helped with roster and other information; Paul D. Schneider and Jane Kremsreiter—and in fact all my close friends—for their moral support (especially helpful after an all-nighter at the computer); and Steve Esposito and Joyce Mooney of Andover Junction Publications, for the use of their facilities and for providing a "home away from home" on book-related trips to the East Coast. Trains are people, too, and thus I would like to salute the *Capitol Limited* and *Broadway Limited* (perhaps my two favorite Amtrak trains) for many pleasant, inspirational hours of riding during book-related travels between Chicago and the East Coast.

And finally, ALL ABOARD AMTRAK would simply not be possible without the tremendous, talented support of the dozens of photographers represented herein. Flip through these 176 pages, and you'll see that their images prove that Amtrak is indeed a colorful subject.—M.S.

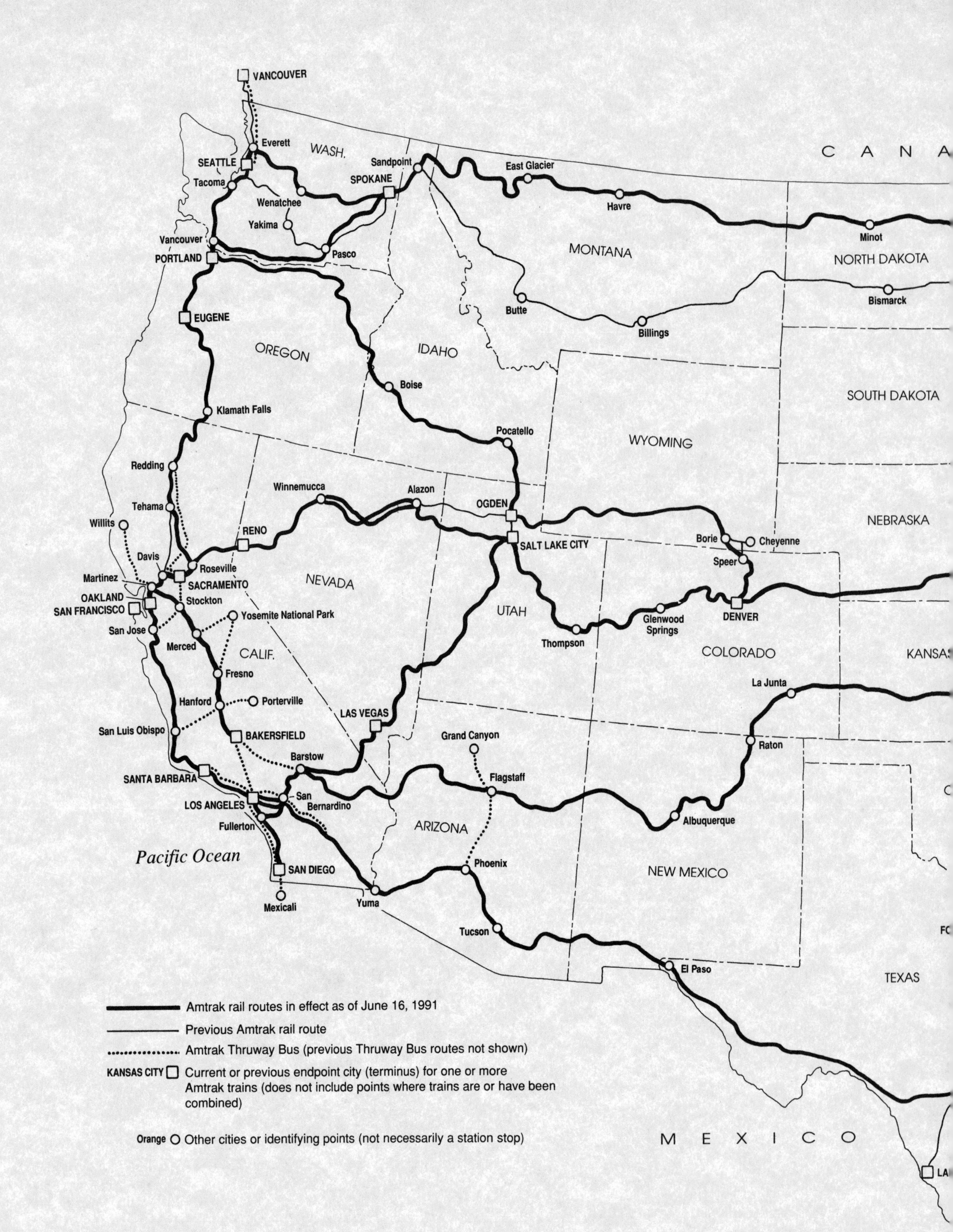
VANCOUVER
Everett
WASH.
SEATTLE
Sandpoint
East Glacier
C A N A
Tacoma
SPOKANE
Wenatchee
Havre
Yakima
Minot
Vancouver
Pasco
MONTANA
NORTH DAKOTA
PORTLAND
Bismarck
Butte
EUGENE
Billings
OREGON
IDAHO
Boise
SOUTH DAKOTA
Klamath Falls
Pocatello
WYOMING
Redding
Winnemucca
Alazon
Tehama
OGDEN
NEBRASKA
Willits
RENO
Borie
Cheyenne
SALT LAKE CITY
Davis
Roseville
Speer
Martinez
SACRAMENTO
NEVADA
OAKLAND
Stockton
DENVER
SAN FRANCISCO
Yosemite National Park
Glenwood Springs
San Jose
UTAH
Merced
Thompson
COLORADO
CALIF.
KANSAS
Fresno
La Junta
Hanford
Porterville
LAS VEGAS
San Luis Obispo
BAKERSFIELD
Grand Canyon
Raton
Barstow
SANTA BARBARA
Flagstaff
San Bernardino
LOS ANGELES
Fullerton
ARIZONA
Albuquerque
Pacific Ocean
SAN DIEGO
Phoenix
NEW MEXICO
Mexicali
Yuma
Tucson
El Paso
TEXAS
Amtrak rail routes in effect as of June 16, 1991
Previous Amtrak rail route
Amtrak Thruway Bus (previous Thruway Bus routes not shown)
KANSAS CITY Current or previous endpoint city (terminus) for one or more Amtrak trains (does not include points where trains are or have been combined)
Orange Other cities or identifying points (not necessarily a station stop)
M E X I C O